AND THAT'S THE GOSPEL TRUTH

Jack McArdle ss.cc

And that's
the Gospel truth

REFLECTIONS ON THE SUNDAY GOSPELS

Year C

the columba press

First published in 2000 by
the columba press
55a Spruce Avenue, Stillorgan Industrial Park,
Blackrock, Co Dublin

Cover by Bill Bolger
Cover photograph by Marie McDonald
Origination by The Columba Press
Printed in Ireland by Colour Books Ltd, Dublin

ISBN 185607 307 6

Contents

Introduction

The four gospels are spread over a three-year period, so that we are presented with every part of all four over those years. This is Year C, which, in case of doubt or confusion, begins on the First Sunday of Advent, and will be back in circulation three years later.

In presenting these reflections, I have a hope in my heart, and a prayer on my lips. I know many people who are reflective and contemplative by nature, and the word of the Lord is a personal word for them. They would like to know what the Sunday Readings are beforehand, so they can prepare their hearts to welcome that word. They also continue to ponder that word throughout the following week. They are too mature in their Christian responsibility to settle for sitting back, and leaving it all to the preacher. The church that is being reborn today is one in which each of us must share equal responsibility. We are no longer like the FA Cup Final in Wembley, where nearly one hundred spectators, badly in need of exercise, are sitting down very comfortably, criticising twenty-two pressurised human beings, badly in need of a rest! In today's church, we are all invited to get down out of the stands.

This book is not written for homilists, even if a few of them have a peep or two! It is written for the ordinary punter in the pew. It is written for the small groups in parishes who meet during the week to reflect on the Readings for the following Sunday. It is written for the house-bound. Indeed, it is written for anyone who needs material for reflection, and who benefits from being presented with material that has some structure and order to it. There is no reason why someone should not pick up this book, and open it at any chapter, irrespective of what time of year it is.

The lay-out and structure of what is presented is purely arbitrary, and need not be adhered to in any way. It is presented with one intention, and that is, with a genuine desire to be most helpful. To know that it helps someone will give me great joy. My decision to confine myself to the gospel of each Sunday was made in the context of my own work-load, bearing in mind the limits of time available to both writer and reader.

P.S.: A special word of thanks to Diane Porterfield, Geneva, N.Y., who keeps me supplied with stories, several of which are included in this book.

FIRST SUNDAY OF ADVENT

Gospel: Luke 21:25-28, 34-36

Theme

Today's gospel parallels the events of Christmas, for which we now prepare. If, when Jesus came at Bethlehem, the people were not ready to receive him, then, when he comes again, they will have no excuse, because he has come to prepare them for that Second Coming.

Parable

We are just getting used to the new Millennium. One of the many new changes we will have to come to accept has to do with cars. For the first time ever, cars of a certain age, are subject to inspection. When it comes to the time to renew the tax on these cars, they will have to be subjected to a detailed examination first. People in possession of such cars have been given plenty of notice. They are even advised to have the car serviced before submitting to the inspection, as this will save them both time and money. Needless to say, many people have already been caught unprepared, and all that can be heard from them is the unfairness and injustice of the system!

Teaching

Jesus tells us to 'watch and pray'. There is a certain level of alertness that is part of being a Christian. 'Jesus of Nazareth is passing by.' The moment of grace is NOW. If I am not present in the 'now', then I am not at home when Jesus calls. At the end of every day, I can look back, and see the many opportunities the day had afforded me to say the good word, or to do the good deed.

Jesus reminds us that 'that day', as he calls it, will come upon us all. It must not find us filled with the worries of this life. We are a pilgrim people, on our way home. 'Where your treasure is, there will your heart be also.' There is some excuse for people not being ready to greet Jesus when at first he came. There will be no excuse, however, for those of us who have heard the Good News, not to be ready when Jesus comes again. That 'readiness' is called prayer, which is a way of being in the watchtower, of being on guard, of being in a sense of readiness and expectation.

Jesus tells us that his Second Coming will be heralded by signs, turmoil, and wide-spread upheaval. While this will strike fear in the hearts of the citizens of this world, it should be an occasion for great rejoicing among the members of his Kingdom. The kingdom of this world, and the kingdom of Satan will have come to an end, and his victorious Kingdom will be established for all eternity. It will be the beginning of eternal glory and rejoicing for all the children of God.

Response
We are now beginning a four-week period of preparation for Christmas. On that first Christmas night, there was many a heart, and many a home closed against him. We are now given yet one more opportunity to declare where we stand. We prepare for Christmas in so many many ways. There is a lot of time and money that goes into that preparation. There is nothing wrong with this, as long as we remember that 'Jesus is the reason for the Season'.

Salvation is not something I receive when I die. Rather it is the opportunity to begin again, any day I choose. The only 'yes' that God is interested in is my 'yes' of now. God's grace is always available to us. He doesn't give me anything, but he offers me everything. The offer is made anew with each new day. I can live today on my 'yes' of today.

As I journey on my life with Jesus, as he leads me back home to the Father, I become more and more aware of his accompanying presence, and I live with the constant knowledge of that presence. This awareness is expressed through prayer, which is not necessarily saying prayers. It is to have a praying heart. It is to have a constant awareness that Jesus is among us, within us, and that every day is Christmas. The manger is in my heart, and every time I go down into the heart I meet Jesus there.

Practical
Today's gospel is a wake-up call. It would amaze any one of us to discover how much of ourselves is dormant. Did you hear about the bishop who dreamt he was preaching a sermon, and he woke up to discover that he was?! Have you ever discovered yourself beginning a decade of the Rosary, and then find yourself at the Gloria, without any awareness of what happened in between? Today's gospel calls on us to extend the antennae in our heads, as it were, to be alert, and to be aware of what's going

on. John Lennon tells us that 'life is what's happening when you're making other plans'.

The secret of this alertness is to live in the now. There is no reality outside of now. Yesterday is gone, and will never return. To-morrow does not exist. The only reality is now. God is totally a God of now. 'I am who am.' When I was a child we had a wireless (radio), and, because we did not have electricity, it was run on two batteries, one a 'dry'(or ordinary) battery, and the other a 'wet' battery, which was made of glass, and filled with acid. This battery required regular charging. Another thing about the wireless was that it had a drifting dial. We received just one station, and, as the station faded away on occasions, it was necessary to turn the dial slightly to return the wireless to that station. In a way, we all have a drifting dial, and to live in the now entails tuning our attention, to bring ourselves back to the proper wave-length.

Advent is a time of wonderful blessing and renewal. It requires, of course, our own personal investment. We have to take advantage of this opportunity to prepare our hearts anew for the coming of our Saviour. Incarnation is not a once-off event that happened many years ago. It is an on-going evolution going on within the heart of every Christian. It the result of God's offer, and of our acceptance. God's offer is constant, daily, minute by minute. Our acceptance must be the same. It is not a question of preparing for Jesus' Second Coming at the end of time. My future is in the now. It involves wakening up, tuning in, and saying 'yes'. It is deeply personal, and it is very very real.

Story

A young lady was walking through the park, when she became conscious of footsteps behind her. She hastened her step, only to become aware that the person behind had begun to walk faster also. Obviously, she was quite worried, and she decided to face the situation head-on. She turned around to discover a young man walking briskly behind her. She asked him if he were following her, and, if so, why? The young man was embarrassed, as he began to explain why he was doing what he was. He told her that he had noticed her pass this way every day, that he had become infatuated by her, and that he just had to meet her. The young woman remained silent, while the young man poured out his heart about how much he loved her, and there could be nobody else in the whole world that he could possibly love like he loved her. Retaining her composure, the young woman said

'My sister is much more pretty that I am, and she is coming up there behind you.' The man turned quickly, only to discover that there was no one coming. 'You're only making a fool of me', he said. 'There's nobody coming behind me.' The young lady replied very calmly 'Yet you looked around! If you loved me like you said you did, you would not have looked around to see my younger sister!'

SECOND SUNDAY OF ADVENT

Gospel: Luke 3:1-6

Theme

At a time when we are preparing our hearts for Christmas, we read of John the Baptist preparing the people for the coming of Jesus.

Parable

Sept '79 was an historic occasion for Ireland. Pope John Paul II visited Ireland, and all of everyday life came to a stand-still for the duration of his visit. As I now recall that occasion, the strongest memories I have are connected with the work that preceded his visit. Special Masses, all-night vigils, prayer groups, were the order of the day. There were four places in the country where the Pope would celebrate Eucharist, and address the crowds. These places were decorated, corralled, and fully equipped to cater for the many thousands expected. Local communities were organised for mass transport to and fro. I myself was very involved in this preparation, giving talks, conducting vigils, etc. The visit was a wonderful success, and a time of much and many graces for the Irish nation. I have never doubted that the preparation was a very vital part of the success of the Papal visit.

Teaching

John's message was a call to turn from sin, and be ready for God's forgiveness. There was a Saviour coming, there was a Redeemer coming. In order to be saved, it is necessary to acknowledge my sinfulness, and my need for salvation. In order to be redeemed, it is necessary to acknowledge the fact that I am in bondage, and in need of being set free.

In many ways, John the Baptist is an image of the church. At a later time, John pointed to Jesus, and encouraged his disciples to follow him, and become Jesus' disciples. (On occasions, unfortunately, the church could be accused of pointing to herself as the source of salvation). During this Advent season, the church concentrates on preparing us to celebrate the coming of Jesus as our Saviour. We must heed that call, and prepare our hearts for this great occasion.

We are called to straighten out our lives. To fill in the valleys, and to level the mountains and hills is about ensuring justice for all of God's people. In today's language, we refer to this as providing a level playing field for all, so that everybody has access to the goods of this world. The final words of Isaiah in today's gospel tells that 'And then all people will see the salvation sent to us from our God.' This is the direct result of making straight the ways of the Lord, filling the valleys, levelling the mountains, straightening the curves, and making smooth the rough places. We can all identify these areas in our lives.

Response
The only way I will ever be able to respond to the word of God is to accept that it is a personal word for me. Today's gospel contains a message for me. I am the one who is asked to turn from my sins, to turn to God, and to prepare the way for him to make his home within my heart. I am the one who is asked to ensure fair play and justice for others, so that I can see the salvation sent from God.

What exactly does 'turning from sin' mean? If I am conscious of anything in my life that is in conflict with my Christian vocation; if I am aware of any pattern of behaviour, relationship, or deceit in my life that is not according to the will of Jesus, then I must get rid of it. 'If your hand sins against you', says Jesus, 'cut it off. It is better to enter heaven with one hand than to end up in hell with two'. Usually there is little difficulty identifying something in my life that should not be there. We all have a conscience, that still silent voice that reminds us. When I was a child, I had a dog that looked guilty anytime he did something wrong! One look at him, and you knew he had been up to something. When approached, he lay on his back, expecting a slap. When he received a pat, or a friendly stroke, he immediately jumped up all over me, because he knew he was forgiven.

John the Baptist's time was very limited, just as the season of Advent is quite short. There is little time for procrastination. All diets begin on Monday! Today's gospel calls for action now. Surely I cannot presume on the number of Advents left in my life. With the call to respond comes the grace needed to make the response. This is a precious moment of grace that must not be neglected.

Practical
There would never be a war if somebody somewhere was prepared to say 'Sorry, I'm wrong'. There may be somebody in your

life to whom you owe those words. It is relatively easy to say 'I did wrong', because I then can go on to tell you who was responsible for making me do the wrong. (It is never me!). It requires greater honesty and maturity to be able to say 'I was wrong'. Give some thought to this today.

Filling the valleys, levelling the mountains, straightening the crooked road, preparing a pathway for the Lord … this is all part of my preparation for Christmas. This involves decisions, and these decisions come out of the context of the realities of my life. God is always calling on me to respond to him. Responding to him is to become responsible. I have responsibility for my actions, and become willing to face up to the truth. There is a tendency to look for a softer, easier way. Part of the human condition is an inability to understand the human condition. Lucy said to Charlie Browne 'Charlie Browne, do you know what's wrong with you?' 'No', replied Charlie, 'tell me'. 'What's wrong with you, Charlie Browne, is that you don't want to know what's wrong with you.'

Most churches have a Service of Reconciliation during Advent. In a way, we can think of this as 'Confession without the shopping list'. To people of my generation, it may appear all too simple, all too easy. This is to totally misunderstand the thinking behind the Reconciliation Service. Sin has a community dimension. When I do wrong, I offend the community in general, through an individual, or through a group. Because there is a community dimension to my sin, there must be a community dimension to my repentance. That is why the public acknowledgement of our sinfulness, that is part of the Service of Reconciliation, is much more preferable to going into a Confession box and whispering in the dark. In the season where we are told about 'peace on earth to those of good-will', it is very important that I harness my good-will, and ACT on it.

Story
Jim had always been a quiet man. His voice was gentle and pleasant, and he had a sincerity about him that held you when he spoke to you. He seemed to have a constant sense of being in contact with God, and of God's presence in his life, and in the world. He had absolutely no aggression in his personality, but he was always deeply upset by reports of injustice, ethnic cleansing, and the flow of refugees, in search of safety and security.

Jim got cancer. From the very beginning, he was totally aware of his situation, and he insisted on being kept informed of

every step of the prognosis. He retained his dignity, his composure, and his peace of mind. He was very realistic about life and
about death. He spoke openly about how he felt, and what he
thought. Most impressive of all was his attitude towards death.
Whenever I was with him during his final weeks, I always felt
that his whole life was a preparation for what was to come. It
was obvious that he had made a direct connection between the
first coming of Jesus, and his return to call Jim home. He was
ready, and he had a sense of waiting patiently. He spent a lot of
his time, while he still had the energy, in reaching out to others,
in sorting out his affairs, and in preparing his wife and family
for what lay ahead.

I was with him when he died. He died as he had lived, with
peace, calm, and dignity. When I read today's gospel, I think of
Jim. He represents for me what today's gospel is all about. My
own personal reinforcement of the gospel message has come
from the people I have met who are living the message.

THIRD SUNDAY OF ADVENT

Gospel: Luke 3:10-18

Theme

Today's gospel is a gem, because it is full of practicalities. When they heard John speak, people from different ways of life came to John and asked him 'What should we do?' His words had obviously touched their hearts, and they were ready to respond. It is reasonable to assume, by the nature of their questions, that they were prepared to listen to his answer.

Parable

A friend of mine is a member of AA. He is now a fully convinced and convicted member, after a long period of rationalisation, self-justification, and denial. For most of his first year there was a raging battle going on within him. He could not identify with the others, and, because he had not done all the crazy things the others had done, he continued to deny that he really was an alcoholic. By sticking with the programme, however, and by continuing to attend the meetings, he gradually came to a point where he was ready to ask for help, to take his focus off the others, and to ask himself 'What do I have to do to gain sobriety?' It was only then that his recovery had begun. The message had got through to him, and he was ready to make a personal response to what he was hearing.

Teaching

Today's gospel contains some very simple questions, and some very direct answers. There are several occasions in the gospels when someone asked Jesus what should he do. On Pentecost morning, the people asked Peter what should they do to receive the Holy Spirit. Pilate asked Jesus 'What is truth?', and then he walked away, because he probably didn't want to hear the answer. We are speaking about truth here. In other words, if you don't want to hear the answer, don't ask the question. Denial of the truth is very much part of our human condition. Part of our sinful condition is that it blinds us to that very condition. That's why it's so much easier to see the faults of others.

John himself was very open and truthful when it came to the question as to whether or not he was the Messiah. John had never any doubt about his role. He was sent to prepare for Jesus, and, once Jesus had arrived on the scene, John's role was over. 'I have to decrease, if he is to increase.' John knew his place before God, and he had no tendency to try to play the role of God or of Messiah. That is humility in the truest sense. It is stating things as they are, and it is living in, and with reality.

The most important thing about John's announcements was that he saw them as Good News. He was very definite about the good times up ahead. It was part of the Jewish tradition that a Messiah would come some day. Even today, Jews are still waiting for that Messiah. John was a specially anointed prophet, who had a clear and definite vision about what was unfolding. Calling on people to repent, to change their lives, to get their lives in order was the perfect introduction to the themes Jesus would pick up on, when he came. Just as John highlighted the need to acknowledge sin in our lives, so would Jesus emphasise his offer of forgiveness for sin.

Response
Supposing you went up to John the Baptist, and asked 'What should I do?' What do you think his answer might be? It is interesting to note that each group who asked this question in today's gospel was told something about what they did for a living. To the tax collectors he replied that they should not extort more money than was due. To the soldiers he said that they should not accuse people of things they know they didn't do. I don't think it would require any deep or prolonged reflection for any of us to come up with what John's answer to us might be.

If we are honest, it must surely amaze us at times how much we take for granted. We know that Jesus will come again, but, in reality, that is not his Second Coming. His Second Coming is when he enters the heart of each of us, and sets up his Kingdom there. For us, the final coming will be the Third Coming. What I'm driving at here, is that it is so essential that we take him seriously. Advent is a precious time, a time of grace. It will pass us by, leaving us untouched, however, if we do not make a personal response to it. This is our third week of Advent, of preparing for Christmas. How do you think the preparation has been going?

When we follow the advice of the Baptist, and the Messiah arrives in our heart, then we, in turn, can become like the Baptist in the lives of others. I am not talking about preaching, or gathering followers to listen to my message. Life is made up of relationships. How I function in my relationships is a wonderful opportunity to touch the hearts and lives of others. My life is my message, and I speak clearly of my values by the way I live that life, by the way I relate to others. Looking seriously at my relationships is certainly one good way to prepare my heart for Christmas.

Practical
Supposing you were to take five minutes out today to sit with the question that you posed to John the Baptist… To sit sincerely with the question, in peace and quiet, without any pressure or guilt-trip… It would be interesting to reflect on what comes to mind. It is obvious, of course, that I would do this after a whispered prayer to the Holy Spirit to enlighten me. I strongly suggest you do this.

John tells us that the Messiah will baptise us with the Holy Spirit and with fire. Through his Spirit, he will enkindle within us the fires of divine love; he will stir up within us a zeal and enthusiasm for things of God. Most of us, I'm sure, have been baptised with water. Our experience of living the Christian life may not be very exciting or energising. I'm sure you have heard the phrase about 'having fire in your belly'. Once again, here is another suggestion for a five-minute time of stillness: Open your heart, and ask Jesus to complete your Baptism of water by baptising you with the Holy Spirit. Ask with a strong sense of expectation…

How real does the sense of Good News ring in your heart? Familiarity can breed contempt. The opposite to love is not hatred, but indifference. Without knowing it, I can easily slip into an indifferent mode, where nothing is really passing my head, and entering my heart. A life without reflection is a life that's not worth living. Indifference usually comes from the absence of reflection. Even as children, we excused our wrong-doings by saying 'Oh, I never thought'! There is just over one week to Christmas. It would be wonderful to make this a time of reflection. How to do this would be up to each individual. Reflection is a condition of the heart, and I can reflect in the midst of throngs. There will, however, be those few quiet moments that each of can steal from our schedule, no matter how hectic that schedule might be. If I am too busy to reflect, then, indeed, I am too busy.

Story
I believe there is a great need for us to hear the truth, to see the truth, and to speak the truth, without waffle, hearsay, or 'woolly thinking'.

A young lad was doing his homework, as his dad watched television. 'Dad', called the boy, 'where did I come from?' The father was unprepared for the question, as he hummed and pondered. 'A stork brought you', came the answer at last. A few minutes later came another question. 'Dad, where did you come from?' Once again the father was slightly flustered, and then he replied 'Santa brought me'. The young lad continued writing. Just as his dad was beginning to relax, a third question came. 'Dad, where did grand-dad come from?' The father was running out of ideas by now, but then he reverted to the old reliable. 'He was found under a head of cabbage.' By now the father was quite pleased with himself, and the young lad finished his writing, closed the copy, and went to bed. As the father was reflecting on the string of questions, he got a bright idea, and he went over to the table, got the young lad's copy, and read what he had written. Imagine how he felt when he read 'As far as I can ascertain, after persistent questioning, there hasn't been one normal birth in this family for the past three generations'!

FOURTH SUNDAY OF ADVENT

Gospel: Luke 1:39-45

Theme

Today's gospel contains a simple but beautiful story. Before Jesus comes to the rest of the world at Christmas, Elizabeth has the extraordinary privilege of having him come to her. This is Elizabeth's Christmas Day, and, of course, once again, Mary is instrumental in that happening.

Parable

I was ordained a priest at the age of 41(and I'm neither a Jesuit or a slow learner!). At my first Mass, I had a song that was sung at two different parts of the Mass, and it was actually printed twice in the Mass leaflet for the occasion. It had a personal importance for me, and I needed to stress that fact. It was called 'The Visit', and it was about Mary visiting Elizabeth. 'Be brave little mother, for the burden you bear, 'cause it's Christ that you carry every-where, everywhere.' I thought that the image of Mary visiting Elizabeth, and bringing Jesus to her, would be a wonderful model for me in my role as a priest. Mary did what I would hope to do as a priest. I can use this same model for any Christian, whose role is to be a Christ-o-pher, or a Christ-bearer.

Teaching

Christianity is not about producing nicer people, with better morals. I could be a pagan, and be a good person. It is not about prayer and fasting; I could be a Muslim, and do all of that. Christianity is about a person, Jesus Christ. I have to meet Jesus before I can follow him. There are many different ways in which people in the gospel met Jesus. One man got down out of a sycamore tree. Another man was lowered on a stretcher through a hole in the roof. In today's gospel, Elizabeth met Jesus, while he is in the womb of his mother. In fact, John the Baptist, also in the womb, showed clear signs that he was in the presence of the divine. It is interesting to note that, in all our debates about the viability of the unborn, that it was an unborn baby who first re-sponded to the presence of the Saviour.

When I was a child I thought that Mary visited Elizabeth, be-cause Elizabeth was old and frail, was going to have a baby, and needed someone to care for her. I don't see it that way now.

Mary was in the midst of the most extraordinary experience of her life. Since the angel appeared, until now, her heart was bursting with prayer, praise, amazement and wonder at the goodness of her God. She certainly couldn't talk to her neighbours about it, because it would be unreal to expect them to understand. In all the world, at that time, there was only one other human being who was having an experience similar to her own. She just had to meet with Elizabeth. They had so much to share. Elizabeth was filled with the Holy Spirit, and her baby leaped with joy. Mary poured forth the Magnificat prayer, one of the most beautiful prayers of praise ever to come out of a human heart.

Elizabeth paid an extraordinary tribute to Mary, 'All these things happened to you because you believed that the promises of the Lord would be fulfilled.' Mary had been told that 'nothing is impossible with God', and she believed that. Jesus said that 'the sin of this world is unbelief in me', and 'when the Son of Man comes, will he find any faith on this earth?'

Response
Today's gospel marks the beginning of a new way of being a pilgrim people. In the words of the song, from now on, 'You'll never walk alone' anymore. Like Mary, I, too, can bring Jesus into every situation I enter. 'I will never abandon you … I will not leave you in the midst of the storm … I will be with you always…' Incarnation is not a once-off event, but is repeated again and again within the heart of every Christian. Like Mary, once I say my 'yes', the Holy Spirit comes upon me, the power of the Most High overshadows me, and the one who becomes incarnate within me is the Son of God.

Today's gospel just stops short of the Magnificat, which was Mary's response to the greeting of Elizabeth. To magnify the Lord is to make him bigger. The bigger your God, the smaller your problems. Some people have a very small God, because they seem to have mighty problems. Mary had a very clear vision of the width of the gap between herself and God. 'He that is mighty has done this thing to me … He raised up the lowly …' It is a special grace to know my place before God. Humility is nothing more than the truth, than seeing, and accepting things as they are.

There was something in common between the experiences of Mary and Elizabeth, and they had a lot to share with each other.

One could easily imagine the atmosphere of prayerful praise that was part of their time together. In miniature, it is the ideal model of the Christian community, where people come together to share a common message, and to respond to a common call. Each individual is still very unique, while completing the unity of the body. When one reflects on the situation between the various Christian churches, it is, indeed, sad that, while sharing so much in common, it is the differences that are most highlighted.

Practical
The journey of Mary to visit Elizabeth is one of the symbolic journeys in the gospel. It is the life of the Christian in summary. This can become part of my prayer, as I set out each day. I can offer myself as someone who is willing, and who wants to bring Jesus to others today. My prayer could be 'Lord, may your presence within me today touch the hearts of those I meet, either through the words I say, the prayers I pray, the life I live, or the very person that I am.'

A committed Christian is never alone, but is always in the presence of the Lord. I know an elderly lady, living on her own, and she is in constant conversation with Jesus all day long. She loves gardening, and she is chatting away to him, as she weeds, trims, or plants. I have often come within a yard of her before she became aware of my presence. I have spoken to her about this, and she is so clear about the fact that she is not alone, and how she is constantly aware of being accompanied.

For those of us brought up on promises, it would be a good thing to reflect on the words of Elizabeth to Mary in today's gospel 'All these things happened to you because you believed that the promises of the Lord would be fulfilled'. The greatest promise I could make to the Lord is not to make any more promises! How much better it would be if I listened to his promises, and began to act on them. There are hundreds of promises in the gospel; more than one for every day of the year. At the time of writing this I am also in the process of writing a book, with a promise, a reflection, and short prayer, for every day of the year.

Story
It was a Charismatic Prayer Meeting. There was a goodly crowd there, and there was no shortage of contributions by way of prayers, readings, testimonies, etc. One man stood up to tell his story. He said he had been a wife-beater, a drunk, a child moles-

ter, a cheat, etc. When he was finished he announced to all and sundry that he wanted to publicly thank God here tonight that, during all those years, he had not lost his religion! He may not have brought Jesus to others, but...

CHRISTMAS DAY

Gospel: Midnight: Luke 2:1-14
Dawn: Luke 2:15-20
Morning: John 1:1-18

Theme (of Morning Gospel)

Today's gospel is pure poetry. It is as if John just opened his mouth, and poured out all the joy, wonder, and gratitude within his heart. It is a summary of the gospel, of Incarnation, and of the blessings that Jesus' coming has brought us. The other gospels give us some glimpses of that joy, whether it's with angels, shepherds, etc.

Parable

When I think of today's gospel, I think of a friend of mine who is an artist. What I associate most with her work is her extraordinarily effective use of colour. Her most abstract painting would hold your attention, as you study the shades, highlights, and interplay of colour, all resting peacefully with each other, and combining to present a kaleidoscope of colour. To me, John succeeds in doing that in today's gospel. It is a gospel I would have to read again and again, with pauses for reflection, before I would even begin to catch the beauty and the richness of it. It is interesting to reflect on just how many famous and priceless pictures of the stable, the shepherds, the star, etc,. there are throughout the world today. Many a gifted artist has endeavoured to capture that moment, and hold it before our eyes for reflection.

Teaching

Christmas is an occasion of genuine celebration for the Christian. It celebrates the fact that God came to dwell among us, and to journey the road of life with us. It marks the beginning of our journey to redemption and salvation. It is a time when freedom is announced to captives, and when new hope is offered to those who sit in darkness, bereft of all hope.

John's gospel is like the backdrop to the accounts of Luke. Luke is the only writer who gives us some detail of the birth of Jesus. He tells us about there being no room in the inn, and how it happened that Jesus came to be born in a stable. One of his greatest gems is his account of the shepherds. The most important part of this story is that, even though they were told the good news by angels, they said 'Let us go to Bethlehem, and see for ourselves this news that the Lord has given us.' That journey to Bethlehem, to see for ourselves, is part of the journey of every Christian.

'He came onto his own, and his own received him not. But, for those who did receive him, he gave the right to become children of God. All they had to do was to trust him to save them.' Those sentences are at the centre of what today is all about. They was many a heart and home closed to him that first Christmas night, and that is still the case today. The greatest blessing for us, of course, is that we are given yet one more opportunity every moment of every day. Today's gospel is something that is happening for us today.

Response

It helps make the gospel more realistic and authentic if I remind myself that the gospel is now, and I am every person in it. This is my Christmas Day. It is as if I were born this morning, and this is my first opportunity to be alive on such a day. As I grow older, I will hear the story in school and in church. Sooner or later, however, like the shepherds, I must be ready and willing to 'go to Bethlehem, and see for myself'. That is a journey of faith, where I no longer believe something just because someone else told me. There is a story in the gospel about the woman at the well, who ran off, collected some of her friends, and brought them to meet Jesus. There is a very significant line at the end, when her friends turned to her and said 'Now we believe, not because you told us, but because we have met him ourselves.'

By coming here to church (or by reading this now!), you are showing that you have your priorities right. Jesus is the reason for the Season. With all the hoopla that surrounds Christmas today, when the ads on the telly begin months in advance, it is difficult to keep the priorities right. By all means have a good day, have a good dinner, and enjoy whatever gifts you receive. The whole concept of Christmas is based on gift, and on giving. The Father gives us the greatest gift he possibly could give us. Jesus comes to give us life, redemption, and salvation for our sins. When I buy something that is a gift for another, I always make sure that the price-tag is removed. God's gifts have no price-tags. A gift, by definition, is something that is free.

The door of the human heart has but one handle, and that is on the inside. The human heart is the manger of today. For all the hearts and homes that have been closed against Jesus since that first Christmas night, we open up our hearts to him today. This is a day when we receive gifts, and it would be odd, indeed, if we failed to accept the greatest gift of all. Much of what we receive as gifts are toys, food, or clothes. The time will come when the toys are broken, the food is eaten, and the clothes are worn. The gift of Jesus in our lives is on-going and eternal.

Practical

Part of the ritual of being present at a Christmas Mass, especially for those with children, is to pay a visit to the crib. These few moments can be a time for heart-felt prayer. They can also provoke and evoke some serious reflection to carry into our day. Whether you have children with you or not, I would suggest that you spare a minute or two to visit the crib. All of us have spent many an idle moment staring at all the goodies in the shop windows over the past few weeks. Surely, then, the crib deserves a few moments of our time.

Of all the gifts we may give or receive today, it is important to remember that the greatest gifts in our lives are people. We don't throw our Christmas presents in the bin because we don't like the wrapping in which they came. We often, however, judge and reject people by the colour of their skin, how they dress, their age, or some other external dimension.

While I wish you a 'Happy Christmas', what I really mean is that you, as a Christian, may be a great source of love and blessing in the lives of others today. This is a special day, and, in a way, it gives us some clue to what every other day should/could be like. For those of us who want, every day is Christmas Day. Today can be what you want it to be. It can be a genuine Christian celebration, when I experience, and pass on to others, the blessings of this time. It is an opportunity not to be missed. Make the most of it.

Story

The following story is told by a mother as having actually happened to her:

It was Sunday, Christmas. Our family had spent the holiday in San Francisco with my husband's parents, but, in order to be back for work on Monday, we found ourselves driving the 400 miles back to Los Angeles on Christmas Day. We stopped for lunch. The restaurant was nearly empty. We were the only family, and ours were the only children. I heard Erik, my one-year-old,

squeal with glee. 'Hithere', the two words he always thought
were one. 'Hithere', and he pounded his fat baby hands –
whack, whack, whack – on the metal high chair. His face was
alive with excitement, his eyes were wide open, gums bared in a
toothless grin. He wriggled and giggled, and then I saw the
source of his merriment. I gasped with shock, as my mind
couldn't take it in all at once.

A tattered rag of a coat, obviously bought by someone else
aeons ago, dirty, greasy, and worn; baggy pants; spindly body,
toes that poked out of would-be shoes, a shirt that had ring-
'round-the-collar all over, and a face like none other, with gums
as bare as Erik's.

'Hi, there, baby! Hi there, big boy! I see you buster!' My husband and I were mortified and embarrassed, and we suggested
that we should leave. Just then our meal arrived. The banging
and the noise continued. Now the old bum was shouting across
the room. 'Do you know 'peek-a-boo'? Hey, look, he knows
peek-a-boo!' Erik continued to laugh, and to answer 'Hithere!'
Every call was echoed. Nobody thought it was funny. The guy
was a drunk and a disturbance. I was embarrassed. My husband, Denis, was furious. Even our six-year-old asked 'Why is
that old man speaking so loudly?'

Denis went to pay the bill, telling me to meet him in the parking lot, with the children. 'Lord, just let me get out of here before
he speaks to me or to Erik', I whispered, as I bolted for the door.
It soon was obvious that both the Lord and Erik had other plans.
As I drew closer to the man, I turned my back, walking to side-
step him, and any air he might be breathing. As I did so, Erik, all
the while with his eyes fixed on his new-found friend, leaned
over my arm, reaching with both hands to a baby's pick-me-up
position. In a spilt second of balancing my baby, and turning to
counter his weight, I came eye-to-eye with the old man.

Erik was lunging for him, arms spread wide. The bum's eyes
both asked and implored 'Would you let me hold your baby,
mam?' There was no need for me to answer, since Erik propelled
himself from my arms to the man's. Suddenly a very old man
and a very young baby were embraced in love. Erik laid his tiny
head against the man's ragged shoulder. The man's eyes closed,
and I could see tears hover beneath the lashes. His aged hands,
full of grime, and pain, and hard labour, gently, so gently, cradled my baby's bottom, and stroked his back. I stood awe-
struck. The old man rocked and cradled Erik in his arms for a

moment, and, then his eyes opened, and set squarely on mine. He said, in a firm commanding voice, 'You take good care of this baby, mam'. And, somehow I managed 'I will' from a throat that contained a stone.

He pried Erik from his chest, unwillingly, longingly, as though he were in pain. I held my arms open to receive my baby, and, again the man spoke: 'God bless you, mam, and thank you. You have given me my Christmas gift.' I said nothing more than a muttered 'Thanks.' With Erik in my arms, I ran for the car. Denis was wondering why I was crying, why I was holding Erik so tightly, and why I was whispering 'My God, forgive me. Lord, please, please forgive me.'

Erik is the Jesus I'm speaking about today. Are you willing to let him hug you?

FIRST SUNDAY AFTER CHRISTMAS (THE HOLY FAMILY)

Gospel: Luke 2:41-52

Theme
Today's gospel is about the loss of Jesus, and how he was found in the Temple. It is a simple story, but there are some beautiful and simple lessons in it. We can strongly identify with Mary and Joseph, because we have all experienced that sense of loss from time to time.

Parable
One of my earliest memories of my mother's simple piety was to watch her while she searched for something she had lost. St Anthony was called in straightaway, and, if the object was found, she owed Anthony a few bob! While involving St Anthony, however, her audible prayer was 'Jesus was lost, Jesus was found. Jesus was lost, Jesus was found … etc.' It was like a mantra, but she was completely convinced that the outcome would be good. (I must confess that, when my own back was to the wall, and I had lost something precious, I just swallowed my pride, and repeated her mantra!).

Teaching
This is a lovely little human story, with profound lessons. Jesus is a personal God. He is actually among us, as real as you or I. I may not be aware of his presence, I may not see any evidence of his presence; I may not hear his voice, or have any sense of personal association with him. I just presume he is somewhere within the community. It may be some consolation to all of us to remind ourselves that Mary and Joseph made that mistake! They presumed he was somewhere in the crowd, and they arrived home before they realised he was not with them. (When a little boy in school was asked what Mary and Joseph did then, with total conviction, he replied 'They went down to the Temple and said three Hail Marys to St Anthony'!).

Today's gospel lifts the veil a little bit for us. What seemed a very ordinary little lad is found in the Temple discussing profound questions with the experts of the day. One of my earliest memories as a child is a sense of great joy that he was able to put these know-alls in their place! I really don't see any good reason why this should have happened in the first place. One possibility

I can accept is that only God can do God things. Only God can speak God's word, and reveal his mind. In that case then, it matters little how young or how old the speaker is, because it is God speaking through them. 'Out of the mouths of infants thou hast perfected praise.' I certainly don't think that Jesus was fully aware of his mission yet, no more than I was when I was twelve. I think this would have been a gradual revelation, through his baptism in the Jordan, and his many hours of prayers with the Father on the mountain-side at night.

When Jesus told Mary and Joseph that he had to be about his Father's business, they didn't understand what he meant. Immediately, however, he resumed his normal place within the family, and, as a family, they got on with life, like any normal family. We are told that Jesus grew up to be what we would describe as a very likeable young man, 'beloved of God, and of those who knew him.' Even on a human level, with the parents he had, it would be difficult to imagine anything else.

Response

It would be a mistake to think that Jesus, or, indeed, Mary and Joseph, really knew who Jesus was, and what his mission was. They were very ordinary people, who were destined for an extraordinary mission. Mary never wrestled with mystery. We are told that 'she kept these thoughts, and pondered them in her heart.' Time, in reflection and prayer, would unveil all the mystery. She didn't claim any inside track with God. She always waited for the Spirit to make the first move.

Later in life, Jesus showed a great zeal about the Temple, and he went there on a regular basis. Tradition has it that Mary would have almost been reared in the Temple. It was a place towards which religious Jews felt a natural gravitation. On the occasion of today's gospel Mary, Joseph, and Jesus were there for the Passover festival. They seemed to be very strict about all the Jewish traditions, as we see in the stories regarding the Presentation in the Temple, the circumcision, etc. It is interesting to see how Jesus will seek to challenge the authenticity of some of those festivals, at a later date, and how he will clear the Temple of much of its 'merchandising', with his whip of cords.

Jesus is a personal God. It is not enough to assume or presume that he is somewhere in the Community. Throughout the gospel, his questions are quite direct and personal 'Who do you say that I am? Will you also go away? Do you love me? ...' There is a way in which I immerse myself in the community, so that I am deeply aware of his presence. As a church, we provide the body, and he provides the Spirit. If the Spirit of God is present and active within the community, then, surely, I should have some personal sense of that.

Practical
The most consistent way to deal with the gospels is to see each event as something that is happening now, and to see myself as being every person in it. As a Christian, I travel the road of life with Jesus. Sometimes I lose sight of him, and, like the disciples on the road to Emmaus, I fail to recognise him. When he walked on water, his apostles thought he was a ghost, and at the tomb, Mary Magdalene thought he was a gardener. 'In this is eternal life, to know you, the one true God, and Jesus Christ whom you have sent.' This was the prayer of Jesus to his Father. He also says 'I am the good shepherd; I know mine, and mine know me.'

The mystics and spiritual writers often refer to the 'Dark Night of the Soul'. It is a time of inner darkness, when I have absolutely no sense of God's presence at all. St Thérèse of Lisieux spent long periods in this darkness towards the end of her life. It was her crucifixion, and, like Jesus on the cross, she could cry out 'My God, my God, why have you forsaken me?' We can easily get bothered when we lose this sense of God; we blame ourselves, and become troubled with guilt.

The last paragraph of today's gospel speaks about what we call the 'Hidden Life' of Jesus. These were the years up to the age of thirty, before he began his public mission. His life is very ordinary. In fact, when he began to preach and work miracles, those who grew up with him in Nazareth were puzzled, and said 'Where did this man get all this power? We have known him and his family, and he's just one of ours.' Most of our lives are very ordinary and everyday. It is at such times that the Kingdom grows within us. Jesus speaks of the farmer sowing the seed, and then moving away, and letting the earth do the rest. The Kingdom of God is built up by countless tiny acts, most of which are hidden. 'Life is what happens when you're making other plans.'

Story
When I was growing up in the country, there was a man who was classified as being 'simple'. He was to be found in the front row of church, chapel, Orange hall, or 'meeting house'. One day he was on the main street of the local town, listening to an evan-

gelist preacher, who addressed all who cared to listen from the back of a truck. He was talking about 'finding the Lord'. Our friend was at the front of the crowd, and he had his usual vacant grin, which the preacher may have interpreted as some sort of religious trance! Anyhow, as he thumped his bible, he turned to our friend, and asked him 'And you, sir, have you found the Lord?' To which our friend replied 'Naw. Have ya lost him?'

For once in his life, our friend was brilliant...

SECOND SUNDAY OF CHRISTMAS

Gospel: John 1:1-18

Theme

This gospel is pure poetry. It is as if John opened his mouth, and let the Spirit of God within him pour out the sparks of the furnace within his heart. It is hard to grasp the profound nature of what he writes, compared to the letters he wrote at the end of his life, which can be summarised in one sentence: 'Little children, let us love one another, because God loves us.' This is written with the total conviction of who Jesus is, why he came, and what happens if we are open to his message. At the end of his gospel, John will have to admit that, if he wrote down all the things Jesus did and said, the whole world couldn't contain all the books. John is known as the beloved disciple, and it is obvious that his heart is overflowing with love, gratitude, and joy, because of the Jesus about whom he is to write in the following pages of his gospel.

The heart of the message is that Jesus came to his own, the Jews, but they did not accept him. The message is now offered to all of us, and, for those of us who do accept it, Jesus will allow us full membership within the family of God. This privilege is pure gift, and has nothing to do with merit, birth-right, or achievement.

Parable

When I was a kid we had a popular song for all singalongs called 'All me granny has left you is her old armchair'. It was about the jeers and sneers of family members directed against the one who was left an old armchair, while they shared her house and property. The part of the song that always gave me great joy was when the one who received the chair discovered that all of granny's savings were carefully concealed within the chair, and, that he turned out to be the lucky one; something that wiped the sneers off the faces of the others, and filled them with a jealous rage.

A poor way to illustrate today's gospel, but I'm sure you get the idea. In John's day, for example, Jesus had left them nothing tangible beyond the memory of a man who had died as a public criminal, and, I'm sure, in the eyes of John's family, he was seen

34

to be really foolish to have followed such a one, and he deserved
nothing but disdain.

Teaching
I like the following statement: 'For those who do not understand, no words are possible, and for those who do understand,
no words are necessary.' That is part of John's problem in
today's gospel. While he witnessed Jesus healing the blind, he
himself had come to see much clearer. All of the miracles Jesus
worked for him were within him. Jesus was, indeed, the light
that had come into the world, and, John, as one of his followers,
had been handed the torch to carry that light to others. John the
Baptist was not the light, nor is John the Evangelist claiming that
he is the light. The role of one was to prepare the way; the role of
the other was to proclaim the message, and guide others to the
Way, which is Jesus.

From the very beginning, Jesus was not accepted. John
would later write in one of his letters 'You are children of God.
Only those who are of God will listen to his voice. The proof that
the word is from God is that the world will not listen to it.' The
Word became flesh... Word can mean many things. It can be a
word in a dictionary: it can mean a message as in 'Did you get
any word from John yet?'; it can mean a promise as in 'I give you
my word on that.' Jesus is the Word of God, he is God's message, God's statement, God's promise. Jesus wants decisions,
not discussions. 'You are either for me or against me' he said.
One of the ways of not getting around to doing something is to
talk about it long enough. Debates and discussions can turn the
flesh back into word again, and, what is a reality, becomes a the-
sis or a theory; something involving mental assent, which has
nothing whatever to do with faith.

The Law was given through Moses, and, by the time Jesus
came along, the people were totally hamstrung by the love of
law. This law was studied and taught by the Scribes, imposed by
the Pharisees, and scrupulously obeyed by the people. Jesus
came to replace this love of law with the law of love. John is really
excited about that, as we see in the last paragraph of today's
gospel. Many years later, as an old man in exile on the island of
Pathmos, he had simplified the gospel message to one simple
truth: 'Little children, let us love one another, because God loves
us.' (Do you remember hearing words like that from Mother
Teresa?)

Response

There are none so deaf as those who don't want to hear. You could be sitting there wondering what I'm going to say, while I'm up here wondering what you're going to hear, and we can all forget that only God can speak God's word, and only those who want to hear will actually hear that message.

There are two parts to the history of salvation: What Jesus did, and whether we accept that or not. He came to his own, but they weren't interested. For you, for me, for any or all of us gathered here today, however, it is our moment of decision. The only YES God is interested in is my YES of now. I cannot live today on a YES that was said on my behalf at my Baptism. For those who did receive him he gave the right to become children of God. All they had to do was to trust him to save them. That is the offer that is made to us today. God doesn't give me anything; He offers me everything.

In the beginning was the Word... John also knows only too well that, at the end, the Word will still be there. Jesus is the Alpha and the Omega, the beginning and the end. In other words, no matter whether people accept or reject his word, no matter what way the world chooses to behave, no matter how bad things might appear, at the end of time Jesus will be Lord; the kingdom of this world and the kingdom of Satan will have come to an end, and there will only be the Kingdom of God, which Jesus came to establish. (It is significant that the last Sunday of the church calendar is the Feast of Christ the King). It's like knowing the result of the race before you go into the bookies. You can have no excuse for not being on a winner. God won't send you anywhere when you die. Rather will he eternalise the decisions and directions you take now.

Practical

Give some serious thought today to the YES of your Baptism, to ensure that you personally have taken full responsibility for it, and that you are a member of the Christian family by deliberate choice, and not by some coincidence or accident of birth.

If the Word becomes flesh, if Jesus takes on our human nature, then, surely, he has taken on your human nature. This should lead to some serious reflection along the following lines: If Jesus has taken on my human condition, then I am faced with a serious situation. He can take over and effect only that which I allow, and the limits to what he can do in and through me, are set by me. The implications of such a possibility are frightening. There is nothing automatic about God. He will not enter where he is not welcome. And he needs my goodwill as the foundation for all his work in me. Did you hear about the man whose beard went on fire, and he prayed it would start raining? He himself wasn't prepared to do anything …

Story
There once was a little boy who wanted to meet God. He knew it was a long way to where God lived, so he packed his rucksack with biscuits, several cans of coke, and he set off on his journey. When he had gone about three blocks he saw an elderly lady. She was sitting on a park bench, watching the pigeons. The boy sat down next to her, and opened his rucksack. He was about to take a drink from a can of coke when he noticed that the little old lady looked hungry, so he gave her a few biscuits. She gratefully accepted, and smiled at him. Her smile was so wonderful that he wanted to see it again, so he offered her a can of coke as well. Once again she smiled at him. The boy was delighted.

They sat there all afternoon, eating and smiling, without saying a word. As it began to grow dark, the boy realised how tired he was, and that it was time for him to go home. He got up to leave, but before he had gone no more than a few steps, he turned around, ran back to the old woman, and gave her a big hug. She gave him her biggest smile ever.

When the boy arrived home, his mother was surprised by the look of joy on his face. She asked 'What has made you so happy today?' He replied 'I had lunch with God'. Before his mother could respond, he added 'And you know what? She's got the most beautiful smile in the whole world.'

Meanwhile, the old lady, also radiant with joy, returned to her home. Her son was stunned by the look of peace on her face. He asked 'Mother, what has made you so happy today?' She replied 'I ate biscuits and drank coke with God in the park today.' And before her son could reply, she added 'And you know, he is much younger than I expected!'

Not everybody recognised Jesus when he came …

BAPTISM OF THE LORD

Gospel: Luke 3:15-16, 21-22

Theme

Today's gospel witnesses to the handing over of the mission from John the Baptist to Jesus. No, John was not the Messiah, Jesus was. Both the Father and the Spirit bore witness to that fact.

Parable

For those of us who have grown up with the experience of infant Baptism, it is that little bit more difficult to grasp the immense significance of the Sacrament. Baptism was intended for adults only. In the time of Jesus, it had to do with repentance, and turning from sin, which certainly should not be a call made to new-born babies! I had the privilege of bringing groups on pilgrimage to the Holy Land on several occasions. One of the highlights of our trip was a Service of Reconciliation on the banks of the Jordan river, after which each person (appropriately dressed!), was fully immersed in the waters of the river for the forgiveness of sin.

Teaching

Today's gospel is where the Saviour meets the sinners, where the Divine meets the human. Jesus joined the sinners at the river to be baptised. In other accounts, we have John protesting that it is Jesus who should be baptising him. John was a prophet, and, with the insight of the prophet, he went through with the ceremony. Immediately his action was confirmed from on high, and his best suspicions of Jesus were proven to be correct.

We are told that 'the heavens were opened'. This is significant in that it is a reversal of the effects of original sin, when the heavens were shut. When Jesus will have completed his mission on Calvary, we are told that the veil of the Temple was rent in two. In other words, we now could come into the Holy of Holies. The voice of the Father, and the visible presence of the Spirit was clear proof that full connection has been established between heaven and earth.

John made a very clear distinction between his form of Baptism, and the Baptism that Jesus would made available to us. John's baptism was for the forgiveness of sin. Jesus would baptise with the Holy Spirit and with fire. He would anoint us, make us holy, and enable us to share in the fullness of the Divine life.

Response

It is strange that Jesus had already spent thirty years on this earth by this time, with nothing extraordinary happening. He was being prepared for his mission, by living and experiencing the ordinary everyday hum-drum life of those around him. While being divine, he put his divinity to one side, and lived a full human existence. He would be guided by the Father in everything he said and did. He must have spent long periods in prayer, which, for him, was listening.

While he was preparing himself for his mission, John the Baptist was preparing the way for him. They were cousins, of the same age, and their first meeting was extraordinary, in that they both were in their mothers' wombs at the time of Mary's visit to Elizabeth. John's father, Zachary, prophesied about the coming Messiah. He said that he would visit those in darkness and in the shadow of death, and that he would guide our feet into the way of peace, so that 'free from sin, and saved from the hands of our foes, we might serve him in holiness and gladness all the days of our lives in his presence.'

At the beginning of creation, God took the clay, and breathed his Spirit into it. Once again, as in a new creation, the Spirit comes upon Jesus, and John tells us that Jesus will make this possible for every one of us. It is a new creation; it is salvation, which is not something I get when I die, but the grace to start again any day I choose. Being called to share in the life of divinity is to be called to share life with the Father, Son, and Spirit. All three persons of the Trinity are represented in today's gospel.

Practical

I conducted an adult education course recently, and the theme for eight nights was Baptism. Because most of us were baptised as infants, we discovered that we didn't know a great deal about Baptism. We knew the externals, the water, candles, oils, etc., but we had to spend quite a lot of time trying to come to grips with what Baptism really implies for any one of us. Quite a lot of our time was spent on prayer, reflection, and silences. This is mystery, and we depend totally on the Spirit to reveal this to us. One thing we did discover was it was time well spent, because our understanding of Baptism was the foundation of much of the rest of the gospel message.

Those of us who were baptised as infants had no input into the process. That is no longer an excuse today. I can renew the commitments of my Baptism any day I choose. My Baptism gives me certain rights. Through it I am enrolled in the family of God, and I am a member of God's Kingdom. The Kingdom now is what we call heaven later on. I could be greatly blessed if I renewed my Baptism commitment every single day.

My Baptism brings me under the Niagara of the Father's love. I, too, can hear the Father say of me 'This is my beloved child...' The Spirit is poured out upon me once again. I am anointed and empowered through my Baptism. I can sally forth into each day with the prayer 'Lord, may your Spirit within me today, touch the hearts of those I meet, either through the prayers I pray, the words I say, the life I live, or the very person that I am.' My Baptism gives me a whole new focus and purpose in life.

Story
A pig and a chicken were out for a walk one day. The pig wasn't too bright, and tended to repeat everything that others said or suggested. The chicken remarked 'Those are very nice people down in that house down there.' 'They are, indeed,' replied the pig, 'they are very nice people.' 'They are very good to us,' continued the chicken. 'They are, indeed,' replied the pig, 'they are very good to us.' 'Do you know what I was thinking?' asked the chicken. 'No,' said the pig. 'What were you thinking?' 'I was thinking that we should do something for them.' 'That's a very good idea,' replied the pig, 'I think we should do something for them. What did you have in mind?' 'I was thinking,' said the chicken, 'that we should give them something.' 'A brilliant idea,' said the pig, 'I think we should give them something. What did you have in mind?' 'I was thinking,' said the chicken, 'that we should give them bacon and eggs.' The pig quickly stopped in his tracks, and said 'Definitely not! For you that's only a slight inconvenience, but for me it's a total commitment!'

Baptism is intended to lead us to a total commitment, and our acts of Christian charity should be seen as anything but slight inconveniences.

FIRST SUNDAY OF LENT

Gospel: Luke 4:1-13

Theme

This is the story of the temptation of Jesus in the desert, a story which is included in the gospels for the first Sunday of Lent for Years A & B as well (cf.). Jesus has just been baptised. He has joined with public sinners in a very public place. He has taken upon himself the whole burden of human sin, evil, disobedience, and pride. Immediately he is tested by Satan, who will never, and who never does miss an opportunity to stop or destroy the good. Jesus was led by the Spirit into the desert, so the temptations, as it were, were part of his baptism. He had been baptised with water, and he would now be baptised with fire.

Parable

We are all familiar with times of testing. When we buy a new car, we insist on test-driving it. Soldiers and marines go through very severe tests before being sent to the battle zone. The whole process of training in any field of learning, be that medicine, science, religion, etc. contains an endless battery of tests that tell as much about the personality of the student, as it does about his knowledge of the subject. Every marriage has its testing times; those times when the level of commitment is put to the test, and where the strength of the bond of love is fully revealed, whether it be strong or weak. It is a fact of life that good will always be tested by evil. If an undertaking, which is purported to be good, doesn't come under attack of some kind from somewhere, then, its value should be reassessed. There is not a saint in heaven, or a truly great person on earth who has not, or does not attract some vicious slander, or find their paths strewn with obstacles. Jesus joins that group in today's gospel.

Teaching

Right from the beginning of his ministry, Jesus is immersed in his humanity. We are all familiar with being tempted. Temptations are tailor-made to our natural weaknesses. A temptation for one person would not be a temptation for another. From a very early age children show traits of character and personality flaws that are unique to each. With one lad, you could leave money lying around the place, and he would never think

41

of touching it. With another, you couldn't leave a thing out of your hand, for fear he might lift it. A bottle of whiskey would be too much for one person, while not holding the slightest interest for someone else. We are all uniquely different, and a temptation is like dangling something very attractive outside the windows of our souls, when such an item or thought appeals directly to some weakness within.

How does all of this apply to Jesus in today's gospel? As far as Satan was concerned, the whole purpose of the exercise was to discover if Jesus were God, or merely just an ordinary selfish, weak, human being. Straightaway I must stress that yes, Jesus was a human being just like the rest of us. The big difference is that he had the Spirit within, after his baptism in the Jordan river. This inner strength would be stronger than any human weakness. (This Spirit is now available to all of us, of course, but, back then, Jesus could not give that Spirit to others, because he himself had not yet overcome the evil one, and achieved the victory). St John says 'Little children, there is a spirit within you that is greater than any evil spirit you will meet on the road of life.' In today's gospel, Satan selected the three great human weaknesses of appetite, power, and pride. Jesus responded to each temptation in a way that would show the whole direction of his mission. He checked Scripture, and quoted what God had said. He himself had come to do the Father's will, and he was not prepared to do anything unless the Father told him. That is why he quoted the word of the Lord on each occasion, as a direct rebut to each of the temptations.

We are told in Scripture that Jesus was like us in all things but sin. He was tempted as we are, says Paul. He was accused of being a glutton, a drunkard, a friend of tax collectors and sinners, and someone with whom no religious Jew should have any contact. He never denied any of their accusations, but he challenged them 'Who can accuse me of sin?' He certainly experienced all of our human weaknesses. I honestly believe that if there is one single weakness within me that Jesus did not personally encounter, experience, and overcome, then I am outside the scope of salvation. Jesus came on earth to take care of the weeds among the good wheat, which God had sown, the weeds of sin, sickness, and death. He did battle with all three evils, and overcame them, one after another. Today's gospel marks the beginning of that battle.

Response

Jesus is our Moses, who leads us through the desert of life, through the Red Sea, into the Promised Land. Scripture tells us that Jesus came to do and to teach. He washed the feet of his disciples before he asked them to wash one another's feet. In Scott Peck's book *The Road Less Travelled*, he begins with the sentence 'Life is difficult'. He goes on to say that if we accept that fact, then, life won't be too bad, because we will not be surprised or taken unawares when it does get difficult. There are many tensions in life. I can experience the tension between what I want to do, and what I ought to do; between what I want and what I need; between how I am and how I think I should be. Learning to live with the tensions is the very essence of life. If you ever waken up some morning, and discover that your life is exactly the way it should be, then, please don't move … just wait for the undertaker!

Human appetites are good, and like everything else, they can be abused. There is a whole question of relationship here. Some people find it impossible to relate properly to alcohol, to food, to sex, to power, to wealth, etc. It is as if some power has taken over inside that propels them towards destruction, through addictions and compulsions. They experience a powerlessness, even if they refuse to admit it. In today's gospel, Jesus, literally, had the world at his feet. He wasn't depending on Satan for any of the power and the glory. He had come with a mission, and his mission was to set up the Kingdom on this earth. This Kingdom would be diametrically opposed to the kingdom of Satan, which is based on power, pleasure, and pride. Jesus taught us to pray to the Father 'The kingdom, the power, and the glory are yours…' In himself, and in his message, he was, indeed, a sign of contradiction, as Simeon had foretold about him.

If I look at the life of Jesus as my model for living, what can I learn from today's gospel? I certainly have my own share of temptations. When faced with a temptation, Jesus responded with a word from Scripture, with a directive from God, as to what he should do. I have something called a conscience, and it is part of who and what I am. I could write the Ten Commandments myself, without ever learning them at school. I know it is wrong to steal, to kill, to tell lies, to be jealous, or to be ungrateful. When I was a child, I had a dog that looked guilty whenever he did something wrong! Any parent can look at a three-year-old, and know that he has been up to something he shouldn't. The call of the gospel is a call to be honest, with my-self, with others, and with God. Only the truth will set us free. A temptation, by definition, is a lie. Adam and Eve fell for the lie in the Garden, and, as it were, came under new management. They hid, and we're hiding since. A bully is a coward when faced up to. So is it with temptations. If I take to myself the power of the Spirit which is mine through Baptism, then, I, like Jesus, will ex-ercise that full authority he speaks about. I have given you full authority over all the power of the evil one. Nothing shall harm you...

Practical

There is an ideal level of freedom to which some people aspire, and it includes the freedom to name, claim, and tame their demons. This begins with honesty to one's self, because the biggest lies I tell in life are the ones I tell myself. I can never hope to be honest with someone else until I begin to get honest with myself. Please take a few quiet moments today to reflect on how honest or dishonest you are with yourself. Selfishness, and self-will run riot, can justify anything...

Being totally honest with yourself, would you admit to an area of your life where you are in some form of bondage, whether that be an addiction, a relationship, a pattern of behav-iour, etc. Would you like to be free of that? One thing you just have to accept: on your own, you just don't stand a chance. This is where the Spirit and Power of God comes in. Remember that the Spirit led Jesus into the desert, and it was from that Spirit that his strength came. The Holy Spirit is like Popeye's spinach for all the many things that are impossible for us. There is noth-ing impossible with God.

The gospels provide us with a way of life, with a way of wholesome living. I think it should be necessary for the Christian to be familiar with the words and teachings of the gospels. Traditionally, Catholics have not been good at indepen-dent use of Scripture, because of the old fear of a too personal in-terpretation, or an inability to understand. Traditionally, the task of knowing and explaining the Scriptures was the preserve of the preacher and the teacher. That must not continue. In today's world, there are many excellent translations of the gospels available, from the larger editions to pocket editions. How am I to know the Scriptures if I never take the book in my hands? It would be a wonderful sign of growth in Christian maturity if I had my own copy of the gospels, and, on a regular basis, I took time out to read, and reflect on sections of it. Like Jesus, in today's gospel, I, too, will be able to face the temptations of life by referring to the teachings of Jesus. The Word of God is shot through with Power, and Satan is totally subject to the power of that word,

Story

Peter (not his real name) is an alcoholic. He himself compares alcoholism to travelling on a train or bus, where I have a choice of getting off at any one of the stops or stations, or of continuing right on to the terminus. Peter continued drinking till he reached the terminus. He lost his wife, children, home, job, and, eventually, he lost everything else, from self-respect to the will to live. He ended up sleeping in doorways, stealing whatever or wherever he could, or begging for a few pence from passers-by, totally immune to the looks of scorn or disapproval he received from them. He had a wild beard, and a mop of shaggy, dirty, tangled hair, and he smelled to the high heavens. One Saturday afternoon, he was sitting on a footpath, propped up against a lamppost, with the remains of a bottle of cheap wine in one hand, and the other hand held out to passers-by. A young woman passed by, turned around, and put a 50p coin on his hand. She then continued her journey. Peter was rivetted with a sudden flash of recognition. It was his own daughter, and she hadn't recognised him. He tried to call out, or to stand up, and he could do neither. He literally crawled around the corner on all fours, and into the parking lot behind the building. Then he fell on his face, and cried out to God from the depth of his soul 'Please, please help me!'

Something happened right then, and he doesn't know to this day what exactly it was. To make a long story short that was over twenty-five years ago and Peter hasn't had a drink since. He struggled to a hospital, and had himself admitted to the unit for alcoholics, where he dried out. Over the years since then, he regained everything. His wife has died recently, and his whole life is taken up with his four daughters and six grandchildren. You wouldn't be speaking to him for two minutes before you'd be shown photographs of the children. It is said that if you want to really appreciate something, have it taken away from you, and then returned.

Peter is one of the most convinced people I know about the Power of God that is within all of us. Because of his experience, he is afraid of nothing, and is prepared to take on the world. His God is real, tangible, and accompanying. His faith is certainly not in himself, and if you attempted to compliment him, he will quickly remind you of what his life was like when he was in charge. Through his recovery programme, based totally on spirituality, he knows where the power is, where God takes over, and does for us what we never could do for ourselves. He likes to say 'The only difference between me and all the other bums is that I know where the bread is.'

SECOND SUNDAY OF LENT

Gospel: Luke 9:28-36

Theme
On this Second Sunday of Lent each year the gospel is always about the Transfiguration of Jesus, of which we have several accounts in the gospels. Today's account is from St Luke. Once again, we read of Jesus bringing Peter, James, and John to one side. We are told that Jesus was praying, which seemed to be quite a familiar scene to the apostles who accompanied him. This time, however, something happened. The veil was lifted, and they got a glimpse of the divinity of Jesus. Moses and Elijah appeared to him, and they seemed to be talking together. Peter, as usual, was right in there with a suggestion: This scene is so beautiful, that he wanted to build some sort of accommodation so that they could continue to live there. Moses and Elijah disappeared, however, and, in the midst of some sort of dark cloud, they heard the Father's voice announcing 'This is my Son, the Beloved. Listen to him'. Everything then returned to normal, and the apostles kept the event a secret for a long time after it happened.

Parable
After Mass each morning, Padre Pio used go up to the gallery in the church, where he spent a long time in silent prayer. There was something about the way he prayed, and his whole demeanour during prayer, that people flocked just to watch him. He was totally unaware of this, but, on the occasions when he became aware, he was very annoyed, and he pointed to the tabernacle as the place to which their attention should be directed. We have all come across these occasions when someone seemed to be in such deep meditation, that we felt guilty if we had to intervene and distract them. We feel we are in the presence of someone who is in the Presence of Someone, and that someone is God. Moses was told to remove his shoes, because the ground on which he walked was holy ground. There are people who can go into a church and just sit there, without saying a word. They experience a quiet tranquillity, and a sense of God there, and, like Peter in today's gospel, they just want to stay there.

Teaching

Coming aside is one way of thinking of prayer. It is those pockets of silence we find in our busy schedules, and it can occur in the midst of throngs. It is good, though, to come aside on a regular basis, to be alone. It is not easy to be alone, because I am never less alone than when alone. It can be so much easier to become aware of God's presence when I take time out to be alone. I think it is reasonable to say that Jesus was a very busy man. The amount of work and travel he packed into his three years of public ministry is phenomenal. Yet, again and again in the gospels, we are told that we went aside for long periods of time, and, on other occasions, he brought a few, or all, of his apostles to a place of quiet where they could be alone.

Jesus had come with a mission. Part of that mission was to fulfil the promises of the prophets, and to complete the work of God's leaders from a previous era. It makes sense that he should be seen in the same cameo as Moses and Elijah, because there was a very direct connection. Moses was the lawgiver, and Elijah was the prophet, and Jesus had come to complete the work of both. The entrance of the Father's voice into the scene is as if the Father was so pleased that he could not hold back his pleasure and approval for what he witnessed. By comparison with the view the Father had, the vision of the apostles was very dim and dull indeed. However, it is hard to imagine that one could spend much time in the presence of Jesus without getting a glimpse of something very unique, and of coming to experience a deep sense of awe and reverence in his presence.

The first thirty years of Jesus' life is what we call his hidden life. We know little or nothing about those years. From a human point of view it was so ordinary that those who knew him then were amazed when he began to display a power that was out of the ordinary. On the other hand, because he had come to do the Father's will in everything, and because he never said anything unless the Father told him, it is reasonable to presume that he spent a great deal of that time listening to the Father, which is the essence of prayer. Prayer is much more about listening than speaking. Speak, Lord, your servant is listening, and not Listen, Lord, your servant is speaking. The apostles saw Jesus perform some very impressive signs and miracles, from calming the storm, to healing the blind, to raising the dead. Yet, in the final analysis, when they were alone with him, they simply asked 'Lord, teach us to pray…' To be with him when he prayed, and to see the priority he gave to prayer, must have stood out as being high in the impression he made on them, and in the influence he exerted on them.

Response
It can be difficult to find time for prayer. That is true, but it can be so much more difficult if I don't understand what prayer is, and what I'm supposed to be doing at such times. Let us look at what we do know. Prayer is a relationship, and continuing in prayer is to deepen and strengthen that relationship. Life itself it all about relationships, and there is not a problem in life that is not a relationship one. I am not getting on too well with God, with others, or with myself. Building a relationship requires time and effort. It requires a lot of listening, and a lot of honest sharing. It is built on mutual trust and respect, and it is dynamic, in so far as, if it's not going forward, then, you can be sure, it's going backwards.

I believe that each one of us feels called to come aside from time to time, to reflect on our lives, to get in touch with our inner selves, and to listen to our inner voice. In the rat-race of today, it might be difficult to hear that call, to admit to hearing that call, and, especially to making the time to answer that call. Such goings-aside were very much part of the training of the apostles. It was at such times they saw him transfigured, as in today's gospel, or they saw him in agony in Gethsemane. It was at such times that he explained the parables to them, and he taught them to pray. It is very difficult in today's world to get a few moments of quiet, on one's own. Every kitchen has a radio playing, there's a TV on in the living room, and, as people walk around, many of them carry walkmans, and have earphones on their heads. (Could these things be called brain by-passes?!)

God's real work in our hearts is done in the very ordinary events of life. Peter wanted to build a structure so they could stay on the mountain. He enjoyed the rapture and the glimpse of glory. The building of the kingdom of God, however, has two characteristics. It is made up of very small acts, which are largely hidden, like the grain of mustard seed Jesus spoke about. Jean Vanier, one of the well-known Christians in today's world, said that the quiet prayers and actions of totally unknown people bring about the greatest movements for good in the history of the world. We all have a part to play in this, and every one of us can, and must make a contribution to this work. If I really want peace in the world, then, I must begin with my own heart. It is

from there that Jesus can begin to bring peace to those around
me.

Practical
Martin Luther King spoke of having been to the mountain. This
is a way of saying that, like Moses, he had gone to meet God,
and from there he could get a much clearer view of what was
happening on the ground below. Life is like a beautiful tapestry,
but the view I have is from underneath, where all I can see are
threads going every which way. Only God can see the other
side, and appreciate the beauty of the scene. Only if I spend
some time with God, only if I am prepared to go down into my
heart, in moments of quiet, will I ever get a glimpse of the God-
view of things. We live in a very materialistic world, where time
is of the essence, and achievement is the name of the game.
Wasting time with God would be one way to describe prayer. In
any meaningful relationship I have, I must surely find time to
waste with and for the other. A time when nothing is actually
achieved, but a time which is truly precious.

Did you ever ask yourself if you like your own company?
Are you at ease with yourself? The surest way of driving someone insane is to lock that person in solitary confinement long
enough. A life without reflection is not worth living. If you believe in Incarnation, then, no matter where you go, no matter
where you are, Jesus is there with you. The kingdom of God is
within you. Sometimes we hear of an alcoholic doing what is
called a geographic. 'If I go to live in Canada or Australia, everything will be different.' Unfortunately, what is within also travels to that new place, and life there becomes all too like the life
that was before. On the other hand, no matter where I go, or
where I am, the Spirit of God is within me. I don't have to go
aside to find the Lord. Rather I go aside, so that, in the silence
and quiet, the Lord may find me. He may get my attention, and
have access to my heart. Then, and only then, will I experience
just how present he is in my life.

If you get a chance, sometime, just check on your priorities. I
mean take any twenty-four hours out of a week, and see where
most of your time and money went. You may not discover anything very startling, but it may help point to your order of priorities. We all know how easy it can be to arrange our schedule so
that we can watch Coronation Street or a football match on television. The more important the attraction is to us, the more ef-

fort will go into ensuring that it is not neglected. I ask you, please, to give serious consideration to taking a few moments out of the busiest day to be alone with the Lord. In the past, it was easy to slip into a church on the way to work, or on the way home. Nowadays, unfortunately, most churches are locked during the day. This means that I just have to find another special place, which I might well call my prayer place. It might be in a room, in a particular armchair, sitting in a car, or when I'm out for a walk. Don't worry about what to say at such times. Just show up, be there, and, as in today's gospel, let Jesus reveal his presence to you.

Story
The young mother, with her little four-year old son, called into the church. She was saying her prayers, while he was running around investigating everything in sight. He pointed to a statue and wanted to know who that was. His mother told him that was Holy God. To another such question the mother said that it was Holy God's mother. Finally he made his way into the sanctuary, where the light was streaming through the stain-glass windows. He held out both arms, as he moved backward and forwards, fascinated by the colours that were reflected on this hands and clothes. He looked up at the windows, and asked his mother who they were, and she said that they were the saints.

The following day, in play-school, the teacher was telling them about the saints. He got all excited, as he interrupted her to tell her that he knew who they were. When asked who they were, his answer was very simple, and given with great confidence 'They're the ones who let the light shine through'.

Today's gospel gives us a glimpse of Jesus' glory, but it also shows the possibility for every Christian, who is called to reflect the face of Christ to others.

THIRD SUNDAY OF LENT

Gospel: Luke 13:1-9

Theme

In today's gospel, Jesus is trying to draw his hearers into the middle of things. Rather than looking on, and debating why this is happening, or why that happened, he asks them to look at themselves, at their own situation, and become more concerned with what's happening or not happening there. He uses an illustration to show them how many chances they are getting, how patient and tolerant God is with them. He goes on to say that this will not go on indefinitely, and that, sooner or later, they will be responsible, and will be held responsible for what they have done, and for what they have failed to do.

Parable

My own mother could always be drawn on an incident that happened to her, as she tended the garden. She liked gardening, and, within reason, she could be said to have had green fingers. She had her own favourite plants and flowers, and these were always in a place that was in full view of all passers-by. One year she had a real problem with a row of sweet-pea she had sown. They appeared above ground, but never showed any hope that they were going to come to anything. She gave them her attention every single day, buying nutrients for them, watering them regularly, and adjusting the rods that help keep them in an upward position. Despite her best efforts, they continued to remain sickly, forlorn, and, indeed, a serious blotch on her otherwise well-kept garden. One day, in total frustration, she just pulled them all up, and threw them over the hedge into an adjoining field. She replaced them with some other species of flower. And here's where the analogy with today's gospel ends! Imagine her amazement, then, when, some weeks later, she was in the adjoining field, and her attention was drawn to a beautiful selection of very pretty and very healthy sweet-peas, growing close to the hedge, just beside her front garden. To the day she died she wondered just how that could have happened. I myself don't have the answer. All I know is that something happened, something changed, and the result was totally different.

Teaching

Salvation is a word that is often used in connection with the work and mission of Jesus. It is not exactly the same as Redemption, which means to buy back something or someone who is enslaved, owned, or in bondage to another. Salvation is not something I get when I die. It is the grace I get to start again any time I so choose. This is a vital concept for us, because, as humans, we will always continue to fail and to fall. If there was no such thing as salvation, then when we fall, we would stay down, and there would be no come-back. St Augustine says that our glory consists not in never falling, but in getting up every time we fall. To get up and start again is heaven; to stay down is hell.

Jesus compares himself to a vine, and we are the branches. The branches draw their life from the vine, and it is the branches that produce the fruit. He said that we didn't choose him, but he chose us, and he appointed us to bear fruit, fruit that would re-main. Today's gospel speaks about a fig tree that did not pro-duce fruit. Producing fruit was the whole reason and purpose of it being planted in the first place. God gives me nothing for my-self. He doesn't give me my gift of speech to go around talking to myself! As a Christian, I am called into the service of others. It is in giving that I myself receive. There are three groups in every society. There is a small group that cause things to happen. There is a larger group that watch things happening. And then there's the largest group who haven't a clue what's happening! Christianity is more about walking the walk than talking the talk. It is about action, and not just ideas.

It is never too late for God. The only 'yes' in my life that God is interested in is my 'yes' of now. He is totally a God of now. 'I am who am.' In today's gospel, the fig tree is given every oppor-tunity, and more and more time, in the hope that it might pro-duce fruit, and give some return for the work put into its cultiva-tion. The gardener asks for one more year, for one more chance. Earlier we are told that the owner of the farm had come again and again to see if there was any fruit on it, but each time he was disappointed. Remember this is a parable, and not a true story. The reference to time is stressing a very lengthy time; something like a life-time. If the Father is the owner, and Jesus is the gar-dener, and we are the fig tree, then we can view the situation from three different view-points. While the Father is looking for some response, Jesus is pleading for one more chance, and we, on the other hand, may be happy to go along with the idea that, yes, we must do something, but not yet. Why do today what I can put off till to-morrow? All diets begin on Monday. Jesus tells other parables, like the one about the servants or the foolish virgins who were caught unawares when their master returned.

Response

The gospel is an invitation, with RSVP written all over it. Not to respond is, in itself, a response. Jesus says 'I will not have to judge them. The word I have spoken to them will be their judge. If I had not come and spoken to them, they would have an excuse for their sins.' By coming to church here this morning, there is some evidence of response on our part. Mere presence, of course, as you know, would not be enough, but, at least we have made a start.

Christianity is about walking the walk, and not just about talking the talk. Faith is not some sort of mental concept up in my head, like, for example, knowing that Jesus is God. Satan knows that too! Faith has more to do with my feet than with my head, when the message has come through the heart, down to the feet, that inspires some sort of stepping out, leading to Christianity in action. Remember, I am responsible for what I do, and for what I have failed to do.

The inspiration for this response is the work of the Holy Spirit. Just as Jesus was led by the Spirit into the desert, or into the Temple, so can I be led into actions, decisions, conversions, and renewal, when I am ready and willing to be led by the Spirit of truth. Notice I use the word ready, because, if I am ready, I will hear and heed the prompting of the Spirit; and if I'm not ready, I'll hear nothing, because there are none so deaf as they who don't want to hear.

Practical

Any one of us here can think of some one thing in our lives that we are going to get around to some time. Notice my use of the words get around to? Please give some thought to this, and, maybe, who knows, maybe, today I may head straight towards it, and do it!

Time and tide wait for no one. The clock ticks away. Mondays come, and the diets will all begin next Monday! The road to hell is paved with good intentions. I could well end up as someone who nearly did something worthwhile with my life. Life is now. Life is what's happening when you're making other plans.

Many of us remember Retreats when we were in school, or, perhaps occasionally since then. A Retreat is a time when I can get away from the ordinary everyday schedule of my life, and take time out for reflection, prayer, and teachings on the gospel message. It is important to remember that I can do this any day I wish. We all can find those few quiet moments for reflection. It is out of such times that a response can come to the message I hear. Finding the time is a test of how seriously I take the message of Jesus, and how real he is in my life. If I am too busy to have these times, then, in truth, I am too busy. Prayer is giving God time and space in my life. There will be no response from me if I don't take time out to listen to him.

Story

A man returned to his car in the parking lot of a supermarket, to discover that the side had been badly dented by some other car. Naturally, he was very upset. He was somewhat relieved, however, to see that there was a note under one of the wipers. At least, whoever was responsible had owned up, and there was a chance that the other person's insurance would take care of the damage. He opened the piece of paper, and it read 'The people who saw me bumping into the side of your car are watching me now. They think that I am leaving my name and address for you, when you arrive. They are wrong!'

Day after day after day, you and I can go through the motions...

FOURTH SUNDAY OF LENT

Gospel: Luke 13:1-3, 11-32

Theme

Today's gospel contains a core message of the teaching of Jesus, which we call the story of the Prodigal Son. It could also be called the story of the Forgiving Father. In itself it is a summary of the whole gospel. Please notice how today's gospel begins. All the outcasts of his day flocked around Jesus, and he welcomed them, and he sat down to eat with them. It was when the religious leaders complained about this that Jesus responded with this story. It was a very strong, a very brave, and a very clear response, that left them in no doubt about where he stood regarding such people. What really drew the wrath of the religious leaders was the implication that this was how God felt towards them also. It was this definite attitude of Jesus that brought about his death, because, in the eyes of the religious people of his day, this was reckless disregard for law.

Parable

Imagine the following scene in a court-room. There is a young man in the dock, charged with murder. In front of him sits a judge who will decide the appropriate punishment, if he is found guilty. To his right sits the jury, who will decide on his guilt or innocence. Around him are the legal eagles who will argue the law, with all of its sections and sub-sections, one trying to prove his guilt, and the other his innocence. In the main body of the court are journalists who are looking for a story with a catchy headline for the papers on the following day. Present also are the curious, drawn here to look at him, to listen to all the gory details, and to have some sort of Peeping-Tom role in the goings-on. In the back of the room sit his parents. They see everything everybody sees, and they hear everything everybody else hears. Try to imagine, if you can, the difference between what is going on in their hearts, and what is happening in the hearts of those around them. Their real pain lies, not in believing that he is innocent, but in knowing that, of all the people in the room, they are the only ones who would love to give him another chance. They experience powerlessness, because they have no role to play, their feelings are not part of the proceedings, and they desperately cling to the slimmest hope that, maybe, just maybe, their son may get another chance. Imagine their joy if the case was dismissed, and their son turns around to face them …

Teaching

If Jesus were on this earth for three minutes, instead of thirty-three years, he could have summarised his message through the use of this story. The Prodigal Son got it wrong, very wrong. To this day the Jews consider pigs as unclean. For this young man to end up feeding pigs was bad enough, but to end up sharing their food with them was Skid Row to the highest degree. This boy had really hit bottom, and, in human terms, there was no hope or future for him. There was one thing that saved him. He remembered. He remembered what it used to be like. This set in motion a whole line of thought that brought him to his senses. In other words, he opened his eyes and saw, he opened his ears and heard, he reached out his hand and touched his surroundings, and he smelt the stench of the situation in which he was. In other words he came to his senses.

He headed for home, for the only place where he had ever experienced love. The love was still there, and his father rushed out to meet him. No condemnation, no lectures, no scolding. Just a warm hug. The son had prepared a speech, but he had only begun when his words were swallowed in his father's embrace. A festive meal was prepared, he was dressed in the finest clothes, and, very significantly, his father ordered that he be given new sandals. The significance of this was that sandals were worn only when one headed off on a journey. This was the father's way of saying that the welcome was so unconditional that, if his son so chose, he could head off again on his travels.

And then there was the second son. A lot of people would feel sorry for this guy. After all, he had remained at home, had worked hard, had earned his crust, trying his best to be everything a son was supposed to be. One can understand his anger and his resentment. However, the father, who is love personified, while accepting that the son returning from the fields has been a good son, is quite definite that the son in most need is the one who should get the most attention. Because he is coming from the angle of real love, there is absolutely no question or discussion about which son deserves or does not deserve a celebration. Love is unconditional, it cannot be earned. Because the father in the story is intended to represent God the Father, there is a powerful message here for all of us. The lesson is so clear that it is one gospel that requires very little explanation. It does, however, require a very definite response.

Response

When Adam and Eve fell for the lie in the Garden, they came under new management. They came under the sway of the father of lies. One could imagine the gospel as Jesus running after them, inviting them to return to the Garden, where the Father has a big hug waiting for them, even if they have got pig's food all over their faces. The gospel is a message to all of us to come home; to come home to truth, to love, to forgiveness, to belonging to the family of God. For someone that could mean a complete turnabout of the direction in which their lives are going.

Coming home to God is to experience his hug, and to know that I belong. Conversion literally means to turn around in a different direction. It can happen to anyone that life can take a turn for the worse, and I can find myself turned back into myself, where my selfishness and self-will run riot is dictating the journey. When I become aware of this, like the Prodigal Son, I can come to my senses, and decide that there is no future for me down that particular road. The alcoholic in recovery knows all about this.

It is interesting to note that it is the son who stayed at home that causes the father most problems. In a way, he represents religious people, who have become self-righteous. The Pharisee, in another gospel story, tells God how good he is, and he then proceeds to compare himself to the publican, whom he looks upon as a sinner, and unworthy to be in the same place as himself. It is as if he would want God to expel the publican from the Temple, because he was not worthy to be there. Religion becomes dangerous and destructive when it leads to this kind of judgement and self-righteousness. Once again, I remind you, that this is exactly what Jesus is teaching in the story presented to us today.

One final thought: In the normal course of a lifetime, I may well find that, at various times, I have been the prodigal son at one stage, and the self-righteous son at another. The prodigal could well be lurking within me, awaiting my forgiveness. The love of the father is directed towards getting one to embrace the other. Make friends with your shadow.

Practical

I can put myself in the place of each person in today's story.

I can be the prodigal son. There may be areas in my life that are not compatible with being a member of the family of God. What am I going to do about it? With what decisions will that face me? If I really want to come home to the forgiving Father, and to experience his hug, then there are certain decisions I must make right now.

I can be the self-righteous brother. I may have the tendency to look down on someone else, because that person is not as good as me, or behaves in a way of which I disapprove. I may have cut myself off from a family member because of behaviour that I saw as bringing disgrace to the family. I have to ask myself, honestly, what the Father in today's gospel might have to say to me on that one.

I myself can be the forgiving Father. That is the ultimate target for the Christian. As I said earlier, I can be any one of the persons in today's story, and, no doubt, I have been one or both of the sons at various stages in my life, but being the forgiving father is the person I must strive to become. Experiencing my own forgiveness and rehabilitation with God can contribute enormously towards generating that same spirit of forgiveness within myself.

Story

I remember meeting a missionary priest, home on holidays, from Nigeria, where he had spent the previous twenty years. It was obvious he had a great love and respect for the people among whom he had lived and worked. On the first Saturday of each month a group of flying doctors arrived. The priests and his co-workers went out into the bush in their jeeps beforehand, and rounded up as many as they could find who were in need of medical attention. Because of the nature of things, the doctors cared for one particular problem on each separate occasion. For example, on this particular Saturday, they were operating on harelips and cleft palates.

That afternoon, the priest noticed one young lad coming out of the clinic, after having had plastic surgery for a harelip. He was amazed at the wonderful job the surgeons had performed. The young lad's father sat under a tree, while his mother and the rest of his family were chatting with others somewhere else within the mission compound. The lad approached his father, and, as was the custom, bowed before him, and the father placed a hand on his head, without making a single comment. His mother and the others appeared, and when they saw the transformation effected by the doctors, they were wild with delight, as they hugged the boy, examined his lip, and drew the attention of others to what indeed was a surgical miracle. Meanwhile, the father sat beneath the tree, showing absolutely no sign of emotion of any kind. The priest was watching the whole scene, and the attitude displayed by the father really annoyed him. He approached the man, and asked him 'Are you happy with the job the doctors did for your son?' 'Oh, yes, I am', came the reply. 'Well', said the priest, with not a little sarcasm, 'you sure haven't showed much sign of your satisfaction.' 'I love my son', the father replied, 'and if I got excited, and showed any great sign of emotion at what has happened to him, that would show him that I didn't real love him when he had a harelip. Nothing has changed in my love and my attitude towards him.'

FIFTH SUNDAY OF LENT

Gospel: John 8:1-11

Theme

Like last Sunday's gospel, today's gospel makes a very clear statement of where Jesus stands relative to sin and to sinners. It is the story of the woman taken in adultery. Jesus does not condemn her, but he adds 'Go and sin no more'. In other words, while not approving of the sin, he very definitely refuses to condemn the sinner. Once again, we come up against the conflict between the love of God, and the demands of the law. According to the law, this woman should be stoned to death. From God's point of view, however, it's just not as simple as that. If the law was fair and consistent, then there should have been a man condemned to death as well, because she wasn't committing adultery on her own! One of the more precious nuggets in today's gospel is the challenge to the others about whether any of them was in a position to condemn her, or anyone else. There is a powerful message in today's gospel.

Parable

It is some years ago now when I actually witnessed the following scene. I saw a mother with a son about six years of age, and a daughter of about four. The young girl was crying because her brother was after hitting her on the head with his school bag. The mother lifted the young lad off the ground, gave him a sharp smack across the face, with the words 'I'll teach you not to hit anyone smaller than yourself!'

We are all familiar with the concern of parents and teachers about the young people in their care taking drugs. This is correct and acceptable, but only up to a point. Many of the same adults can spend quite a lot of time and money buying and using alcohol, cigarettes, stimulants, and other addictive products. If they themselves fail to see the contradiction inherent in their behaviour, they should not expect the younger generation to be as blind as they are.

Teaching

Law, in itself, is good and necessary, but its only purpose is to protect from harm. For example, it is wrong to drive down the main street of a town at ninety miles an hour, except one is dri-

ving a vehicle involved in some emergency service. Law is there
to protect, not to control. The religious leaders of Jesus' day used
the law almost exclusively as a method of control. In the past,
the church has been guilty of the same misuse of law, but, thankfully, that is changing today. However, we still have a long way
to go until love takes precedence over law within the structures
of the church.

The gospel tells us that Jesus was writing with his finger in
the dust. We don't know what he was writing, but it is reasonable to assume that he was signifying the need to update the
law, and write something new. The writing in the dust wouldn't
last long, because the first gust of wind would totally obliterate
it. The woman standing beside him was more important than
any written words, and the law of God that is written within the
hearts of all God's creatures is something that will never be
blown away. I sometimes think that, perhaps, writing in the
dust was Jesus' way of letting them know that he wasn't about
to take them too seriously. They had come to him, in the first
place, because they were anxious to get him to do or say something that would trip him up, and give them an excuse to condemn him. He wasn't going to play their game, but, as they insisted, he turned on them and treated them as they rightly deserved. The kind and compassionate Jesus could easily be
stirred into resounding condemnation by the trickery and
hypocrisy of those whose only love was power and authority.

Guilt is not from God. In the last book of the Bible, called the
Book of Revelations, or the Apocalypse, we are told that Satan is
the accuser of our people. He accuses them night and day before
our God. In today's gospel Jesus says neither do I condemn you,
and in another place he says that he had not come to condemn
the world, but to save it. Guilt is a very dangerous emotion. A
leading psychiatrist said some years ago that he could discharge
two-thirds of his patients that day if he could get them deal with
their guilt. Most of the guilt has its origins in religion, because of
the inability of weak human nature to strictly adhere to thousands of regulations, rules, and commandments. We sin because
we are weak, not because we are evil. It is ironic that, in today's
gospel, and in many other passages of the gospel, Jesus accuses
the religious leaders of their legalism, hypocrisy, and sham;
while telling a prostitute or a public sinner 'I do not condemn
you'. Our church has not been good in this area, and many of us
grew up in a church where sinners were condemned off the

altar, were threatened with hell fire, and were even excluded from church altogether. If some unfortunate person, because of a brain-storm, or a total inability to cope, committed suicide, such a person was excluded from a church funeral. It is amazing just how far we wandered from the simple message, like the one in today's gospel.

Response

I can place myself in the presence of any one of the people in today's gospel. I am the woman being stoned to death. I, too, have broken God's law, and, perhaps, some of the laws of the land. She is deserted because only those who really love us will stick by us when the going gets tough. She is like a fox with the hounds baying at her heels. She is like one of those in a scene from a Wild West movie, who is going to be lynched by the mob. If she committed adultery, then where is the man she was with? For every unmarried mother in our society, there is an unmarried father. We know nothing at all about her background, her upbringing, or the circumstances of her life. If we take time out to think, however, we might be able to look out through her eyes, and see life from her perspective. There but for the grace of God go I is a very wise saying indeed.

I may well be among those who are ready to stone her to death. She doesn't fit into my expectations of what a person should be. She is different from me, and it is not very likely that she could ever be persuaded to see things my way. One of us has to be wrong, and it certainly cannot be me. Pride is a very frightening and destructive thing. It allows for no opinion but ours, and of no way of being, belonging, and behaving than what we accept as normal. It is truly frightening when one human being sits in judgement on another, when the only crime is that one is different from the other. We have laws of the land, and we have legal systems. When administered fairly, they give equal rights and protection to the accused and to the accuser. Even this is fraught with danger, and we have all witnessed examples of where justice was not seen to be done. That included innocent people being condemned to lengthy periods in prison, but it has also included a guilty person walking free. Most of us are not involved in the legal profession. We all, however, can easily put ourselves on the seat of judgement, and become judge, jury, and executioner for someone whom we don't really know, and about whom we certainly don't have all the facts. Judge not and you will not be judged, condemn not, and you will not be condemned is the simple instruction of Jesus to his followers. If I am compassionate, I will receive compassion, and the measure which I mete out to others is the measure I myself will receive in return. Judgement of others is a luxury most of us can't afford. If anyone among you has not sinned, let that person throw the first stone.

The other person I can be in the story is Jesus. That is a choice I have in life. The moment I begin to be Jesus to others, I will begin to see Jesus in others. My Christian vocation faces me with the same question in each and every situation: What would Jesus himself do in a situation like this? That is my term of reference, and his teachings are my guidelines. Again and again, it is important to stress that, by myself, I just don't have what it takes to treat others as Jesus would treat them. This is where the Holy Spirit comes in. The same Spirit who came upon Mary, upon Jesus, and upon the Apostles in the upper room. Only God can do a God-thing. To err is human, to forgive is divine. Without the power of God's Spirit in my heart, I haven't a hope of ever becoming a Christian, of ever having a forgiving heart, or of ever overcoming that pride, arrogance, and self-righteousness that bedevil us all.

Practical

There are many practical lessons to be drawn from today's gospel. All judgement belongs to God. There are times, because of responsibilities I have in life, when I have to form opinions, and express opinions about people for whom I am responsible. This is very different from sitting in judgement on someone, when their behaviour is none of my business. There is an Indian prayer which goes something like this: Lord, please don't let me judge my brother until I have walked a mile in his moccasins. 'Live, and let live' is a very good slogan to guide me.

Quite often what annoys me about others is when their behaviour reflects weaknesses I myself possess. When you point a finger at another, you are pointing three fingers at yourself. If you could imagine a slide projector in your head, and it projects onto the face of others the very weaknesses and failures that you yourself experience. That is the wonderful spiritual dimension of movements like Alcoholics Anonymous, where the alcoholic can enter a room full of people, and be absolutely sure of empathy, compassion, and total understanding. The whole recovery programme is dependent on the healing that results from the non-judgemental acceptance of others. As human beings, we all could benefit from being in such a recovery programme, because, like alcohol, life itself is something over which we are powerless, and which we are unable to manage.

As you come before the Lord today, put yourself in the place of the woman in the story. It is quite possible that much of the condemnation is coming from within yourself. We can often be our own most rigid and intolerant judges. If I cannot forgive myself, I will probably not be too generous in my forgiveness of others. I often imagine that, before I am really ready to celebrate the Sacrament of Reconciliation('Confession'), I should be willing to look at myself in the mirror, and give myself absolution first, before coming to the Lord for forgiveness. Otherwise I am asking God to do something that I myself am unwilling to do.

Story
A woman brought her daughter to Mahatma Ghandi one time, asking him to place his hand on her head, to recite a prayer over her, and to free her from an addiction she had. Ghandi asked what the addiction was, and the mother said that her daughter was addicted to sweet things, like sugar, sweets, sweet cakes, etc. Ghandi thought for a while, and he then asked the mother to bring her daughter home, and to return one month later. This seemed strange, but the mother did what she was asked. One month later, she arrived with her daughter. Ghandi placed his hand on the young girl's head, prayed a prayer over her, and he then told the mother to bring her daughter home, because, from now on, everything would be OK. The mother, more puzzled than annoyed, asked Ghandi why he was able to do something this day, and not on the previous occasion. Ghandi smiled, as he told the mother that, up to one month ago, he, too, was very fond of sweet things!

PASSION (PALM) SUNDAY

Gospel: Luke 22:14-23:56 (If Mark 14:1-15:47, see Year B)

Theme

This is Luke's account of the passion and death of Jesus. What makes it different from the accounts in the other three gospels is that, for one thing, there is much more space given to the role played by Peter in the whole scenario. Luke never actually met Jesus, and it is generally accepted that his gospel is strongly influenced by his association with Peter. Peter got it wrong many times, and Luke's gospel recounts most of them. Standing out, also, is the role of Judas, although, unlike Peter, who repented and wept bitterly, this gospel spares us the details of how Judas ended. I suppose it is fair to say that each in his own way had aspirations of grandeur. They were determined to look after number one, no matter what happened. I'm not sure that either of them understood what Jesus meant when he spoke of those who are the greatest in his kingdom. This account is filled with many and diverse personalities, from Herod to Pilate, to the two men being crucified with Jesus, and, of course, there was Barabbas. It would prove worthwhile if I took time out to reflect on the role of each, and to see each one against the role of Jesus, who is at the centre of the story.

Parable

Karla Tucker was executed in Huntsville, Texas, at the end of January, 1998. She had spent fourteen years on death row, after being found guilty of the murder of two people. Her execution was an occasion that showed up what is best and what is worst in the human condition. While her pending execution evoked world-wide condemnation, it also galvanised those who favour capital punishment. On the night of her execution, a large crowd gathered outside the prison. Some carried placards calling for an end to capital punishment, while others dressed up in death-the-reaper costumes, demanding that she should die. The official announcement of her death brought tears to some, and brought cheers from others. Even the next-of-kin of the victims were divided; some demanding revenge, and others who became her friends, and who were genuinely impressed by her extraordinary Christian conversion. Once again, as with today's gospel, it would be a very worthwhile exercise to examine the stances, the motives, the roles, and the responses and reactions of all those involved. This would range from a Governor who hopes to be US President some day, to the feminists who were caught between their stance on equal rights for women, and the outcry against her death, just because she was a woman.

Teaching

In the midst of all the many scenarios being acted out around him, stands Jesus, the innocent one. Each of the others has a personal agenda. It is very important that we see Jesus as standing out from all that surrounds him. He said that he had come to fulfil a mission, and he could not be at peace until that mission was completed. His is the centre and key role, and all the other persons revolve around that. His mind is fixed and firm. His mission is one of love, and there is no road so lonely as the one of unreciprocated love. In a most extraordinary way, his mother, while not understanding, would have been the only one to be unselfish and humble enough to be there; to share the pain, and to cling to the hope that all of what is happening is part of a plan that is beyond her comprehension. Those with a hidden agenda could not possibly see beyond their own immediate interests.

Jesus had told the story several times of the farmer, the king, or the landowner who sent servants to collect that which was owed. On each occasion, the servants were rejected and maltreated. One man sent his son, and he was killed. This is where that story is being fulfilled. It is a case of not liking the message, so you shoot the messenger. If you listen to the message you will have to change many things in your life. If you are a self-righteous Pharisee who is perfect in your own eyes, then, of course, you have no need to change. Yes, indeed, Jesus hadn't a hope in such surroundings. And yet it is important to remember that he lived with hope, with love, and with total faith and trust in the Father. It is interesting to note that today's gospel ends with the words 'When the captain of the Roman soldiers handling the execution saw what was happening, he praised God, and said "Surely this man was innocent". And when the crowd that came to see the crucifixion saw what happened, they went home in deep sorrow.' Innocence will out...

Peter is not the only moral coward in this story. It is interesting to see the bind in which Pilate found himself. Herod found nothing wrong, but, because he was a selfish bully, and Jesus refused to perform for his entertainment, he set out to make a complete mockery of him. Pilate, on the other hand, clearly saw that Jesus was innocent, and was of a mind to let him go. Because he was such a moral coward, and because of his own self-interest, he bowed to the demands of others, and made a decision which was not according to his own conscience. In the words of today's gospel 'the crowd shouted louder and louder for Jesus' death, and their voices prevailed'. Once again, moral courage and integrity lost out, the bully prevails, and the innocent suffer. This is a scenario we see repeated again and again in the very days in which we live.

Response
Jesus said 'you are either for me, or against me. They who do not sow, scatter'. In the last book of the Bible, called the Book of Revelations, or the Apocalypse, the Lord says 'I wish you were either hot or cold, but, because you are lukewarm, I will begin to vomit you out of my mouth'. In our day, and in our words, that means 'you make me sick'. Strong words from God! Jesus is totally and completed committed to what is best for us. He is completely on our side. He awaits our response, because, without that, all his efforts for us are in vain. The gospels tell us that he went back to Nazareth earlier on in his ministry, and 'he could not work any miracles there, because of their lack of faith'.

We can condemn the men and women of violence, but we must admit that they are committed to whatever they believe in. It is significant that today's gospel tells us that 'Then a mighty roar rose from the crowd, and with one voice they shouted "Kill him!" We are all familiar with gangsters, drug barons, and dictators meeting a violent death. They who live by the sword shall die by the sword. These people had a goal, whether it be power, control, wealth, or whatever, and they followed that right up to the moment of their death. Why should Satan have all the best music?! Despite the mob violence involved in today's gospel, there are people whose hearts were touched, and who were changed for the better in the midst of it all. Peter wept bitterly, as he repented of his cowardice, and he would eventually die for Jesus. One of those being crucified with Jesus asked for help, and was offered heaven right there. The captain of the Roman soldiers saw what had happened, and he turned to God in prayer; while those who witnessed the execution went home visibly upset, and, one can surmise, were profoundly effected for the rest of their lives.

I know we are all very human, and nothing is as simple as it seems, but it seems a contradiction that a Christian should read the Passion narrative, and not be involved. All of this happened because of me. If I were the only person in the world, all this would have had to happen, if I were to be saved. Jesus came that we should have life, and have it to the full. To enter into the fullness of life, it is necessary to pass through the gates of death. Jesus is our Moses, leading us through the desert and the Red Sea into the Promised Land. He tells us that if we want to be disciples of his, we, too, should take up our cross and follow him. 'If you follow me', he said, 'you will not walk in darkness, but will have the light of life'.

Practical

Above all days in the year, this is one week when I should take a few moments out to read the gospel narrative on my own, and to reflect on it. I am suggesting to you that you should do that, and I leave it to you how and when to do it. One practical obstacle to be overcome might be to get your hands on a copy of that gospel. This may not be easy, because the leaflets here in church may be needed for the next Mass. However, your very efforts to ensure that you get a copy for your personal reading will, in itself, be a test of your commitment.

Shakespeare says that fear makes cowards of us all. Moral courage is the highest, and, therefore, the rarest form of courage. I believe it is reasonable to presume that every single one of us comes up against that barrier from time to time. Young people experience the pressure of the peer group, and become involved in activities that they themselves would not have chosen. I can be caught in a wrong relationship, and I may want out, but I am afraid of the anger or outburst of the other if I follow my conscience in the matter. On the job scene, just because others take short-cuts, or help themselves to bits and pieces of property, which, in effect, is stealing, I may not be able to take a stance on the issue. I may either turn a blind eye, or become involved myself. It is a well-known fact that, once someone becomes involved with gangsters, mobsters, or paramilitaries, it is virtually impossible to get free again. Many a person has paid the ultimate price for trying to regain their integrity and freedom. Whenever I am authentic, I am mediating life to those around me; and whenever I am inauthentic, I am mediating death. Look at the lay-out of today's gospel, and see how Jesus stands out against the events and the people involved.

One week from today is Easter Sunday. We celebrate the triumph of Jesus over the final enemy, death. It is only correct and just that, if I wish to join in the victory, that I should contribute something to the battle or the struggle. There is no sharing in Easter without some role in the events of Good Friday. This is not to say that I have to, or can earn salvation. Far from it. It does mean, however, that I must be called into a decision-making situation relative to Jesus. Paul says that it is Jesus' blood and our faith that combine to produce our salvation. There is nothing automatic about God. When we speak about Jesus in the Mass, for example, we use the past tense. Dying you destroyed our death, rising you restored our life ... By your cross and resurrection you have set us free... In other words, Jesus has completed his part of the formula of salvation, and the rest is up to me. We are entering into Holy Week. It is a sacred time, a time of decision, a time for involvement. Just as at Christmas, this too requires my yes, my personal decision to be part of the events I commemorate, celebrate, and reflect on. Please make sure that your participation throughout this week is active; that it is something that draws you into the main-stream of salvation. This could range from the quiet prayer to the Sacrament of Reconciliation, from reflection on the events to the decision or decisions required to avail fully of the benefits and blessings resulting from those events.

Story
He was a criminal, and was well known for his criminal record. He was on death-row, and there wasn't a hope of a reprieve. The day of his execution was approaching, and there was nothing he could do but wait. His date with destiny finally arrived. He sat in his cell, awaiting those dreaded footsteps, that would indicate that they were coming to get him. The man's name was Barabbas.

He could hear the growing commotion in the court-yard above, and he presumed that it was the crowds coming to witness his public execution. The howls of the mob grew louder, and there was a sense of some great activity. And yet, they still hadn't come for him. This puzzled him, especially because the commotion up in the court-yard seemed to have died down, and it seemed that the people had all gone away. Finally, after what seemed like hours, they came for him. This was it. The soldiers opened his cell door, and, instead of grabbing him, and dragging him out, one of them told him that he was free to leave, and that he should go home now. There is no way Barabbas could accept this. There just had to be a catch somewhere. Surely the mob was waiting to tear him to pieces, or to stone him to death. He refused to budge, so the soldiers grabbed a hold of him, and threw him outside the cell. There was nobody there. He skulked in the shadows, and remained motionless. He remained thus for a long long time, afraid to move, lest his presence might be noticed, and he would draw the crowds down around him. It was hours later when he spotted a former associate of his passing by. He felt safe enough to attract his attention. When the man approached, Barabbas asked him what was happening. The man replied 'Do you really not know what happened here today?' Barabbas shared his total confusion and ignorance of what had been going on. The man beckoned Barabbas to follow him. They walked some distance outside the town. The man drew Barabbas' attention to three crosses on a distant hill. 'Do you see that middle cross there?' he asked. 'Yes, I do', replied Barabbas. 'Well', said his friend, 'take a good look at the man on that cross, because that cross was meant for you, and he took your place. You really are free, so, if you take my advice, get out of here, go home, and consider yourself one of the most fortunate people on this earth.'

EASTER SUNDAY

Gospel: John 20:1-9

Theme
This is St John's brief account of the resurrection. He had already devoted several chapters to the Last Supper, the final discourse of Jesus, and to much detail about his death. The bottom line is that Jesus is alive and well, and John puts that truth as simply as he can, including his own personal experience of that morning. For him the resurrection is a central and crucial fact, and he feels no need to do anything but tell us what he himself experienced.

Parable
I had often heard of Niagara Falls, the Grand Canyon, or the Eiffel Tour. What I had was factual or academic knowledge. When I visited these places, and saw them for myself, I had crossed the line into experiential knowledge. Experiential knowledge is not something that can be taught. The only way I could share such knowledge with you is to bring you to share the experience. Quite a great deal of our religion has to do with academic knowledge, where we learned catechism answers, and memorised whole passages of the gospels. Bill Wilson was the founder of Alcoholics Anonymous, together with a man called Bob Smith. One day Bill was in the horrors, when he fell on his knees, and cried out 'God, if you're there, please help me!' Suddenly the room was filled with a bright light, and Bill just sat there, filled with awe. Eventually, as it were, the light entered his heart and soul, and he came out of that room feeling totally changed, exclaiming 'Now I know the God of the preachers.' It is in that way that we can read John's account of the resurrection.

Teaching
Right from the beginning, I need to stress that the resurrection of Jesus is the core truth of the Christian message. Christianity is not about producing nicer people with better morals. I could be a pagan, and be a nice guy. It is not about prayer and fasting. I could be a Muslim, and fast for a month at a time, and pray several times a day. Christianity is about a person, Jesus Christ, and what comes to us, as a result of what he has done, and made possible. Death entered the human mix at the time of the Fall, and was not part of God's plan or creation. It is important, therefore,

that we see and believe that, because of the resurrection of Jesus, death is no longer an enemy, but a means of entering into that third and final stage of life. We are all familiar with birth, when the baby passes from the womb life to the womb of life. For the Christian, death is moving from the womb of life into the fullness of life. It is only in death that I can become all that I was created to be. It is through death, and what Jesus made possible for us, through his death, that we can return in triumph to the Garden.

I know it's unfair to Mary Magdalene to smile at her predicament! However, she does remind me of many a person in the church after the changes from Vatican II began to take effect. Up till that time, everything was so predictable. Even the Mass was in Latin, no matter what country you visited. Some people don't like change, even though life itself is about a constant change. 'They have taken him away, and I don't know where they've put him' reflects the comments of those who say that they're not sure what's happening anymore. It is vitally important to remember the following comment: There are only two things that matter, i.e. Jesus Christ, and his message. Jesus is the same yesterday, today, and always, and not one word of the gospel has changed. Surely everything else should be open to change, if that is seen as necessary? 'The Sabbath is made for the people, not the people for the Sabbath', Jesus tells us. A law or custom should never become an end in itself. Because of the resurrection of Jesus, everything has changed, and nothing could remain the same again. People who are afraid of change can often be those who like to live with certainties, with situations over which they have control. This is usually evidence of insecurity, and a lack of hope that, even if I were to die this moment, the world could continue OK without me.

It is interesting to reflect on the interaction between John and Peter in today's gospel. It is generally accepted that John was one of the youngest of the apostles, and Peter is generally depicted as being weather-beaten, and showing the wear of the years. Whatever the reason, John got to the tomb before Peter, but, because Peter was the one Jesus had put in charge, John stood to one side, and did not enter the tomb until Peter had first done so. There is nothing profound to be learned from this, and yet it does contain the ingredients of obedience, humility, and proper order. Jesus was quite ordered in how he went about things, despite the fact that, compared to the Pharisees, he appeared to be reckless, irresponsible, and without boundaries. Time and time again in the gospels, we read how he put structures in place in the course of his undertakings. Before feeding the hungry thousands, he made them sit in groups of fifty on the ground. He sent disciples on ahead to prepare for the Last Supper. He cleared out the house of Jairus, except for the immediate family, before he raised the young girl from the dead. Again and again this pattern is repeated. It is important to remember, however, that structure and proper order is not authority, but is a means towards efficiency. Within the parish here, we are continually trying to build structures of service, to contribute towards greater effectiveness, and greater involvement of individuals. Of necessity, this involves greater and lesser degrees of responsibility. No responsibility, no commitment. Like a body we move together in some sort of mutual interaction and responsibility to one another. Each has a role to play, and like vital parts of the engine of a car, if one is not available, the engine cannot function. Forming Christian community is a very powerful image of the reality behind what happened that first Easter morning. Like the body of Jesus, we, too, will have the wounds, but if you ever come across the body of Christ without the wounds, then you can be sure it is a phoney.

Response
The call of resurrection is a call to new life. It involves putting to death those things in us that are not life-giving, whether that be addictions, pride, arrogance, or other destructive behaviour. So great and so real is this change that it is significant that no one recognised Jesus after the resurrection. Mary thought he was the gardener, Peter thought he was a ghost, and the disciples on the way to Emmaus thought he was a stranger passing through. The beginning of this process was the willingness of Jesus to go through the gates of death. Anybody could give up smoking, drinking, sexual misdemeanours, etc. if there was no struggle or pain involved. Everybody wants to go to heaven, but nobody wants to die! And I'm speaking of life on this earth. We all want a share in Easter, but it's the Good Friday bit that scares us off. The following phrase from the letter to the Hebrews is something that should be a rule of thumb for every Christian: Because of the joy that lay in the future, Jesus willingly went to his death on the cross... This is what is often called 'the short-term pain for the long-term gain', and every recovering alcoholic, or any-

one who has given up on nicotine, can tell you exactly what that means.

Resurrection is something that I can actually experience within myself. When I go to the trouble of battling the traffic to visit a friend in hospital, I experience a real sense of worth and of well-being as I come out of the hospital. The happiest people on earth are the givers, because they alone are the real receivers. I give you a watch for your birthday. Some years from now both of us will be dead, and someone else may have the watch. It matters nothing about the watch. The real value of the exercise is that I learned to give, and you learned to receive. That was the real gift at the time, and not even death will take that away.

Jesus said that he came that we should have life, and have it more abundantly. I believe that this offer is for now, rather than something I get after I die. I further believe that there is nothing I'll get when I die that I'm not offered now. I would go so far as to say that our concern should not be about life after death, but about life before death. Everybody dies, but not everybody lives. Some people settle for existing, and when they do die, it would require a doctor's certificate of death to verify that fact, because there was never much life there in the first place! Some people could have the following words on the headstone of their grave: Died at forty, buried at eighty!

Practical

Resurrection implies new life. This is the gift I receive every morning I waken up. Today is a totally different day from yesterday. Part of something being a gift is that someone gives, and someone else receives, and there is no price tag attached. If there is a snag it is that God gives me nothing for myself. He doesn't give me my gift of speech to go around talking to myself! If he gives me the gift of life today it is because I can be a life-giving person to someone else. If I leave this church with a willingness to do that, then, you can be sure and certain, that the Lord will put in your day the people for whom he wants you to be his touch-person.

I often imagine that the one person who was least surprised on Easter morning was Mary. Without needing to understand, she just knew that all would be well, and that goodness will always have the final victory, even if evil seems to triumph for a while. Easter is about hope, and the only real sin for the Christian is not to have hope. Jesus triumphed over sin, sickness, and death, and, in the words of Paul 'having given us

Christ Jesus, will the Father not surely give us everything else?' There is great need for people of hope in today's world, and in today's church, because the doomsday prophets never had it so good! St Peter wrote these words to the early Christian community: 'Always have an explanation to give to those who ask you the reason for the hope that you have.' Peter had experienced, witnessed, and lived through many a failure, so his point about hope is more important because of that.

Easter is a time when all of nature is blooming, when the death of winter has passed, and when everything comes alive again. It would be really sad, indeed, if my inner spirit did not experience some of that reawakening. There is a movie called 'Awakenings', which depicts people with mental disabilities displaying glimpses of very intelligent life inside, and the ability, willingness, or otherwise, of those around to respond to that. Each of us, because of our Baptism, has the potential for divinity within us, in so far as we are invited to share directly in the life of the Trinity. Responsibility is about responding to something, and each of us must take personal responsibility for the gift of Easter, and what it offers and holds for us. You can walk out the door today, and today can be just another yesterday, or you can reflect seriously on all that you have heard, and, somewhere, within your soul or your spirit, you can say yes. We will celebrate the results of that yes a few weeks from now, when we celebrate the feast of Pentecost. The stone was rolled away from the tomb for Jesus on Easter morning, and the doors of the Upper Room were flung open for the apostles at Pentecost.

Story
A man was standing on the parapet of a bridge, and was going to jump into the raging waters below. The police and rescue services were present, endeavouring to prevent him jumping. One brave policeman made his way along the parapet, and succeeded in getting close enough to engage the man in conversation. Very patiently, and very gently, he succeeded in getting the man's attention. He even succeeded in making a pact with the man. The man would get five minutes to explain to the policeman why life was so difficult, and why he didn't want to go on living, but then he must listen for five minutes, while the policeman explained what was good about life, and how important it was to live it to the full. The man began. He was in full flight, and his five minutes were up, but the policemen couldn't stop him, as he rattled

off one problem, obstacle, and life-burden after another. The policeman finally got his attention, and he began to list all the positive things about life, and why it was worth living. After he listed two or three, he found it increasingly more difficult to think of other reasons. Eventually, he gave up, reached out his hand to the man, and the two of them jumped!

The blessing of Easter is HOPE. Jesus overcame the final enemy, and, by his cross and resurrection, he has set us FREE...

SECOND SUNDAY OF EASTER

Gospel: John 20:19-31

Theme

Today's gospel describes one of the more significant appearances of Jesus after his resurrection. Remember, he spent forty days with them, because it was of central importance that they know, beyond all doubt, that he had, indeed, overcome death, and that he was, indeed, alive. Thomas, like many of us, just refused to believe until he got some proof, or until someone convinced him that it was true. This is his big moment. Jesus was more than willing to oblige, because, once again, I stress that Jesus didn't want any of them to be in any doubt. They were to be his witnesses throughout the world, and they could hardly give any great credible witness if they themselves were unsure.

Parable

We are all familiar with Commissions and with Boards of Enquiry. Let's suppose that, back then, there was one set up to enquire into the whole question of whether Jesus had risen from the dead, and was really alive. There would be a judge on the bench, and there would be advocates for and against the subject of the enquiry. Most of the enquiry's time will be taken up by witnesses. Mary Magdalene is called. She had known Jesus for several years, and was one of his inner circle of friends. Her evidence was laughed out of court, because, when she met him after his resurrection, she thought he was the gardener! The next group of witnesses were even more ridiculous, and unworthy of belief. They claimed that an angel had told them that Jesus was alive! This was getting both unbelievable and ridiculous at the same time. The next two told how they had travelled with him to Emmaus, and they thought he was a tourist from elsewhere. When asked if they recognised him, they said they finally did so when he broke a piece of bread! This was turning into a complete farce! And then came Thomas. He looked around at the legal eagles, the scoffers, and the cynics. Then he spoke. 'I know how you feel, and what you must think. I was exactly like you. There was no one could convince me that Jesus had risen from the dead, and was, indeed, alive. I demanded proof, and I got that proof.' He then proceeded to tell them what had happened to him. Thomas turned out to be the only credible witness in that room to the fact that Jesus had actually risen from the dead.

Teaching

There are many gems in today's gospel. We notice that the apostles were still in hiding, because they were afraid. Once Jesus appeared among them his first words were 'Peace be with you'. His mission was continuing. He showed them his wounds, to re-enforce the reality of his presence, and he repeated the greeting 'Peace be with you'. Jesus understands the apostles' anxieties, confusion, and bewilderment at all that was going on, and he was extremely patient with them, and sensitive to them. Certainty and faith don't go together, because if you have one, you don't need the other. The Apostles were caught somewhere in the middle. Up to this time they had lived with certainties. Jesus was the Messiah, the long wait was ended, and the good days were coming. Now all that had been was stood on its head. Oh, yes, he was now appearing to them here and there, now and again, but it would take much more than that to rebuild their shattered dreams.

In the midst of today's gospel, we could easily miss one very important point. Jesus breathed on them, as a symbol of giving them his Spirit, and immediately, he asked them to forgive others. I have often heard this quoted as part of the church's teaching on Confession, or the Sacrament of Reconciliation, as it is now called. I don't accept that as valid. I believe Jesus is saying very simply something like the following: 'You are the one that was hurt. The hurt came through you, so the forgiveness must go back through you. If you refuse to forgive, you are blocking my forgiveness to that person. When I forgive you, I do so in the expectation that you will forgive others. I taught you a prayer in which you ask my Father to forgive you as you forgive others. Please don't get in the way of my forgiveness of others. You ask me to make you a channel of my grace. I certainly wish to make you a channel of my forgiveness. If you forgive, you yourself are forgiven.' Is it possible that there is someone who is dead for years, and who is not yet fully within the presence of God's glory, because I still have unforgiveness in my heart towards that person? I don't know the answer to that question, but I believe it is a question that should be asked.

Thomas asked for a sign, and Jesus was quite prepared to meet him where he was at. This was not just to indulge Thomas, because he was stubborn, but to assure him, because he was unsure. Thomas was honest, and he was in touch with his feelings. He was not prepared to go along with something that seemed totally crazy, just because other people told him. He was unsure, he was confused, he was hurting deeply. He obviously loved Jesus, and, because of what had happened, he was totally distraught. So what! The others had seen Jesus, but what help was that to Thomas? It is obvious, also, that Jesus loved Thomas, and he understood him more than anybody else. If Thomas wanted a sign, then Thomas would get a sign. Once he had witnessed the sign, a prayer came from the depths of his heart 'My Lord, and my God', and this is a prayer that is used to this very day.

Response
Faith is a funny old thing, if I may use the expression! Unlike Thomas, we have not seen, and yet we are asked and expected to believe. At least that is what it looks like on the surface. In reality, that is not so. I can get all the proof I want that Jesus is alive and well, and living in me, if I myself am alive and well, and living in him. I am living thousands of years later, Pentecost has happened, and the message of the gospel, and the person of Jesus has been debated and written about in every language on the globe. What signs do I want? What signs do I need? The atheist would believe if you could furnish the concrete facts, and satisfy the arrogance of pride, that needs to subject everything to the microscope of its inspection, and to be given its approval. Faith requires a generous dose of humility, and a large amount of common-sense. Every time I buy a car, every time I enter an operation theatre, every time I board an aeroplane, I continue to make acts of faith in someone or in something. Without faith, I would end up doing nothing. No one would get married if they didn't have faith in themselves, in each other, and in the love that binds them.

We are a resurrected people. In simple English, Jesus took on human nature, with all its weaknesses of sin, sickness and death; these were nailed to the cross with him; they died with him; and now they are no longer enemies of destruction, but can be turned into opportunities for good, for wisdom, for compassion, and for faith. When I say that Jesus took on human nature, I mean, of course, that he took on your human nature, my human nature, the nature of the person in front of you, and that of the person beside you. We become a resurrected people when we accept the simple fact that, yes, Jesus did overcome death, that he is very much alive, and that we share in the results of that victory when we trust Jesus to effect those results in us. We ask him for that full and abundant life that he came to offer. We take him at his word, when he tells us that 'They who eat my body, and drink my blood, have everlasting life, and I will raise them up on the last day'. All Jesus asks is that we believe him. 'The sin of this world is unbelief in me. When the Son of Man comes, will he find any faith on this earth?'

When I spoke about forgiveness just now, it must surely have hit us just how central and essential this must be in the mind of Jesus. He himself, while dying on the cross, was praying for those who were killing him. The whole gospel is about forgiveness. The story of the Prodigal Son summarises the central message of the gospel. This could also be called the story of the Forgiving Father. Our God is a forgiving God, and love is best expressed through forgiveness of others. If you love those who love you, what reward can you expect? Even the pagans do that, don't they? At different stages of my life I may have been the Prodigal Son, or the self-righteous unforgiving son, but my call is to become like the forgiving Father. St John says 'In this is love, not that we love God, but that he first loved us. Little children let us love one another, because God loves us.' If we are to be children of God, and if we dare pray the prayer that Jesus taught us, then we must accept full responsibility for displaying our Christianity through our loving forgiveness of others.

Practical

There are a few words we should all consider for a moment. Whether we say 'Lord, by your cross and resurrection, you have set us free', or 'Dying, you destroyed our death, rising you restored our life', or simply 'My Lord and my God' ...no matters which formula we choose during this Mass, we should seriously question ourselves as to how much of that is coming from our heart, or are we saying it just because it is written on a page in front of us?

I'm sure it's reasonable to presume that every one of us could take pen and paper right now, and write out the name of someone against whom we have a grudge, a resentment, or against whom we experience anger and unforgiveness. Some of us have been deeply hurt, and it is not easy to forgive. Indeed, there are times when I am convinced that I will never be able to forgive that person. To err is human, to forgive is divine. While we're at it, I'm sure each of us could turn over that same piece of paper,

and write down the name of someone who may be finding it
well nigh impossible to forgive us. In death, we have to let go of
everything. The journey of the Christian is to do the letting go
along the journey of life. Letting go of unforgiveness, resentments, the need to be right, the need to be always proven right,
etc. There is an endless list of things of which we can begin letting go right now, and not hold onto them until it's too late. Did
you ever hear someone say 'It would kill me to have to do that'.
There is always an element of dying in forgiveness ... dying to
my pride, my arrogance, to my need to always have the victory,
the upper-hand.

Faith will always be accompanied by doubt. If there was certainty, there would be no need of faith. Jesus compares faith to a
tiny grain of mustard seed, that continues to germinate and
grow, and ends up as a large tree. Incidentally, mustard seeds
are actually so tiny that it would be impossible to examine them
without the benefit of a microscope. Faith grows through exercise. Like a child learning to walk, talk, read, or write, I can become a person of deep faith only if I practice it, and continue to
apply faith to everything I do. When my faith, which is a response to God's love, makes its way down into my feet, then,
every time I step out in faith to do or say something, my faith
will continue to grow. It may sound stupid, but the Lord likes to
be involved in all that we do, right down to looking for a parking meter in town! This is something that the cynic might dis-
miss, but it also something you might try some time! Jesus says
that the mustard seed grew into a big tree, in which the birds of
the air found shelter. My faith can be a great support to others.
When the people lowered the man through the roof, in the
gospel story, we are told that 'Jesus marvelled at their faith', and
he healed the man. We often joke about certain people having a
hot line to God. Maybe, there is something in that! We turn to
others for prayers, and we promise others that we will pray for
them. All of this is good, of course; but, it can also be totally
meaningless, if it is not shot through and through with faith. 'Do
you believe I can do this? Do you want to be healed? Your faith
has healed you. Oh woman, great is your faith. I have not found
faith like this in Israel.' I could go on and on quoting Jesus' reference to faith, and to the necessity of faith. 'Lord, increase my
faith. I believe, Lord, help my unbelief' are prayers directed to
Jesus in the gospel.

Story

A missionary in Africa was translating John's gospel into the local dialect. He encountered many problems finding a suitable word in the dialect to fit the word in the English translation. One such word was 'to believe'. There was no exact word in the dialect, so he approached one of the natives for help. When he explained his problem, the native replied that his understanding, as he listened, was that 'to believe' should be translated as 'to listen with the heart'.

A Short Poem...

As children bring their broken toys with tears for us to mend,
I brought my broken dreams to God,
Because he was my friend.
But, then, instead of leaving him
At peace to work alone,
I hung around and tried to help
With ways that were my own.
At last I snatched them back, and cried,
'How can you be so slow?'
'My child', he said, 'what could I do?
You never did let go'.

THIRD SUNDAY OF EASTER

Gospel: John 21:1-19

Theme

Today's gospel gives us yet another graphic account of an encounter between Jesus and his apostles after his resurrection. It
is as if he doesn't miss a chance to meet them, so that they will
have no doubt whatever that he is, indeed, risen from the dead.
Today we have another miracle, involving a catch of fish, we
have the human touch of Jesus, preparing breakfast for the apostles, and we have the healing of any scars Peter may still have
borne because of his earlier denial of Jesus.

Parable

There is a certain Irishman who is at the top of his profession as
a film-star, enjoying world-wide acclaim. One of the things for
which he is noted is the fact that he never misses a chance to return to the area in which he grew up. When we returns, he becomes
a local again. He attends the local games, and joins the local fishermen. In a way, this helps to make him more REAL. In many
ways, in today's gospel, even after his resurrection, Jesus is back
among the old familiar scenes. He cooks a meal for his friends,
he filled their boats with fish, and he ensured that he was accepted
and loved as someone who loved them and cared for them.

Teaching

Jesus was the meeting place of the human and the divine.
Human powerlessness, when brought to him, was turned into
power, strength, hope, and conviction. If we were to take the
gospels literally, Jesus was a carpenter, and Peter and Co. were
the fishermen. They failed miserably, and so it was left to Jesus
to fill their boats. It was many years earlier when Mary was told
that 'nothing is impossible with God'. Jesus is Emmanuel, 'God
with us'. Sometimes we are pushed to the point of utter failure
and despair before we are prepared, ready, or humble enough to
let him into the situation, and let the miracle happen.

Having Jesus cook breakfast for the Apostles is a lovely
human touch. It is hard to imagine or to remember that this is
the same Jesus who carried a cross to Calvary. We often use the
phrase 'some things never change', and St Paul tells us that
'Jesus is the same yesterday, today, and always'. Just because he

has overcome death, and now enjoys the freedom of a life in which death is no longer a threat or a reality, he still retains that lovely human touch, that down-to-earth relationship with those whom he had already called his friends.

For the ordinary punter among us, Peter is probably one of the most appealing of the apostles. He certainly comes across as being the most human, and, in the best sense of that word, the most ordinary. Just think of the following two points about Peter. When Jesus first saw him, we are told, that 'Jesus looked at Peter', and then he told him that he would be the rock on which he would build his church. Later, when Peter denied Jesus, and ran away, we are told, once again, that 'Jesus turned and looked at Peter'. The thing that struck Peter was that the look had not changed. It was still a look of genuine love, and of friendly invitation. No wonder Peter went outside and wept his heart out. That is the origin of his beautiful words in one of his letters 'Always have an explanation to give to those who ask you the reason for the hope that you have'. Peter had earlier boasted that, though the rest might deny Jesus, he certainly would not. Now it is Confession time for Peter! 'Peter do you still think you're the greatest?' That, of course, is not what Jesus asked him. Jesus had shown that he still loved Peter, and he needed Peter to declare where he stood. If Peter were burdened with guilt, he would hate himself, and, therefore, he would not be in a proper frame of mind to receive love and forgiveness from any-one else, including Jesus.

Response
One point that can go unnoticed in today's gospel is that, despite everything they had been through, the apostles had returned to work, and had decided to get on with it. It is impossible for us to imagine what must have been going through their minds during those days. Life, however, has a way of marching on. It was like the shepherds at Bethlehem, where, it can be presumed that, after being to see the sign that the angel spoke of, they probably returned to their task of minding their sheep. On Thabor, when Jesus was transfigured, and was seen in resplendent glory, Peter wanted to stay there. Jesus, however, had a job to do, and they had to come down off the mountain, and get on with it. While they return to the normal work-style, however, because of their experience, something deep within has changed, and nothing is exactly the way it used to be.

Those of us who were brought up on religion may find it difficult to be constantly conscious of the humanity of Jesus. He came to join us on the journey, and he wants to travel every step of the road with us. He wants to be involved in all that we are, and in everything we do. Throwing a few fish on a barbecue is not something very extraordinary. And yet it is this common touch that Jesus wants us to allow, and to expect in our lives. He doesn't want to be listed under 'Emergencies Only', to be called on when the boat's going down.

As you listened to the gospel, did you notice that Peter never actually apologised, or said he was sorry. In a movie some years ago, there was a line 'Love means never having to say you're sorry'. While this can be true, it could also be said that 'Love means saying you're sorry even when you don't have to'. Jesus said about the woman washing his feet with her tears 'Many sins are forgiven her because she loves much'. Paul tells us that love covers a multitude of sins. Peter could confess his sin, he could grovel, and beg forgiveness, or he could open his heart, ask the Lord to look within, and see that he really did love Jesus. Peter was direct and uncomplicated. He spoke from his heart, and he knew that Jesus loved him. Because of his failures, and the many ways in which he got it wrong, Peter was ideal to be put in charge of others. Earlier, he had recoiled at the idea of Jesus washing his feet, but, once he understood the meaning of what Jesus was doing, he was totally open to whatever it took to be one of Jesus' disciples. Because he couldn't afford to point a finger at others, or to condemn others for the weaknesses of their humanity, he would have the necessary compassion to be a leader. To be a leader, in the mind of Jesus, was one who was prepared to be of service to others.

Practical
In an ideal world, today's gospel is something that each should take away, go off to some lonely place, and spend the rest of this day reflecting on it. There is such a wealth of teaching in it, such a wonderful collection of insights, such a rich source of inspiration, that it would be a great pity to go out the door at the end of Mass, and just forget the whole thing. For example, if I were to ask you to tell me what last Sunday's gospel was, do you think you would be able to tell me? If I approached you with today's gospel within a book in a big red cover, and said to you 'This is your life', how do you think you would react? Just think about that for a moment. Can you see the need to transfer something

that happened back then, and make it part of who I am, what I am, and what I do today?

You came in the door to Mass here this morning? Is that a statement, or is it just something you do on a Sunday morning? We all have failed many times during the past week. Is our coming here today a way of saying 'Lord, you know all things. You know that I love you.' Peter was promoted from being a sheep who followed Jesus to being a shepherd who would have personal responsibility for the welfare of the flock. Do you experience yourself as a sheep, who is just a follower, or do you experience within you some desire to give practical service within the community?

There is one little item in today's gospel to which I have not yet referred. At the end of the gospel, Jesus indicates to Peter the kind of death he would die to glorify God. What did Peter do? He turned to John, pointed to him, and asked Jesus 'What about him?' Good old Peter! The everyday human being right up to the last! Jesus is a personal God. He speaks to you. He asks 'Who do you say that I am? Do you love me? Will you also go away?' His words are spoken to you. Have you ever listened to a homily, and you wished that such-a-one was here to hear this?! Live and let live is a very wise bit of advice. Each of us must take responsibility for ourselves. When you go out of here today, think of some one thing you will do today because of the fact that you were part of this worshipping community now.

Story
A man was driving a Hi-ace van into Dublin, and he had got as far as the quays when the van grinded to a halt, and could not be restarted. The man was always very intense and highly-strung, so he got out, kicked the van, swore and screamed, and slammed the keys on the ground. Just then another Hi-ace van pulled up behind him, and the driver got out to enquire what the matter was. The first guy said that he had a van load of monkeys that he was bringing to the zoo, and he had to have them there at three o'clock. The other man said 'Sure, that's no problem. I'll take them to the zoo for you.' 'You will? Oh, Lord, that's great. Here, let me give you some money for that.' He reached into his pocket, took out fifty pounds, and gave that to the driver. The monkeys were quickly transferred, and off he went. The broken-down van was towed to the nearest garage, and about an hour and a half later, it was on the road again. The driver was going up the North Circular Road, when, what did he

see but the other van, coming from the other direction, with the windows open, and the monkeys hanging out the windows, eating bananas, with balloons on strings flying in all directions! He was absolutely furious, as he did a U-turn, and followed the van, until he got him to pull over and stop. With a flow of strong language, he asked the man what on earth was he doing? He had asked him to bring the monkeys to the zoo, and he couldn't even be trusted with that. The other guy was completely laid back, and very relaxed, as he assured him that, of course, he had taken the monkeys to the zoo. In fact, he was there even before three o'clock. But, because he had some money left over, he thought he should give the monkeys a treat, so he bought them some bananas and balloons!

It may not have much to do with the resurrection(!), but, as an Easter people, we are expected to live with hope and tranquillity...

FOURTH SUNDAY OF EASTER

Gospel: John 10:27-30

Theme

This is what is normally called Good Shepherd Sunday, a day when we pray especially for vocations to priesthood and Religious Life. Today's gospel states very clearly just how much we mean to Jesus, and how he takes full responsibility for looking after us. He tells us that we are safe, really safe, when we are in his care.

Parable

Some years ago, a book was written, and later made into a movie, called 'Not Without My Daughter', which describes how a mother travelled to the Middle East to get her daughter back, after she had been abducted, and brought there by her Arab father. It is a gruelling story of hardship, danger, and many narrow escapes. There was something within the mother which drove her to face up to, and to go through any and every obstacle to retrieve her child. She had already been given custody, but the father had kidnapped the child, and had escaped out of England. The whole story is about the love within the heart of the mother, which drove her to attempt the impossible, and to go through whatever it took, to get her daughter back. To read today's gospel message certainly comes alive in the story of this mother, who was literally prepared to die, and did actually narrowly escape such a fate on several occasions, in her determination to rescue her daughter.

Teaching

Knowing Jesus and knowing about him are two different things. One is mental or academic knowledge, while the other is experiential knowledge; it is something which I myself have experienced. In today's gospel, Jesus says that his disciples know his voice, they know exactly what he is saying, and they obey him.

God is Father, and he has given Jesus responsibility for all his children. Jesus takes this responsibility seriously. He accepts full responsibility for us, just as the role of being a shepherd included his willingness to die in protection of the sheep entrusted to him. The people who listened to Jesus were very conscious of the role of a shepherd, and of the strong bond that developed between a shepherd and his sheep.

Unlike the ordinary shepherd, Jesus tells us that no one will take his sheep away from him. The Father, who entrusted the sheep to him in the first place, is infinitely powerful, and those who are under his protection have no need to fear. If God is for us, who can be against us?

Response
I come to know about Jesus by reading books, listening to sermons, studying theology, etc., I come to know him when I fall on my knees before him, and accept him personally into my life. From that first Christmas night until now, there have been many a home and many a heart closed to him. I open my heart, invite him in, because I am a sinner and he is a Saviour, who came looking for sinners. Nothing dramatic happens. I just continue, day after day, to say 'Yes' to him, and then, one day, I realise the miracle has happened. The coin has dropped, the lights inside have come on, and now I know what no book or sermon could ever tell me.

There are people who just don't want to go near a doctor. There comes a time, however, when I have no choice. I realise the seriousness of my situation, I accept that I have no option, and I agree to do whatever it takes to remedy the problem. Coming to accept my sin and brokenness is not easy. Part of sin is that it tends to blind me to its existence. Jesus said that the Spirit he would send would be a Spirit of Truth, who would lead us into all truth, and the truth would set us free

If Jesus is to be a Good Shepherd for me, then I must be willing to follow him. Following him implies several steps. Firstly, I must get to know exactly what he has to say to me. This is much simpler than it may seem. We have all heard sections of the gospels read. I must ask myself honestly when I have actually listened. I can reflect on what I hear, I can ask the Spirit to touch my heart through the word that I hear. All of this is part of what is usually called Incarnation, when the word becomes flesh; when the word that I hear becomes part of the person that I am.

Practical
We are all familiar with points in our lives when we didn't have any great sense of direction. We weren't sure which direction to take, which decision to make. This is where Jesus as Shepherd comes in. 'They who follow me shall not walk in darkness, but shall have the light of life.' Lord, lead me in your ways, and guide my feet into the ways of peace...

Let me ask you a straight honest question: Is your Christian belief of such a nature that it involves a personal relationship with Jesus, and, therefore, gives you a deep sense of personal security? Read today's gospel again. Do you actually feel safe in the care and in the promises of which Jesus speaks today?

Where does the Father come into all of this? 'The Father and I are one', says Jesus. What is your image of God? Have you fully embraced the concept of being a child of God, which makes Jesus your brother? That is a very profound thought, and it cannot or must not be passed over lightly. Reflecting on all of this is real prayer, and that requires time and space in my day.

Story

Mrs Thompson was a primary school teacher many years ago. As she stood in front of her 5th class on the first day of school, she told them a lie. She looked at her pupils, and told them that she loved them all the same. But that was impossible, because there in the front seat, slumped across the desk, was a little boy named Teddy Smith. Mrs Thompson had watched Teddy the previous year, and noticed that he didn't play much with the other pupils, that his clothes were messy, and that he constantly needed a bath. He also could be quite unpleasant. It got to the point where Mrs Thompson would actually take delight in marking his papers with a broad red pen, making bold X's, and then putting a big 'F' at the top of his papers. Part of her work was to review each child's past record. She deliberately put Teddy's off till last. However, when she reviewed his file, she was in for a surprise. Teddy's first grade teacher wrote, 'Teddy is a bright child, with a ready laugh. He does his work neatly, and has good manners ... he is a joy to be around.' His second grade teacher wrote, 'Teddy is an excellent student, well liked by his class-mates, but he is troubled because his mother has a terminal illness, and life at home must be a struggle.' His third grade teacher wrote ' His mother's death has been hard on him. He tries to do his best, but his father doesn't show much interest, and his home life will soon effect him, if some steps aren't taken soon.' Teddy's fourth grade teacher wrote. 'Teddy is withdrawn, and doesn't show much interest in school. He doesn't have many friends, and he sometimes sleeps in class.' By now Mrs Thompson realised the problem, and she was ashamed of herself. She felt even worse when her students brought her Christmas presents, wrapped in bright paper, and beautiful ribbons, except for Teddy's. His present was clumsily wrapped in the heavy brown paper that he got from a grocery bag. Mrs Thompson took pains to open it in the middle of all the other presents. Some of the children started to laugh when she found a rhinestone bracelet with some of the stones missing, and a bottle that was one quarter full of perfume. She stifled the children's laughter when she exclaimed how beautiful the bracelet was, putting it on, and dabbing some of the perfume on her wrists. Teddy stayed backed after school that day, just long enough to say 'Mrs Thompson, today you smelled just like my mother used to.' After the children left, she cried for nearly an hour. On that very day she quit teaching reading, writing, and arithmetic. Instead, she began to teach children. Mrs Thompson paid particular attention to Teddy. As she worked with him, his mind seemed to come alive. The more she encouraged him, the faster he responded. By the end of the year, Teddy had become one of the smartest children in the class, and, despite her lie that she loved them all the same, Teddy became one of his teacher's 'pets'. A year later, she found a note under her door, from Teddy, telling her that she was the best teacher he ever had in all his life.

Six years went by before she had another note from Teddy. He said he had finished his Leaving Cert, came third in his class, ... and she was still the best teacher he ever had in all his life. Four years later, she got another letter, saying that, while things were tough at times, he'd stayed on in school, and would soon graduate from college with the highest of honours. He assured Mrs Thompson that she was still the best and most favourite teacher he ever had in all his life. Four years later, another letter arrived. This time he explained that after he got his bachelor's degree, he decided to go a little further. Once again he said she was the best and most favourite teacher that he'd ever had. This time his name was a little longer. It was signed Thomas F. Smith MD. In another letter, he said he had met this girl, and they were going to get married. He explained that his father had died some years previously, and he was wondering if Mrs Thompson might agree to sit in the place at the wedding that was usually reserved for the mother of the groom. Of course, Mrs Thompson did. And guess what? She wore the rhinestone bracelet, with the stones missing. And she made sure she was wearing the perfume that Teddy remembered his mother wearing on their last Christmas together. They hugged each other, and Dr Smith whispered in Mrs Thompson's ear, 'Thank you, Mrs Thompson for believing in me. Thank you so much for making me feel important, and showing me that I could make a difference.' Mrs Thompson, with tears in her eyes, whispered back, 'Teddy, you have it all wrong. You were the one who taught me that I could make a difference. I didn't know how to teach until I met you.'

FIFTH SUNDAY OF EASTER

Gospel: John 13:31-33, 34-35

Theme
Jesus is about to leave his disciples. It is part of a greater plan than he cannot explain to them, or they could possibly understand. However, he simplifies it by giving them one simple instruction: they are to love one another, and, in this way, they will belong to him, and will be seen to belong to him.

Parable
In our own ways, and in our own days, most of us have sat by the bedside of someone who is dying. Dying is something that I have to do, and no one else can do it for me. Even if the room is full of people, and they are holding my hands, mopping my brow, and whispering prayers to me, death is a journey that I must take alone. In many cases death is followed by a legal declaration of what is to be done with what personal possessions and effects are left behind. In today's gospel, Jesus makes an open and personal declaration of his legacy to them. His legacy is one of love, and this is something that they must share with one another. He himself must leave their sight, but all that he is, and all that he stands for, will remain with them. That is the great scandal of so many Christian churches seen to be fighting over who has, or who has not, the entitlement to that legacy of love. 'My Church has a greater share of his love than yours' is one way of defining the differences that separate the Christian churches. In fact, some churches would claim a total monopoly of that love, to the exclusion of all others.

Teaching
In today's gospel, Jesus is caught in the middle between two loyalties, which, of course, are not at all opposed to one another. To do the Father's will, he must face death, and complete his mission. Death was not part of God's original creation, so through his death and resurrection, when he will be seen to have overcome death, Jesus would remove death as an evil, and turn it into a blessing. He himself was going to cross through the Red Sea of death into the Promised Land, and so come into his glory.

When Jesus had achieved that victory, he could then send the Spirit on his apostles, so that they could live as he lived, and fol-

low the way he had gone. For them he was the Way, and to follow him meant to walk in the light, rather then stumble around
in the darkness. He had returned to the Father, who is Love, and
their love for each other would point to the direction in which
their lives were taking them.

In a way it is sad that Jesus depends on our love for each
other as proof that the Father sent him. In other words, he en-
trusts the credibility of his mission to the witness of our lives.
When the early Christians came on the scene first, they were an
unusual bunch, and not easily understood. They spoke about
following a leader who had been executed as a public criminal,
whom they believed was now alive, and that he was the
Messiah, God's Chosen One. In one way this was a laughing
matter. On the other hand, however, the others watched their
behaviour, and the only comment they could make was 'See
how these Christians love one another'.

Response
When we think of the witness of the lives of some self-pro-
claimed Christians down the ages, who continue to murder and
destroy others in Jesus' name, it becomes more than a scandal.
The title 'Christian' should be used with great delicacy and rev-
erence. I could be a pagan and be a nice person. I could be a
Muslim and do the praying and fasting. To call myself a
Christian is to open myself to the work of God's Spirit, so that
Christ is formed in me. This enables me to become Christ to oth-
ers, and that, in turn, leads me to see Christ in others.

There is a branch of theological science today called
Eschatology. It has to do with the future, like death, heaven, etc.,
which really are present now, but not fully. It implies a time of
waiting for the fulfilment, but it also includes the hope of that
fulfilment. Jesus told his disciples that they could not go with
him. Later on, he told them that he was going to prepare a place
for them, and that he would come and bring them, so that where
he is they also would be. How do you feel, and what are your
thoughts, when you sit alone, and reflect on the possibilities of
the future? Do you find that the words and promises of Jesus
enter into such reflections, or do you just drift towards fear, and
being uncomfortable; something that drives you back to dis-
tracting activity?

Love is a gift. In other words, by myself, I just don't have
what it takes to love others in the way Jesus speaks of here. Love
is a gift of the Spirit. The expression of that love is witness to the

presence of the Spirit. As Christians, we are called to be witnesses. I cannot give what I do not have. The feast of Pentecost is in sight. This is our annual reminder of the beginning of the church, of the beginning of that Christian witness to love which was characteristic of the members of the early church.

Practical
In our hearts we all like to be loved. In fact we all have a need to be loved. Mother Teresa said that the hunger for love is the greatest hunger in the world. God is Love. In other words, the more my heart is open to God, the greater capacity I have for loving others. Human love is very limited, and can be very limiting. It can involve control, possession, dependence, and many other elements of being unfree. I don't think it possible for one human being to really love another with a love that is unconditional, depending only on the human capacity to love.

There is great emphasis in the gospel on willingness, on good-will, on being open. I believe if I have this that God will most certainly do the rest. 'Here I am, Lord' is a prayer that was used by the prophets, and is another way of saying Mary's 'yes' at the Annunciation.

On a human, practical, down-to-earth level, there are people in the lives of most of us, whom we find it impossible, or well-nigh impossible to love. Here is the kernel and the acid test of the whole Christian mission. Don't forget, Jesus even asked us to love our enemies, and many of us find it almost impossible to love some of our friends! If I am willing to go to the heart of the Christian message, and not just see it as some sort of a-la-carte menu, then I come face to face with the simple fact that I don't have what it takes to be a Christian. To accept this simple fact is a moment of profound conversion. Now I am ready for Pentecost; for the miracle that would enable me to follow the example of Jesus, who prayed for the very people who were killing him.

Story
I heard of a young doctor, married, with three very young children. He was in his late twenties when he discovered he had a very virulent form of cancer, and his life was going to be cut short. Up till then his mind was filled with all his hopes and dreams for his children. He would always be there for them. He would watch them play games, attend all school concerts, would be there to ferry them to scouts, girl guides, etc. Now, to

his horror, all of that was to be taken away from him. He was shattered, and was totally unable to come to terms with what was happening.

One day as he lay in a stupor of pain, confusion, and desperation, he came up with a plan that others might consider crazy. He got a few C-90 tapes, got a tape-recorder, and began to pour his heart out on one tape after another. He told his children how much he loved them, how it broke his heart to leave, but how he prayed that he might still be always there for them. He told them of his dreams for them, how proud he was of them, and how important it was for him that they took good care of their mammy.

He talked about the goods and the bads of growing up; how some lives get messed up, and others evolve in a healthy and life-giving way. He warned them of the dangers, and he gave advice about how to avoid the pitfalls. He filled several tapes. There was not a surplus word, because every word came from his heart. At that time the children would be unable to listen to, or understand the contents of the tapes, but he would give them to his wife, and she would judge when the right time was for any particular part of the tape to be played.

The doctor died, and that was about twenty-five years ago. His children have grown up, gone to college, established their own profession, and all three have children of their own now. The one stabilising factor in their most formative years was the long hours spent listening to their dad's tapes. By now, the tapes are worn thin, and copies have been made to pass on to the next generation.

In today's gospel, and in his long discourse at the Last Supper, Jesus has left us with many many C-90 tapes …

SIXTH SUNDAY OF EASTER

Gospel: John 14:23-29

Theme

Today's gospel stresses the central theme of love. God is love. If we love God, we will do what he tells us to do. If we do what he tells us to do, God will make his home in us; all Three Persons of the Trinity. Love is what brings heaven down to earth. Peace is what flows from love, when my relationships are the way they ought to be.

Parable

Obedientia, the Latin for obeying, literally means to hold one's ear against. The first rule of the road that we all learned was 'Stop! Look! Listen!' Before you cross the railway tracks, stop and listen. There may be a train coming. If you hear a train coming, you will obey that reality, and wait until it has passed. During the years in which I was involved in teaching, I was quite familiar with the child who kept getting it wrong, who continued to be called to the Principal's office. Allowing for deliberate cussedness, the main reason for this repetition of problems was that the child hadn't really listened. What had been said on previous occasions had not sunk in. Just because I had said the words didn't automatically mean that those words were listened to. If, however, I could gain the confidence and respect of the pupil, I would have some chance of being heard. We all have people in our lives who get our full attention, just as there are others to whom we don't really tune in. They prattle on, and our attention is elsewhere. This can mean that, because they are not really important to us, what they have to say is not very important either.

Teaching

Faith is a response to love. There are people I do not trust, because I have no reason to believe that they have my best interests at heart. Don't ask me to trust God until you have clearly shown me that God loves me first. 'In this is love', says John, 'not that we love God, but that God first loved us'. When that simple truth makes its way through my head, when I know it, down into my heart, when I believe it, it may eventually make its way down into my feet, when I act upon it. Faith is love in action.

If I have a block of ice, a snowball, and a fist of hailstones, all I have is water in different forms. God is love, and each Person of the Trinity represents a particular expression of love. The Father's love is creative, and it never becomes destructive. The Son's love is redemptive, and there is nothing in us that is beyond the scope of his redeeming love. The Spirit's love is renewing, recreating, making complete in us what was begun by the Father, and reclaimed or redeemed by Jesus; and there is no human weakness where this love cannot be seen and experienced as Power.

'I am leaving you with a gift – peace of mind and heart.' What a beautiful promise, what a very special gift. Peace is not the absence of war. It is the presence of something real and tangible. It is something I can experience, and it results from having my relationships the way they ought to be. I will deal in greater detail with this later.

Response
We are all familiar with invitation cards that have RSVP on them. The person is looking for a response from us. Every word that Jesus speaks is calling for a response. A rule of thumb is to learn to listen, and then listen to learn. Otherwise what Jesus is saying will go completely over my head. Scripture tells us that the word of God does not return to Him until it has achieved what it was intended to achieve. It always gets an answer, even if the answer is no. Jesus said 'I will not judge them. The word I have spoken will judge them. If I had not come and spoken to them they would have an excuse for their sin…'

My response must be practical; it must entail doing something. Believing something up in my head is nothing more than mental assent. Knowing that Jesus is God is not faith. Satan knows that. Faith is not up in the head; it is in the heart, and it eventually makes its way down into my feet. It is only then that I will be prepared to step out, and act on the direction given me by Jesus. The message of the gospel is very simple, very definite, and very direct. There is not one maybe or one might in all the promises of Jesus.

'Remember what I have told you …' Jesus must go so that the Spirit can come to complete his work on earth, and bring us the fullness of grace. It is the work of the Spirit in us that enables us respond to the call of Jesus. There are two parts to the journey of salvation. Jesus travelled the first part on our behalf, and the Spirit leads us through the final part. We cannot travel any part of either journey on our own. The gospels speak of Jesus being led by the Spirit. In almost every sentence in today's gospel, Jesus is speaking about the Father and the Spirit. What's involved here is our full sharing in the life of the Trinity.

Practical

Today's gospel is a teaching. Supposing I was to read it slowly once more, or give it to you to reflect on for a while, what do you think would be its most important teaching for you? There is great emphasis on obedience, on doing what Jesus tells me. This is the proof that I love him, and that his message is getting a response from me. Coming to Mass here today is one of the ways in which you respond. The real response, of course, is in the heart. It is not what I do, but why I do it. I do it because Jesus asked me to do it. This has to do with forgiveness, charity, prayer, and how I treat my neighbour.

Because of your Baptism and Confirmation, you have the Holy Spirit. The problem could be that the Holy Spirit may not have you! How conscious are you of the Spirit in your life? We are all familiar with words and acts that are inspired by a spirit of anger, rage, revenge, hatred, bigotry, or violence. As a Christian, my words and actions should be inspired and 'charged' with the power of the Holy Spirit. This is not automatic, but results from my constant whispered prayers, as I go about my daily tasks. It is not about saying prayers, as much as having a praying heart. Jesus said that the Spirit would remind us. It is important to remember to whisper the prayer first, before I say the word or do the act. In that way the Spirit will be able to work through me. A simple prayer would be 'Lord, may your Spirit within me touch the hearts of those I meet today, either through the words I say, the prayers I pray, the life I live, or the very person that I am.'

Some of our simpler prayers have to do with the Trinity, Father, Son, and Spirit. From early infancy we were taught to bless ourselves In the name of the Father, and of the Son, and of the Holy Spirit. We also pray Glory be to the Father, and to the Son, and to the Holy Spirit. It would be a lovely idea just to take those two short simple prayers, and to repeat them slowly and sincerely to ourselves over a period of time. No doubt we have often rattled them off, without any thought or attention. It would be a very simple way to pray, and it would help greatly to remind us of the extraordinary inheritance that is ours, because of what Jesus has done for us.

Story

This is not so much a story, as a description of a situation. On several occasions I had the privilege of leading a group of pilgrims to the Holy Land. On the first morning in Jerusalem we usually began on the Mount of Olives. From there we walked down a narrow roadway that led down to the garden of Gethsemane. On the way down the hill we turned into another garden, and entered a beautiful little church. The church is built in the shape of a tear, and is called the *Dominus Flevit* (The Lord wept). It marks the spot from which Jesus overlooked the city of Jerusalem, and wept. He said 'Salvation was within your grasp, but you would not accept it. Now your enemies will surround you on every side, and your temple will be left with not one stone upon another'. Recalling these words of Jesus in that place today can be very moving. Behind the altar is a window which gives a clear view across the Kedron valley to the old city of Jerusalem. As you watch, you will notice that every third or fourth vehicle is a security one, containing police or soldiers. It is literally true that their enemies surround them on every side. Within the walls of the old city lie the ruins of the Temple, and this can never be rebuilt. Within the ruins, somewhere, is the part that used be called the Holy of Holies, and no Jew would dare enter those ruins in case of walking on such a sacred spot. They are caught in a catch-22 situation, because, while no Jew may enter, they would never allow a Gentile to rebuild their Temple. Which means, simply, that, after all these years, the Temple is still left without one stone upon another.

There is no peace outside of Jesus Christ. Worldly forces like UN, NATO, etc. can stop wars but they cannot bring peace. The war breaks out further down the road…

ASCENSION OF THE LORD

Gospel: Luke 24:46-53

Theme

In today's gospel Jesus gives his final message, his final instructions, his final promise, and his final blessing to his apostles. It is obvious that they believed they would see him again, because they were filled with great joy, and their hearts were bursting with prayers of gratitude.

Parable

One of the special blessings I have had in life is that I got to work with the terminally ill, the aged, and the dying on very many occasions. There is nothing more touching or edifying that to be with someone who knows where she's going. To hear someone speak with assurance, peace, and calm, about the fact that she is about to take her leave of her family and friends, and go on to the third and final stage of life, can be very moving. To be present with the family members who are also on the same wavelength is even more moving. To them it is *Au Revoir* and not Goodbye. The person is not going away, but is simply going ahead. At an earlier time in the gospel story, Jesus tells his apostles they are sad to think that he is about to leave them. He went on to explain to them why he had to leave, and why it was for their good that he was leaving. He was going, so that the Spirit could come to complete his work. Apparently his words sank home, judging from the reaction of the apostles in today's gospel, when Jesus did finally leave them.

Teaching

Jesus said that he came to do the Father's will. That was the one thing that kept him going, and that he kept his mind on. He had a mission to accomplish, 'and how can I be at peace until it is accomplished?' That mission was now complete. Even on Calvary Jesus prayed 'Father, I have finished the work you gave me to do'. He could now return in triumph, and the third and final part of God's creative plan of love could begin. The first part was creation itself, which was God's great expression of love. When we messed up that one, Jesus came to present a mission of mercy, of salvation, of redemption. When he had completed that, the Spirit would come, and like the breath of God entering

the clay at the moment of human creation, we would be renewed, reborn, recreated. God's plan would be completed.

Jesus knew his apostles only too well. They were ordinary
weak human beings. He advises them to stay in Jerusalem, and
not leave until the Spirit came. The implication here is that, if
they go off on their own, they are sure to get it all wrong. He tells
them that they will be filled with power from heaven. If you
throw your mind back to the Annunciation, you will remember
that Mary was promised that the power of the Most High would
overshadow her. Only God can do God's work. Therefore, those
whom God uses to do his work must be filled with his power,
live and work through his power, and depend totally on that
power.

Before leaving them, Jesus blessed them. They were, indeed,
truly blessed. Even though the Spirit had not yet come, they
were already filled with hope. Their hearts were filled with
prayer and praise. They seemed to have crossed the bridge from
fear and a lack of faith, into a quiet conviction that the Lord
would fulfil his promises to them. Once again, referring to Mary,
Elizabeth told her 'All these things happened to you because
you believed that the promises of the Lord would be fulfilled.'
When the Spirit would come their mission would begin.

Response

In another gospel account of the Ascension, we are told that,
while the apostles stood looking up to the heavens after Jesus,
angels appeared to them, and told them not to be looking up
there. Jesus ascended into heaven alright, but he is also to be
found all around us, especially in the poor, the suffering, the
marginalised, and the down-trodden. The apostles were to look
around them, and concentrate on life down here. The role of the
Christian is not to work to get to heaven, but to do everything
possible to get heaven down here. There are people around me
living in hell. Make me a channel of your peace. It is much more
difficult to get heaven into people than to get people into heaven!

Jesus is our Moses, leading us into the Promised Land. He
tells us that he will come and bring us, so that where he is we
also will be. He says that he will never abandon us. When he
was on this earth, he was Saviour. He wasn't yet Lord, because
he had not yet achieved the victory, and overcome all the power
of the evil one, and all the effects of original sin. Now, however,
when he returns in triumph to his Father, he will become Lord,
and his Kingdom will be established. 'All power is given to me

in heaven and on earth...'. His Kingdom is identified in three simple ways. Jesus is Lord, the power to live in the Kingdom is the Holy Spirit, and all of God's children have equal access to that Kingdom. The most disabled person on this earth is here with as much right as the greatest genius that ever lived.

Jesus calls himself The Way. Notice he doesn't say that he is one of the ways. He is the way, and there is no other. He asked us to follow him, and, if we did that, we would not walk in darkness, but would have the light of life. Following Jesus includes following him through the gates of death into the fullness of life. It is only when I reach that third and final stage of life that I will become all that God created me to be. If you waken up some morning and discover that your life is exactly the way it should be, don't move, ... just wait for the undertaker! You have arrived, the journey is complete, and all the promises of the Lord will be fulfilled.

Practical

Come back to the gospel of today again. Don't take it as something that happened thousands of years ago. Put yourself in today's gospel. You are one of Jesus' followers. His words are addressed to you. Let me read the words Jesus spoke one more time, only, this time, we listen to them as being spoken to us now.

There is one question that merits very serious reflection. Do I really believe that the Spirit of God is within me, and I am filled with power from heaven? Surely if I really believed this, the effect on my life would be profound. I would suggest that it is very important to personalise the reality of Jesus in my life. I have to meet him as Saviour, and experience his love and forgiveness. I have to reflect on his promises, and take them as promises made to me. Who do you say that I am? Will you also go away? Do you love me more than these? Jesus has very personal questions for me, and the more I personalise those questions and his many promises, the more real he will become in my life.

Some people just don't know what to do about the thought of death. Should I look at it realistically now, and face up to its implications, or should I just keep my head down, keep going, and wait till it approaches me? I think it is a mistake to take the gospel as some sort of a la carte menu, where I can choose what suits me, and leave the rest. Jesus has shared in every dimension of human living. He has encountered and overcome the enemies of sin, sickness, and death. He has opened the gates of heaven, and he has offered us passports, visas, and green cards to enter heaven. The gospel is Good News, and was never intended to be turned into good advice. Pentecost is coming soon. This is our chance to open our hearts anew to the fullness of the life, the peace, and the joy that Jesus offers us.

Story

There is a story told about a small town in Germany that was severely blasted during the last war. Some years later, the buildings were restored. One of the buildings was the town's cathedral. When the renovation was completed, it was noticed that a large figure of Christ the King, which stood in front of the cathedral, was still unrepaired, when both hands had been blown off in the explosion. When there was no sign of it being repaired, some people went to the parish priest to enquire if he had any plans to repair the statue. He surprised them all by saying that, no, he was going to leave the statue exactly as it was. He explained that, when Jesus ascended into heaven, he took his body with him. He asked us to provide the body (church?), and his Spirit would provide everything else. He would not replace the hands on the statue, to remind people that Jesus has no other hands but ours, when it comes to continuing the building of his Kingdom here on earth.

PENTECOST SUNDAY

Gospel: John 14:15-16, 23-26

Theme

In today's gospel, while renewing his promise to send the Holy Spirit, Jesus always stresses obedience as a condition for receiving that Spirit. 'As the Father sent me, so I am sending you.' 'I came to do the will of him who sent me ... If you love me, you will obey me...'

Parable

I remember doing some sort of intelligence test many years ago. We were presented with a page of questions. On the very top of the page was one simple instruction 'Please read all questions before you begin to answer.' The natural tendency of many, of course, was to look at the first question, answer it, and continue down the page. You can imagine how they felt when they came to question 12, which said 'And now, having read all the questions, please do not answer the first eleven!' It pays to do what you're told...!

Teaching

Original sin was a refusal to obey. Humans had decided that their way was best, and human pride rejected divine love. Satan (then called Lucifer) was the first to refuse to obey. In the story of the Fall, he figures largely in getting Adam and Eve to follow his example. The life of Jesus would be one of total obedience, 'even to death on the cross'. This way, he would remove the damage of original sin, and restore humanity to its proper relationship with the divine, as creatures before the Creator.

Jesus lays great emphasis on obedience. His very reason for coming was to do the will of his Father in heaven. He calls on us to obey him, just as he obeys the Father. 'As the Father has sent me, so do I send you ... If you love me you will obey me...' He promises the Spirit to those who obey him. If the Spirit is going to inspire, guide, and teach, then, of course, we must be ready to follow. We are told that Jesus was led by the Spirit into the desert, down to the Temple, etc. I cannot be led if I am unwilling to follow...

Jesus links up his work with the initiative of the Father, what he himself has undertaken, and what the Spirit will do to complete that work, when Jesus' task is over. The story of salvation is the story of the Trinity, offering us a share in the life of the Divinity. To bring us into obedience is to restore us to the family of God, and completely reverse the effects of original sin.

Response
Jesus was sent by the Father with a message, and our salvation depends on us listening to, and following that message. The first step is the coming of Jesus. The second step is the message he gives. ('Jesus came to do and to teach'). The final part of the programme of salvation is the coming of the Spirit. 'That we might live no longer for ourselves, but for him, he sent the Holy Spirit, as his first gift to those who believe, to complete his work on earth, and to bring us the fullness of grace.'

It is vital for us to hear the message. 'They have ears, but they hear not ...' With the message comes the grace to respond to that message. His message is of such a nature, that it can only be heard with the heart. 'Unless you become like little children ...' His message is of such a nature that it will never make sense to the intellectual and the worldly-wise ...

The message of Jesus is compared to a farmer going out to sow seed. He throws the seed in all directions, and lets it fall where it will. It is only when the Spirit comes that the conditions will exist for the seed to grow. It is the Spirit who will provide the Spring conditions in our hearts, enabling the seed to sprout, take root there, and produce fruit that will remain.

Practical
Here is a thought that merits some reflection: I have to learn to listen, and then I can listen to learn.' It is not easy to listen. Some people are so much better at listening than others. It is a decision born out of love to decide to try to really listen to others. Real prayer is 'Speak, Lord, your servant is listening', rather than 'Listen, Lord, your servant is speaking'.

Keeping his commandments has to do with loving God and loving others. It is the balance between the vertical and the horizontal. God doesn't want to hear me say to him 'I'm sorry, I love you, thank you, etc...' unless those around me hear it first. Jesus is very clear and definite when he speaks his message. 'If you forgive, you are forgiven. If you show mercy, you will receive mercy. If you show compassion, you will receive compassion. Judge not, and you will not be judged. The measure you use to give to others is the measure used in giving to you...'

Today's gospel gives us much thought for reflection. It is a gospel that needs to be reflected on, and prayed through, until the Spirit begins to reveal its simplicity and its centrality to my heart. Take special care and full responsibility for the word of God contained in these reflections. Carry them with you in your heart, and let them germinate there. If your attitude is right, and the good-will is there, you can be certain that the Spirit will do everything else.

Story
There was a young lad one time who decided to become a saint. He went down to the library, and got several books on the lives of the saints, in the hope that he might find one who could be his role model. He actually chose St Simon Stylites, one of the most unusual saints in the calendar. Simon lived many centuries ago, and the story is that he lived on the top of a very high pillar in the middle of the town square. What drew the young lad to select him was that, well, if you're going to be a saint, you might as well get as much publicity out of it as possible! I mean, everybody in town knew Simon, and everyone knew he was a saint, despite the fact that if he were alive today, he'd probably be locked up!

The problem our young friend had was that there was no pillar down in the middle of the town square. He opted for humble beginnings, so he got a chair in the kitchen, and stood on it. Shortly after that his mother wanted to get to the sink, so he had to move his chair. Then it was his sister trying to get to the fridge, and he had to move again. Shortly afterwards, his brothers came in the back door, bumped into him, and knocked him off his chair onto the floor. Eventually, he had to abandon his efforts, and, as he put the chair to one side, he declared with complete conviction 'No, it's not possible; it's just not possible to become a saint at home'!

The reality is that it is not possible to become a saint anywhere else! Bloom where you're planted, just as the seed of Jesus' message must grow in the heart in which it is planted.

TRINITY SUNDAY

Gospel: John 16:12-15

Theme

In today's gospel, Jesus gives us a brief summary of the connection between the roles of each member of the Trinity in the work of our salvation. Jesus never said anything unless the Father told him to do so. When the Spirit comes, he will follow the same approach, and will not say anything that would contradict anything Jesus said. All three Persons are of one mind and one intent when it comes to what's best for us.

Parable

At the time of writing there is intense negotiations going on to finalise and copper-fasten the peace process in the North of Ireland. There is shuttle diplomacy all over the place, as intermediaries fly back and forth between London, Dublin, and Belfast. The civil servants involved, and most of the politicians, are quite skillful negotiators. The one absolute in all the negotiations is that no one makes a decision, or finalises a deal without first consulting with, and getting the clearance from those whom they represent. It is vital that all the negotiators on any one side be of one mind and one heart, at every step of the way. They would lose all credibility as peace-brokers if they themselves didn't get on together.

Teaching

When Adam and Eve fell for the lie in the Garden, we came under new management. Jesus would call Satan 'the father of lies'. It is more than significant that he should refer to the Holy Spirit as 'The Spirit of Truth'. His Spirit would be the antidote for all the harm effected by the lies and deceit of Satan.

To be guided into all truth is quite a promise. Of ourselves, we could never find this. Part of the damage of original sin is that it blinds us to the reality of our sinful condition. I'm not saying or implying that we are sinning all the time, or anything like that. What I'm referring to here is the exact nature of our weakness and powerlessness. It may sound a contradiction, but there is no greater grace than to have a clear appreciation of just how weak and powerless we are. The result of this is to open us to the power and strength of God. People may believe in God, but they may not be too convinced that they really need him just now.

When Jesus took on our humanity, he put his divinity to one side, and he really did become as we are. In today's gospel, Jesus is speaking of being restored to the glory he had, before he came on earth. The Spirit would glorify him through us. The Spirit would complete the work of Jesus in us, and thus would the name of Jesus become known, and his Kingdom built.

Response

I often reflect on the words of Jesus 'Oh, there is so much more that I wish to tell you, but you cannot bear it now'. Jesus continues to speak to us each day. Prayer is mainly about hearing his voice; it is about listening to him. It is on-going revelation, because I would not be capable of grasping his message in its completeness. It wouldn't surprise me if that revelation were to continue for all eternity in heaven.

One of the conditions for receiving his Spirit is to have a desire, a willingness, a hunger for truth. If I don't want to hear the truth, then even the Holy Spirit cannot reveal that to me. There are none so deaf as those who don't want to hear. 'Lord let me know the truth about myself today; let know the truth about you today.' If I want to know the truth, a good place to start is to ask the Spirit to reveal the truth to me. To be caught in a wrong relationship, in a destructive addiction, in an aggressive pattern of behaviour, is to be caught in a web of lies and deceit. This is to live in denial, because the human mind is quite capable of justifying anything.

To live with the Trinity is to be in very good company! This is what Jesus is offering in today's gospel. I can open my heart to the Niagara of the Father's love, to the redeeming love of Jesus, to the anointing and empowering of the Spirit. According to Jesus, this brings about a conformity of will. Jesus was totally committed to do the will of his Father. The Spirit would complete the work of Jesus. The Father who sent Jesus, and who 'will surely give the Spirit to those who ask him', that same Father spoke out of the clouds on more than one occasion, to confirm the work and life of Jesus. 'This is my beloved son, in whom I am well pleased. Listen to him.'

Practical

It is easy to be practical in my response to today's gospel. Truth is a very special commodity, and there is no way it can be counterfeited. The truth is in our heart if we want to know it. It is so easy for any of us to live in denial, to refuse to accept reality, to attempt to escape from reality. 'The truth will set you free.' If there is one grace I would ask for more than another, it would be the grace to be completely honest with myself, with God, and with others. Please take this thought seriously, and make it your own.

If I pick up a telephone, dial a number, I can reasonably expect a phone somewhere else to ring, and to hear a voice from there. However, if there had been a storm the previous night, and the telephone wires were down, then I could dial away without result. The connection is broken, and there is no way, from where I am, that I can make that connection. The Holy Spirit is the connection when I pick up the phone to pray. By myself I cannot pray; all I can do is say prayers. Always make sure that you plug into the Power of God when you turn to him in prayer.

Jesus speaks about the Holy Spirit revealing to us all about him. In other words, to use the example I used in the last paragraph, the Holy Spirit is like a two-way radio. It is through the Spirit that God speaks to me, and that I speak to God. I open my heart to the Spirit of God. 'Come, Holy Spirit, fill the hearts of your faithful, and enkindle within them the fires of your love.' I cannot make any progress along the road of spirituality without the Spirit working in me. Just like the air I breathe keeps my life-systems going, so the Spirit, the Breath of God, continues to transform me, and to continue the work of Incarnation within me.

Story
When I was growing up in the country, there was a man who used come around from time to time buying hens. He would buy a hen, tie her legs with a bit of string, and throw her into the back of his donkey-drawn cart. One day he decided to give us local yokels a lesson in hen psychology! He took a pen-knife out of his pocket, reached into the cart, and snipped the twine tying the legs of one of the hens. I was convinced that the hen would fly away, but I discovered that the man knew more about hens than I did! The hen was free, but she didn't know she was free, because all the other hens around her were not free! He was convinced that the only time the hen would fly away would be if he snipped the twine tying the legs of all the hens. In that case, they all would fly away.

It is so easy for any of us to forget that we are free; that we have the Spirit who leads us into all truth, and that the truth will set us free...

THE BODY AND BLOOD OF CHRIST

Gospel: Luke 9:11-17

Theme
Today's gospel presents us with the story of one of the miracles of the loaves and fish. It is a very rich and enriching gospel, and there is so much to be gained from reflecting on it.

Parable
Over the past couple of years we have witnessed some awful atrocities, which resulted in thousands of people being displaced, and becoming refugees in a neighbouring country. One of the sights that sticks in the memory is the sight of all the hands reached out as someone passes bread or other food to them. There is never enough, and, even the food they receive is nothing compared to what they deserve.

Teaching
The first point I would like to stress is that Jesus and his disciples were tired and had planned on slipping away quietly for a rest. They did not succeed, however, because the crowds followed them, and caught up with them. The response of Jesus was to welcome them, and to begin teaching them about the Kingdom of God, and he healed those who were sick.

The second point I would stress is that, though the people were hungry, they did not seem to be aware of that. It was the apostles who drew Jesus' attention to the fact that these people needed to go somewhere to get something to eat. They themselves were so hungry for the word he spoke to them, that they forgot all about their physical hungers.

A third point is the response of the apostles when Jesus suggested to them 'You feed them'. Naturally, this was absolutely impossible. They had only a few loaves and fish. Jesus took the bread and fish, and he worked the miracle to feed the thousands. The point he wanted the apostles to learn was that whatever you have is enough, if you just give it to me. One of the saddest phrases in the gospel is to ask, in the presence of Jesus, 'What are these among so many?' How easy it is for any of us to look at the world's problems, look at our own resources, and decide to do nothing, because what we have to offer looks so trivial.

Response

'Not on bread alone do people live, but on every word that comes from the mouth of God.' The greatest hunger on earth is the need to belong, the need to be loved. The people in today's gospel seem to have forgotten all about their physical hunger, in their eagerness to hear the teachings of Jesus. It is interesting to note that, when they caught up with Jesus, he immediately began to teach them. At that stage there was no thought or mention of food.

There would seem to be a direct connection between the words of Jesus and his acts of healing. They always seem to go together. When the centurion came to Jesus about his servant who was dying, he simply said 'Say but the word, and my servant will be healed.' His word is always a healing word. To listen to his word with an open heart is to be open to being healed.

I may not have much, but what I have is enough. 'Here I am, Lord. I'm not much; I don't have much; but whatever I have, I put it at your disposal. Make me a channel of your peace...' Each one of us is uniquely gifted. No one of us possesses the exact same gifts. Some are natural leaders, speakers, organisers, or initiators. God gives us nothing for ourselves. He doesn't give us the gift of speech to go around talking to ourselves!

Practical

It would be a source of much enrichment in my life if I took some time out to reflect on my appetites. We can so easily get into the habit of over-indulgence in matters of food and drink. We can be driven by lust, greed, ambition, or pride. Our will can run riot, and I can become the centre of my universe. Whether I am conscious of it or not, I do have a real appetite for the word of God. It is so easy to become spiritually undernourished. The real Third World can be here in the West, in the midst of all our affluence and wealth. Today's gospel invites me to reflect on where I stand relative to all of this.

Once Jesus comes into my life, I can expect miracles, because 'there is nothing impossible with God'. All he needs is what I have, and what I am. He is always on standby, waiting for a word from me. I can 'mouth' prayers that are meaningless, or I can turn to him with complete confidence, and be open to the infinite blessings that his presence ensures. The choice is mine. The apostles asked Jesus to send the people away, so they could get something to eat elsewhere. In saying this they misunderstood the reality of Jesus. If Jesus was there, the people just could not go elsewhere. 'To whom else can we go? You, and you alone, have the words of eternal life. We know, and we believe that you are the Christ, the Son of the living God, who has come into this world.'

Imagine you were asked to write a prayer in response to today's gospel, what would that prayer be? May I suggest one possible prayer? 'Lord Jesus, as I look around today's world, I see so many of your people without even the basic necessities of life. I also see many trying to meet their inner hungers with drugs, money, pleasure, and power. I can look at myself, and feel helpless and hopeless among such want and deprivation. On the other hand, I can accept you as someone who came among us to rescue us, to redeem us, to do for us what we never could do for ourselves. I can turn the whole situation over to you, make available to you the little that I am and have, and let you do something with me that will make a difference. I cannot make a difference, but you can make a difference through me. Make me a channel of your peace. Where there is hunger, let me bring your food …'

Story
In his book, 'The Fall', Albert Camus tells the story of a man in the legal profession who is visiting a red-light district of Amsterdam. He hears a woman's screams close by, and he suspects that some woman has been thrown into the canal. His immediate instinct is to be cautious. If he runs to her assistance, he, too, could be attacked. He could also be questioned by police, as they arrive, and he ran a risk of having his name and photo in the newspapers. As he reflected on all his options, the woman's screams died down, and he knew by now that it would be too late to attempt anything. Camus' next line is chilling. 'He didn't do anything, because that was the kind of man he was.'

Today's gospel calls on us to do something …

SECOND SUNDAY OF THE YEAR

Gospel: John 2:1-11

Theme

Today's gospel sees Jesus begin his mission. Now, for the first time, Jesus can go public, and we begin to discover the power of God at the wedding feast at Cana. Since Christmas, we have been considering the preparation for the work. This is a very simple, homely setting. It is obviously among friends. Jesus had been invited to the wedding, as had his mother, and his other friends, later to be called apostles. They were having a good time, when the whole scene threatened to turn sour. Running out of wine at a wedding would be like having the reception in Mc Donald's today! The hosts would be the talk of the town for generations to come. Mary was a quiet woman, who listened more than she talked. It was probably she who first noticed the predicament, and there was no way she could stand idly by, and let the unthinkable happen. She went straight to Jesus, and, as was her wont, instead of a big long speech, she simply said 'They have no wine'. Because she was full of grace, totally led by the Spirit, it was almost as if the Father spoke through her, to signal to Jesus that, yes, his hour had come.

Parable

Beneath the driest desert there is plenty of water. The problem is that the water cannot get to the surface. This happens here and there, and each oasis is a vital source of life for those who travel the desert. In today's world, there is plenty of food, but while half the world is dying of hunger, the other half is on a diet, trying to get down the weight. We have all known some unique and special person, someone who always had time for others, who had some endless supply of compassion, of love, and of patience. Their very presence, and their involvement, was the inspiration that gave hope, momentum, and enthusiasm to all undertakings. For such people problems become challenges and opportunities. I believe in miracles, because I have seen Irish mothers work miracles with very limited resources, in the rearing of their children. As at Cana, they might only have water, but somehow, whatever they had, seemed to be enough, because the Lord was always on hand… It's so true when we say that, if you want to get something done, ask a busy person…

Teaching
A beautiful and very simple story. Grace builds on nature. All
they had was water, and whatever any of us has is enough for
God, if we make it available to him. Only God can do God-
things, and a miracle is a God-thing. There are many many
things that you or I cannot do, but someone, somewhere else
could actually do that thing. A miracle, on the other hand, is
something that is beyond the power of human nature, and can
happen only when God intervenes and makes it possible. It is a
very important lesson to learn that I am not God, and that there
are many things in my life that are beyond my control, and require a miracle. God becomes God in my life the moment I get
out of the way, and stop trying to play God. Notice, in today's
gospel, that Mary didn't dare attempt to go the miracle route by
herself!

I always think of Mary as constantly living with mystery. In
other words, she may not have fully grasped the full implications of where life was leading her. She just kept repeating her
YES, and she left the rest to God. This was her prayer from the
time of the Annunciation, on the road to Egypt, at Cana, and on
Calvary. Her instructions were basic, and simple: 'Do whatever
he tells you'. I am not interested in devotion to Mary, when this
puts her on a pedestal, somewhat out of reach of us mere mortals. Rather am I interested in a relationship with Mary, where
she travels the journey with me, and, when I come face to face
with life's problems, she whispers 'Do whatever he tells you'.
Original sin was one of disobedience, and total obedience was
the only antidote for that. Jesus would later say 'If you love me,
you will obey me, and then you can ask the Father for anything
in my name'.

What does Jesus tell me? He tells me that he has come that we
should have life, and that, apart from him, we can do nothing.
He speaks about the Father's love, about his own very strong
preference for the broken and the lost ones, and that the Spirit he
will send will complete his work in us. I could take pen and
paper, and write down the exact promises and teachings of
Jesus. There is not one might or maybe in the whole gospel. His
words are simple, and his word is certain. All he asks is that we
believe him, and then obey him. 'Fill the jars with water' was a
very simple instruction. He asked them to do something well
within their power, and then, to leave the rest to him. He asked
them to act within their limits, but he would not have been free

to help them if they set the limits for what he was to do. Do what he tells you, and then get out of the way.

Response

This gospel is much more than just bailing some friends out of a problem. It gives us a close-up of Jesus at work. The gospel is now, and I am every person in it. We all have situations in our lives that are just as serious as the one facing the bride and groom at Cana. It is quite possible, actually, that the young couple at Cana may not have been aware of their predicament, until they heard what Jesus had done. In our case, however, we must surely be conscious of situations in our lives where we are acutely aware of our own powerlessness, and our inability to manage things. In human language, this is negative and problematic, but in the designs of God, it contains the possibility of miracle, with an opportunity to get a close-up view of the Lord's care in our lives.

Problems and struggles are part of life, and of living. No doubt, this young couple encountered many another problem as they travelled through life. All marriages have problems, and, thankfully, many of them also have solutions and resolutions to their problems. It is reasonable to presume that, when other problems arose in this couple's lives, that they remembered who was there to help them on the day of their wedding. A wedding is for a day, but marriage is intended for life, even if, for various reasons, it doesn't work out that way. Jesus should not be registered in our phone books under Emergency Numbers. He would wish to be involved in all that we do. He wants to walk every step of the way with us. The wedding at Cana was a public celebration of love, and, where there is love, there is God. They who live in love, live in God, and God lives in them.

In the gospel, this miracle is called a sign. Signs, of themselves, don't do anything. A signpost, pointing to Dublin, cannot compel me to go to Dublin. A Stop sign won't stop me, if I choose to keep going. The idea is to read the sign, know what it means, and follow what it says. Every miracle in the gospel is a sign, and each of those signs is intended for us here, right now. People on a treasure hunt follow the signs, and one sign leads to the next. The gospels teach a whole way of life and of living, if I choose to follow the directions they give me. God will not drag, goose-step, or Shanghai me into anything. He will show the way, and invite me to follow. The servants in today's gospel had only to do exactly what Jesus told them, and he took care of the rest. Today's gospel is well worth reflecting on, and it can give much material for prayer.

Practical

Ask Mary to look within your heart, and see what is missing there. Then ask her to go to Jesus and obtain whatever it is you lack. He has no job. She has no health. They have no peace. Thinking of Mary as she is seen in today's gospel can help greatly in developing a very real and practical relationship with her.

Whatever you have is enough. Stop comparing yourself with others. If you are in a wheelchair, and can do nothing for yourself, then let Jesus have whatever little you have, and he will do the rest. Your silent prayer for others could be the most powerful influence for good. Some of the greatest movements for good in the history of the world were brought about by the quiet prayers of totally unknown people. At Cana it was water; later on it was a few loaves and fish. Whatever you have is enough. There is not one person in this church today who doesn't have the material out of which God can work miracles for others.

Life is a journey that is made up of many journeys. Each journey has its own births, deaths, and struggles. Freud said that the test of your maturity is that, if you had a choice, you would want to be the age you are. Old age can be beautiful, when it brings mellowness, wisdom, and quiet contentment. In that sense, the best wine of life is kept till last. The definition of a good life is: When you were born, you alone cried, and everybody else was very happy. Live your life in such a way that, when you die, you will be very happy, and everybody else will be crying! (Mark Twain says that you should live your life in such a way that, when you die, even the undertaker will be sorry!) We can settle for a life-style that is as insipid as water, or we can open our hearts to the abundant life Jesus offers us, and celebrate the gift with ever increasing joy.

Story

John was one of those people who could say 'Thank God, I'm an atheist', and never see the contradiction! He was always attacking Joe about his religious beliefs and practices. Joe took it all in good spirits, because he had his own quiet conviction in his own beliefs, and what he knew of Jesus, and he considered that such attacks were par for the course for those who took Jesus seriously. John was really annoyed that he failed to get a rise out of Joe, and his intellectual arguments were getting him nowhere. One day, in desperation, he tackled Joe about Jesus, asking him if he had ever seen one single sign or evidence of Jesus' presence in his life. He scornfully referred to Cana, and asked Joe about the chances of Jesus turning a glass of water into wine, if Joe asked him. Joe smiled. He himself had been a chronic alcoholic earlier in life, before he met John, and John was unaware of that. Joe simply said: 'I don't want Jesus to turn that water into wine. When I really needed him, I fell on my knees and asked for help, and he turned wine back into water for me. That was miracle enough for me, because it certainly was something I myself could never have done. There was a time when I would have died for wine, and I would have killed for wine, but, thanks to Jesus, all of that hell and misery is completely in the past. The miracle continues, because, today, I'd prefer one drop of water to a whole barrel of wine. No, John, you can laugh and scorn all your like, and it doesn't bother me, because I know that Jesus is with me, and is looking after me.'

THIRD SUNDAY OF THE YEAR

Gospel: Luke 1:1-4; 4:14-21

Theme

Once again, this Sunday, we see the mission of Jesus move on a pace. He is still being led by the Spirit that had come upon him in the Jordan river. He had a message to preach, and a way of life to teach. He had moved away from home, and had made such an impression that word about him had got back to his home place of Nazareth. In today's gospel, he returns to Nazareth. We are told that he entered the synagogue on the Sabbath, as he usually did. The curious onlookers and hangers-on were concerned that, being at home, and being in the synagogue, he would just be like everyone else, and there would be none of the normal excitement and stir that usually followed him wherever he went. They were not to be disappointed, though. What happened was probably something that went away over the heads of anyone who was not familiar with the words of the prophets. Isaiah had stated very clearly the signs that would show when the Messiah had come. Jesus read that passage to them. He then rolled up the scroll, looked around, and announced 'Today these prophetic words come true even as you speak'. Away back in the desert he had locked horns with Satan. Now, in the very heart of their citadel, he was taking on the religious leaders, when he announced that he had come to replace their love of law with a new law of love. This was the beginning of the end for Jesus, but, with typical gospel paradox, that end would just be the beginning.

Parable

Imagine, if you can, that the powers-that-be are trying everything within their power to discredit someone whom they want to get rid of. In that society Christianity is strictly forbidden, so they decided to go that route. They accused him of being a Christian, and he ends up before the court, to face this charge. The prosecutors dug up an old law that forbade good news being preached to the poor, liberty being preached to captives, or freedom being made available to the oppressed. They went to great lengths to collect witnesses, who would show, beyond all reasonable doubt that this man had, in fact, broken this law. One witness accused him of bringing good news to the poor, but when pressed, he just could not provide one concrete example where this actually happened. The most he might ever have done was to talk about doing it. As each witness came along, not one of them could give a single example of where this man actually did any of the things they had heard him speak of. The prosecution's case collapsed, and the man got off scot-free, because there wasn't the slightest evidence in his life that he was, in fact, and in act, a Christian.

Teaching
The gospels of these Sundays are powerful, rich in meaning, and very central to the message that Jesus came to proclaim. The word gospel means Good News, and I will only hear it as good news, if I am ready to hear such news. The weather forecast for tomorrow, no matter what it is, will be good news for some and bad for others. If you are on a camping trip, you will want plenty of sunshine, and if you are a farmer, you are concerned and worried about the lack of rainfall on your newly sown crops. If you are in touch with your own poverty, be that physical, emotional, or spiritual; with your own blindness, whether that be spiritual or pure bigotry and racism; with your own personal bondage, whether that be depression, addiction, or despair, then, and only then, will you really tune in to the Good News of today's gospel.

It is important to remember that the gospel is now, and I am every person in it. Right here, right now, Jesus tells me that these words are being fulfilled even as I listen. The words of Jesus are anointed by the Spirit, and when his words enter the heart, the Spirit enters with them. Words, of themselves, have no value. I meet people who ask me how I am, and I don't tell them, because I know that they really don't want to know! Someone else can ask the exact same question, and, because of the spirit of concern in the question, I will sit down and answer the question (often in such detail they they're sorry they asked me!) I can stand up here now, and you're wondering what I'm going to say, and I'm wondering what you're going to hear! If we are open to the word of God, anointed by the Spirit, then all of us are listening with great openness to what the Lord wants to say to me this morning. God will never disappoint you. If you don't expect to hear something that will profoundly effect your life, then, you can be sure, that you will not hear it. If, on the other hand, you open your heart, with a whispered Speak, Lord, your servant is listening, then you can be certain that your heart will be touched, that your spirit will be healed, and that your day will be anointed.

At the beginning of this gospel, we are told that everyone was very pleased with his teaching thus far. The next sentence in the story, after where today's gospel ends, says that 'All agreed with him, and were lost in wonder, while he kept on speaking about the grace of God.' In next Sunday's gospel, we will read about how this present encounter ended up. Not too well, actually, but you'll have to tune into the next episode next week! Human nature has some in-built resistance to God, that is a direct result of original sin. There is some sort of basic rebelliousness within us; some sort of stubborn pride; some inability to accept and to live within reality. This, again, is another form of the poverty, the blindness, and the oppression spoken of in today's gospel. As a human being, I am subject to the law of gravity. By myself it is impossible for me to lift myself out of the quicksand of my own selfishness. If I were the only human being on this planet, Jesus would still have to come to join me, to lead me, to save me, because, by myself, I just don't have what it takes.

Response
The next time you are at a funeral, pay particular attention to the readings, and to the words that are spoken. These are meant for you, and not for the person who has died! What's the point in reading the gospel to a lifeless corpse in a coffin? The same goes for today's gospel. The people who were in the synagogue all those years ago are well dead by now! Today's gospel is meant for us ... right here, today.

It's not so long ago since we celebrated Christmas. That was good, and all very well. However, it was for bringing a message, like the one in today's gospel, that Jesus came in the first place. Birthdays are all very well, but it would hardly be appropriate to ignore that person until the next birthday comes along. The word of God is always new, it is always present tense, it calls for a response right now. The words of the prophet that Jesus quotes in today's gospel are repeated several times in the gospel. Jesus quoted them to the disciples of John the Baptist who came to ask if he were the Messiah, or should they look somewhere else. Jesus told them to look around, and see for themselves that these words were being fulfilled. When he sent out his apostles, he quoted these words, and told them that their lives should give witness to the reality of these words. If someone from Mars arrived here today, and asked 'Are you Christians, or will I have to look elsewhere?' could we quote these words, and ask him to look around, and see for himself?

The Old Testament is like radio, the New Testament is like television, and the life of the Christian should be live drama. The value of Christianity lies in its witness. You write a new page of the gospel each day, by the things that you do, and the words that you say. People read what you write, whether faithful or true. What is the gospel according to you? Jesus came to do and to teach. In other words, he did the thing himself first, and then he taught his disciples to follow his example. A good example of this was when he washed their feet at the Last Supper. You and I are asked to live the gospel. You may be the only gospel someone will ever read; they may never buy the book.

Practical

The words of Isaiah are so central to the mission of Jesus, that it wouldn't be asking too much that I should make a copy of them, and keep them handy, as a reminder, and as material for reflection. In these days of word processors, computers, etc., it should be relatively easy to have them printed up as a poster for a bedroom wall, or a bathroom mirror. Have you seen the walls of a teenager's bedroom recently?! They speak loudly of where the time, interest, and money goes...

Supposing I asked you to list the areas in your own life where you experience your own personal poverty, your own blindness, biases, and bigotry, and your own bondage to persons, substances, possessions, pride, etc., what do you think you would write? It is easy for us to speak in generalities, but the test of our sincerity is our willingness to mediate that down to the specifics. 'I'm all for motherhood' is grand, just as long as it is someone else.

These words are being fulfilled even as you listen. How would you explain that to a child of seven? What does it actually mean in your own life? If you really believe these words, what should you be experiencing in your life today? It should literally make all the difference in the world, but that depends totally on you.

Story

A man pulled up at a filling station one day to get some petrol. He asked the young lad attending the pumps 'What are the peo-

ple in this next village like?' To his surprise, the young lad asked
him what the people in the last village in which he had stopped
were like. The man replied 'Oh, they were very nice, friendly,
and most helpful.' 'Well, then,' replied the lad 'you'll find that
the people in the next village will be the same.' The next man
who stopped at the filling station asked the very same question.
Once again, the young lad asked him how he found the people
were in the last village in which he had stopped. 'Oh, they were
sour, dour, and unfriendly', came the reply. 'Well, in that case,
you'll find the people in the next village will be just the same.'

Even if Jesus speaks, nothing happens unless the listeners are
prepared to listen …

FOURTH SUNDAY OF THE YEAR

Gospel: Luke 4:21-30

Theme

Today's gospel is a follow-up on the gospel of last Sunday. Jesus is back in Nazareth, and he is speaking in the synagogue. When he quoted the prophet Isaiah, it was OK, and went down well, but when he began to speak a few home truths about the religious people of his day, he was in serious trouble. They tolerated Jesus as long as he knew his proper place. He was a commoner whose family was known to them all, and how dare he attempt to preach to them. We are all aware of artists, actors, singers, etc. who had to emigrate before they got a break-through. It is difficult to break out of the mould among the environment that bred us. No prophet is honoured in his own country. It always amazes me to see people from Japan, USA, Holland, etc. gather for a summer school on the poetry of someone who has limited recognition in the homeland. I often joke that the further away you live, the greater expert you are!

In today's gospel, Jesus is telling them that God cares for all of his people, and that, when it comes to help, he has no favourites. This infuriated his listeners, who considered themselves to have a monopoly on God. They were God's chosen people, and they resented the fact that Jesus was putting them all on the same level. This approach was to get him into a lot of trouble as time went on. He hung around with sinners and outcasts, he touched the untouchables, and he spoke to Samaritans, to pagans, to prostitutes, to anyone he met. He was seen as someone who threatened the very basics of their authority and control, and they tried to get rid of him. However, Jesus would die when his hour had come, and he alone would decide when that was.

Parable

Brinsley Mc Namara wrote a classic story called *The Valley of the Squinting Windows*. It is a great read, and is available today, many decades later. He came from a very rural area of Ireland, and was well known, because his father was a teacher in the local school. His story was such that everybody in the village recognised themselves among the characters of the story. This led to public outrage in his hometown, while the rest of the

125

country was avidly reading the book! The book was burned in public, his family had to leave town, and, to this day, his name still evokes strong reactions among many of the people of that town. What he wrote was too close to the bone. If he had written a book about the people of some other town, he probably would have been hailed as the local literary hero. To this day none of his descendants would dare return to their roots in that town. They did, in a symbolic way, take him outside the town, and threw him over a cliff.

Teaching

God has no grandchildren! We are all children of God, products of his creation. If the Jews could be called God's Chosen People, it is simply because it was through them, and from among them that the Saviour, Jesus, would come. This is, of course, a privilege, but I cannot accept a privilege without accepting the responsibility that goes with it. Scripture tells us that he came onto his own, and his own received him not. Jesus posed a serious problem to the religious leaders of his day. It was all a question of control. They were in full control. The Scribes studied and taught the law, the Pharisees applied the law, and the people's role was to observe the law. This law covered every single area of their lives, right down to deciding how many steps they could take on the Sabbath. By doing this, they had God boxed into their system, and he was totally on their side. For Jesus to say that God had conferred special graces on non-Jews, and to give examples of that, was nothing short of blasphemy to the ears of his listeners. Jesus came to comfort the afflicted, but he also came to afflict the comfortable.

Religion has often shown this ugly side throughout history. We have killed millions in God's name, just because we decided that God thought about them the same way we did. This was the case away back at the time of the Crusades, when we sent armies from Europe to destroy the infidel, or to force non-Christians to accept the Christian faith, or die. This has lasted down to this very day. There is not a war in today's world that does not have some sort of religious connotations to it. It's not so long ago since our Catechisms taught us that outside the Catholic Church there was no salvation!

There is a phrase prevalent today when we say that, if you don't like the message, you can shoot the messenger. This is what happened to Jesus in today's gospel. There are different ways of killing a person. One way is to throw him over a cliff, and the other one is to totally ignore him, and he'll die of loneliness. We speak of the loneliness of the long-distance runner, where someone is totally alone, ploughing a lonely furrow, without any sense of communication with others. Many of our greatest people were like that. They did not conform to our norms, to our way of doing things, and, so, they were ostracised, excommunicated, exiled, or burned at the stake. There is only one God, and that is the God revealed in and through Jesus, and it is very important that we learn from him about a God who is a loving Father, and rid ourselves of our false gods, or stop playing God ourselves. One of the saddest sentences in the gospel is that 'Jesus walked through their midst and passed them by.'

Response
It is central to our Christian lives that we are open to accepting the full implications of Incarnation. As far as his listeners were concerned, Jesus was a neighbour's child from Nazareth, and that was the beginning and end of who and what he was. This is the great paradox of the gospel. It means that God became ordinary, he became like us in all things but sin, he is right here in the midst of us, and can easily go unnoticed. I who write or speak these words am just a human being, no different from everyone else around me. And yet, by vocation, I have been called to proclaim good news, to be God's spokesperson. God is incarnate in each one of us. Jesus didn't come to be locked in a tabernacle. He came to make his home in the human heart, so that, through any one of us, he can touch the lives and hearts of others.

Jesus tells us in the gospel that the truth will set us free. He could also have said that the truth can often get us into trouble! The greatest lies I tell in life are the ones I tell myself. It is said that the essence of proper communication is the ability to combine total honesty with total kindness. Under the guise of being honest, some people can be brutal and very destructive. I could meet someone today who asks me how I think she looks, and I could tell her that she looks awful, and will probably be dead by the weekend! I am being totally honest, but not very kind. On the other hand, to court popularity, or because of moral cowardice, I can give support to something or someone when I know that the cause or the person is totally wrong, unjust, or immoral. Under the guise of being kind, I can be very dishonest.

Jesus didn't mince his words when it came to the message he had to deliver.

One of the great changes within the church in modern times is, where the church had become allied with the political system, such as in Latin America, it is now open in its condemnation of the injustices of such political systems. This has led to the murder or disappearance of many of the more outspoken critics of the system. Archbishop Romero was a popular choice with the politicians until he turned on them, and condemned them for their actions. Romero, Martin Luther King, Ghandi, and many others, paid with their lives for the beliefs that they held and the truth that they spoke. In today's gospel, Jesus was spared death in some miraculous form, because, as he would say later 'No one takes my life from me. I will lay down my life…' At the end, he told his apostles 'Now the hour has come.'

Practical

At the risk of sounding like an old record, playing the same tune over and over again, I want to stress that the words of the gospel today are meant for me today. I'm sure we all have listened to a sermon or a homily, and we wished that such and such a one was here to hear this! We all know someone somewhere to whom these words directly apply. Try and avoid that, please… If you listen for you, then, perhaps, because of your living out that word, the other person may be touched. Sometimes what we do speaks so loudly that others cannot hear what we say.

God's work is always being spoken. The television set or the radio may be switched off, but the programmes are still being broadcast. When we are prepared to listen, you'd be amazed where you'll hear the word of God, and who will speak that word to you. Out of the mouths of babes … Prayer, real prayer, has much more to do with listening than with speaking. Speak, Lord, your servant is listening is much better than Listen, Lord, your servant is speaking. Take the following word of advice, and try it out sometime: Learn to listen, and listen to learn. You may be amazed at the wonderful things you'll hear when you are ready to hear … There are none so deaf as those who don't want to hear.

If God has no favourites, then he has no favourites within you. In other words, if you spread out the canvas of your life before him, the good, the bad, and the ugly, he would have total acceptance for each area. Don't try to put on a pious and holy face when you come before God! He knows you through and through, and all he asks is that you stand honestly and humbly before him. Humility has had a bad press, because it can be interpreted as meaning that I am worthless, useless, and nothing better than a worm crawling around. Nothing could be further from the truth. You are good, because in the words of Herb Banks, God don't make no junk. Humility is nothing more than accepting things exactly as they are. Humility is truth, and the truth will always set us free.

Story
The following is a summary of the comments made about the parish priest in a typical parish:
If his homily is longer than usual, 'He sends us asleep.'
If it's short 'He hasn't bothered.'
If he raises his voice, 'He is shouting.'
If he speaks normally, 'You can't hear a thing.'
If he's away, 'He's always on the road.'
If he's at home, 'He's a stick-in-the-mud.'
If he's out visiting, 'He's never at home.'
If he's in the presbytery, 'He never visits his people.'
If he talks finances, 'He's too fond of money.'
If he doesn't, 'The parish is dead.'
If he takes his time with people, 'He wears everybody out.'
If he is brief, 'He never listens.'
If he starts Mass on time, 'His watch must be fast.'
If he starts a minute late, 'He holds everybody up.'
If he is young, 'He lacks experience.'
If he is old, 'He ought to retire.'
And if he dies? Well, of course, 'No one could ever take his place.'

FIFTH SUNDAY OF THE YEAR

Gospel: Luke 5:1-11

Theme

If you have been following the gospels of the past few Sundays, you will notice that Jesus' mission is brought one step forward today. He has begun to recruit followers, whom he will inform, form, and, eventually transform, so that they will be able to continue his mission when he returns to his Father.

In the old manuals on mental prayer, they spoke of a thing called the composition of place. This was when you closed your eyes, and tried to place yourself within the story, and to imagine what the scene was like. Today's gospel presents a beautiful and simple picture. There is something special about a lakeside, and the presence of the odd fishing boat makes it even more attractive. By now, Jesus had begun to attract crowds, who gathered to listen to his message. (Remember, this was in the days before megaphones, amplifiers, or public address systems!) The nearest thing to a pulpit he could find was a boat, and, so, by pulling out a bit from the shore, his voice would carry much better on the water, and he was free from the pressing crowds.

The next scenario is both simple and central. Peter was beaten, without a fish to show for his work, and, so, the scene was set for a miracle. As usual with Jesus, the result was pressed down and flowing over, as with the wine at Cana, or the baskets of loaves and fish left over after everyone had been fed.

Peter made the first of his many many mistakes. He asked Jesus to leave him, because he was a sinful man. That must surely have brought a smile to the face of Jesus, because it was for such sinful people that he had come. Jesus ignored Peter's remark, by implying that you ain't seen nothing yet. He invited Peter and his friends to join him full-time in the mission he was undertaking. There was something magnetic about Jesus, and, immediately, they abandoned ship, and set off down the road with him.

Parable

Christianity is about attracting, rather than promoting. Throughout history, we read about founders of communities, of Congregations, of Orders. These were people with a vision. They were dynamic, filled with zeal, and had a powerful sense of mission. Such enthusiasm is highly contagious! Such people always attract attention, and this leads to attracting followers. In recent years, we have seen horrible and grotesque aberrations of this, in the form of cults, that was based on mind control, and that led hundreds to their deaths through suicide pacts. It is the duty of leaders to lead, but it is also their responsibility to know where they're going. Like Moses headed for the Promised Land, Jesus was totally open and definite in the direction of his life. He came to do the Father's will, and he was led by the Spirit. Thank God for the many wonderful leaders and founders with which the Lord has provided us down the centuries. Thank God, for the many such people who are alive and active among us today.

Teaching
Something worth noting: Jesus is spoken of as teaching rather than preaching. There is a difference. The art of teaching is to bring the learner from the known to the unknown. Jesus speaks of fish, of sheep, of vines, of trees, of water, etc., all of which would be there within the view of his listeners. The Acts of the Apostles begins by telling us that Jesus came to do and to teach. A cynic described education as a process in which information is transferred from the notebook of the teacher to the notebook of the student, without having passed through the heads of either! Jesus spoke and taught from the heart, and what comes from the heart of the speaker always reaches the heart of the listener. In himself, Jesus was the message, and that was what gave weight and power to his words.

The two ingredients for a miracle are present in this story. The first condition is that Peter is powerless, and, despite fishing all night, he has caught nothing. The second condition is that he believes if he lowers his nets at Jesus' word, things will be completely different. This is the common denominator for all the miracles in the gospel.

I said earlier that Peter made a great mistake when he judged himself unfit and unworthy to be in the presence of Jesus. In actual fact, that is correct, if we fail to understand the purpose of Jesus' mission. He came to call sinners, and Peter could actually have said, with much greater accuracy and truth, 'Lord, please stay with me, because I am a sinful man'. In the past, the church has not been good in its dealing with sinners. With the pulpit thumping, hell-fire, and open condemnation, sinners were left in no doubt that they did not belong! The message that came across to them was 'Depart from us, for you are a sinful person'. Thankfully, because of the renewal that is going on in the church, we are beginning to recapture the mind and the message of Jesus.

Response

Today's gospel begins by telling us that the people had gathered, and were listening to the word of God. 'Word' means several things, from a word in a dictionary, to a message (Have you had any word yet?), to a promise (I give you my word). Jesus is the Word of God, the message and the promise of God. It is very important that we listen. Jesus said, on another occasion, 'They have ears, but they hear not,' and again 'They who have ears to hear, let them hear.' Prayer is not so much me speaking to God, who may not hear, but God speaking to me who may not listen. The essence of real prayer is the ability to be still inside, and to listen to the word of God there. There is a big difference between praying and saying prayers. I could teach a parrot to say a prayer, but I could never teach a parrot to pray.

Language is a strange thing, because it can mean so many different things to many different people. In our language, to fail, to be powerless, to be totally unable to deal with a situation, …all of that is weakness, failure, and cause for shame. In God's language, the very same situations are extraordinary opportunities for grace, and for God to show his power. Peter had failed. He was a fisherman, and, after a whole night's fishing, he hadn't caught a fish. That is failure in anyone's language, especially in the language of a fisherman. The situation was ideal for Jesus to step in, just as he had done at Cana. He is the God of the hopeless, the God of the helpless, the God of the powerless.

Jesus came to look for, to seek out sinners, and to bring them safely home. If he had a hundred sheep, and one went astray, he would leave the ninety-nine to go after the one that is lost. Peter totally failed to grasp that, when he asked Jesus to leave him. The correct prayer would be Lord, please stay with me, because I am a sinner. Please don't leave me, because, apart from you, I'm totally lost. And, of course, the whole message of Jesus is to reassure sinners that he is always there for them. Peter was only too well aware of his brokenness, and many later episodes in the gospel will point to, and confirm that fact. It is significant that Jesus made Peter head of the apostles. The principal of evangelising is that one sinner tells another, just, as with Alcoholics Anonymous, where one recovering alcoholic helps another achieve sobriety.

Practical

Do you own a Bible? I mean a small modern translation, that you would be able to pick up from time to time? There is a huge selection and choice available today, including booklets with daily readings from Scripture. If Jesus came to teach, it is necessary that we should be willing to listen and learn.

I have no doubt that each one of us could come up with something specific in our lives, when, like Peter, we have fished all night and caught nothing. Some area in which we encounter repeated failure. This could be anything from an addiction, to a resentment, an inability to forgive, to a scar of mind or memory which has never healed. This has the potential for a miracle, if I am willing to hand it over. Let go, and let God. There is nothing impossible with God...

Do you experience the sense or awareness of being called? The fact that you are here now, reading, or listening to this, implies that you are responding to something. Vocation is a word that is being given back to the laity, to whom it belongs in the first place. There is no greater call for a human being that to follow Jesus, to become a Christian. Hold on to that word vocation today; turn it over in your mind; make it your own, and develop within yourself a very real sense of being called and chosen. You did not choose me; no, I have chosen you. I have appointed you to go and bear fruit, fruit that will remain. I have called you by name. You are mine.

Story

A woman came out of her house and saw three old men, with long white beards, sitting in her front yard. She did not recognise them. She said 'I don't think I know you, but you must be hungry. Please come in and have something to eat'. 'Is the man of the house home?' they asked. 'No,' she said. 'He's out.' 'Then we cannot come in,' they replied. In the evening when her husband came home she told what had happened. 'Go tell them I am home, and invite them in.' The woman went out and invited them in. 'We do not go into a house together,' they replied. 'Why is that?' she wanted to know. One of the old men explained: 'His name is Wealth,' he said as he pointed to one of the men. Pointing to the other, he said 'His name is Success, and my name is Love. Now go in and discuss with your husband which one of us you want to invite into your home.' The woman went in and told her husband what was said. Her husband was overjoyed.

'How wonderful!' he said. 'Since that is the case, let us invite Wealth. Let him come in and fill our house with wealth.'

His wife disagreed. 'My dear, why don't you invite Success?' Their daughter was listening from the kitchen, and she jumped in with her own suggestion. 'Would it not be better to invite Love? Our home would then be filled with love.' 'Let us heed our daughter's suggestion,' said the husband to his wife. 'Go out, and invite Love to be our guest.'

The woman went out and asked the three old men 'Which of you is Love? Please come in and be our guest.' Love got up and starting walking towards the house. The other two also got up and followed him. Surprised, the woman asked Wealth and Success 'I only invited Love. Why are you coming in?'

The old men replied together 'If you had invited Wealth or Success, the other two of us would have remained outside. But since you invited Love, wherever he goes we go with him. Wherever there is Love there is also Wealth and Success.'

When Jesus called people to follow him, he offered them love, and everything else would follow ...

SIXTH SUNDAY OF THE YEAR

Gospel: Luke 6:17, 20-26

Theme

Today's gospel contains what we call the Eight Beatitudes, or the core Attitudes of a Christian. It contains a recipe for living, and for happiness. It outlines a series of choices, and it gives us a programme for living. Up till this time, the world had been in the grip of Satan, 'the prince of this world'. These new Attitudes, or Beatitudes, are diametrically opposed to the attitudes of the world, or to the teachings of the evil one. Today's gospel is Jesus' Manifesto.

Parable

We are all familiar with manifestos. We have them trotted out during all general election campaigns. They are held up, and proclaimed as the solution for all our problems. We are also familiar with manifestos that seem to disappear once the election is over. The party in power is called on to 'deliver on their election promises'. The fact is, however, that, no matter how much good-will and good intentions were involved, you can be sure that corners will have to be cut, that promises will be reneged on, and that several of the programmes will have to be put on hold.

The big difference in the Manifesto in today's gospel is that Jesus' guarantee and promise goes with it, and as well as offering us the Manifesto, he offers us all that it takes to be able to live up to it. That is something that no earthly power could ever hope to achieve, let alone offer. It is central that we understand the new language Jesus uses; in other words, he gives a whole new meaning to words that we use in ordinary everyday worldly language.

Teaching

The Beatitudes contain the secret of happiness. To be poor in spirit has nothing to do with living in poverty, or without the basic means for normal living. It means that the spirit, the inner me, the real me, is not in bondage to wealth, to greed, or to material things of any kind. I could have a very healthy bank account, and be poor in spirit. I don't need these material things to give me a sense of value, and an assurance of worth. I can clearly distinguish between being rich, and being wealthy. A person could be very very rich, and have very little of this world's wealth. Another person could be really poor, empty, and alone, despite possessing much wealth.

The hunger that Jesus speaks of has nothing to do with food. It has to do with the hunger for freedom, for justice, for fair play, for equal rights, that continues to drive so many extraordinary men and women in today's world. There is a greater hunger than the lack of food. The deepest hungers in the human heart have to do with belonging, self-worth, dignity, and personal freedom.

Those who weep are those who love. Grief is the price we pay for love. If you never want to cry at a funeral, then don't ever love anybody. Jesus wept over Jerusalem, and he wept at the tomb of Lazarus. These were not tears of despair. They were tears of love, of loss, of longing. They were the tears of the one who holds out both hands, but the offer is not accepted, or the tears of loneliness and aloneness that fill the vacuum created by the loss of a loved one.

Good, by definition, will always be opposed by evil. Good that goes unchallenged from all quarters can be very suspect. Jesus met opposition at every turn, and he tells his listeners that if they follow him, they will experience the same. The world cannot deal with the gentleness of the gospel, the turning the other cheek. Such Christian witnesses often end up as Christian martyrs. We have had many such in recent years, Martin Luther King, and Archbishop Romero being among the better known ones. At this very moment, there is someone being killed because of a stance for justice, or for their proclamation of the gospel.

Jesus then uses the worldly meaning of wealth, opulence, pleasure, and flattery, and warns that these do not lead to happiness. If wealth brought happiness, then every wealthy person should be happy. Indeed, if health brought happiness, then every healthy person would also be happy. This is compounded by the fact that Jesus is speaking here of eternal happiness. In another part of the gospel, he speaks of people who have already had their reward. In other words, there's nothing much waiting for them when they leave their earthly pleasures behind.

Response
To become a Christian involves learning a whole new language. My failures and falls can be turned into compassion and under-

standing of others. Love removes all price tags from gifts, and forgiveness is seventy times seven. Richness is not stored in bank vaults, and it's OK for a grown man to cry. Love is the currency, and God is the bank manager, and all loans are gifts, and everything is interest-free.

There are three kingdoms. There is the kingdom of the world, which is a happy bedfellow of the kingdom of Satan, as they espouse the same causes. And then there is the Kingdom of God, which Jesus came to establish. The language of Jesus is different because the priorities and the values are different. In his Kingdom, he is Lord, every human life is precious and priceless, and the Power to live in that Kingdom is the Holy Spirit. Therefore, if we are to live in his Kingdom, we must have full awareness of the conditions for doing so. The Kingdom, the Power, and the Glory are yours... In other words, if I myself contribute to the power, then, I can easily find myself claiming some of the glory.

Witness-value is at the heart of Christian living. Jesus compares the Christian in the world to leaven that is mixed with flour, to salt that is added to food, to a light that enters an empty room. While still a baby, it was said of Jesus, by Simeon, that he would be a sign of contradiction. He himself said in many and varied ways My Kingdom is not of this world. His whole message was diametrically opposed to the teachings and values of this world. I met a man recently who is a member of Alcoholics Anonymous, and he described his experience in a pub the previous evening. He had to attend the particular function, so he was at ease about entering the pub. It was then that his problem started, however. His work-mates just didn't believe him when he said he didn't drink alcohol. After all, he was in a pub, and, to their way of thinking, that was the reason why people went to pubs! There obviously was a clash of understandings between two different ways of looking at the same thing.

Practical

Supposing you took today's gospel as your Manifesto, how would you print it on a wall chart? Do you think it would attract much attention? Please ignore those last two questions(!), and answer the following: What does the Manifesto, or the Beatitudes, mean to you, in your own life?

Can you think of one time when you actually experienced this teaching at work in your life? When you experienced yourself detached from wealthy or worldly ambitions, and yet you knew you were really rich? How involved are you in your community? In every community, there is a small group who cause things to happen. There's a larger group who watch things happening. And, then, there's the vast majority who haven't a clue what's happening. Are you happy to sit back and let someone else fight for the rights of your community?

Today's gospel is not about laying a guilt-trip on anyone. It is OK to have wealth, to have food, to have pleasure, and to enjoy the plaudits of others. The important questions have to do with where the wealth came from, who is being excluded from the food, or who is being used in my pursuit of pleasure? The problem in today's world is that half the population is dying of hunger, while the other half is on a diet, trying to get down the weight. There is more than enough food in today's world for all its inhabitants.

Story
This story is told by a missionary in New Guinea. An old man, a recent convert to Christianity, used to come to the mission hospital every day, to read passages of the gospels to the patients. One day the man was having great difficulty reading. The doctor examined his eyes, and discovered that the man was going blind, and would probably be totally blind within a year or two. After that, there was no sign of the man anywhere within or around the hospital. No one knew what had happened to him. Eventually, a young man found him, and brought the mission doctor to visit him.

The old man explained to the doctor that he was very busy memorising the most important parts of the gospels, while he still could see. The Eight Beatitudes were near the top of his list. 'Soon I'll be back at the hospital, and I'll be able to continue teaching the patients the most important messages of the gospels.'

SEVENTH SUNDAY OF THE YEAR

Gospel: Luke 6:27-38

Theme

Today's gospel summarises something that was very new to the religious leaders of Jesus' day. They had a law which said an eye for an eye and a tooth for a tooth. In other words, they were expected to strike back at those who harmed them in any way. It is in a gospel like that presented to us today that we see just how radical and revolutionary Jesus' teaching must have sounded back then. Indeed, it is still quite revolutionary in today's world, with our dog-eat-dog mentality. The process of salvation which he had come to establish would be based on forgiveness, and, therefore, to be part of, and to belong to that process must put each one of us right out there in the front line of tolerance, forgiveness, and love.

Parable

There is extraordinary power in forgiveness, gentleness, meekness, and love. 'Blessed are the meek' says Jesus, 'they shall possess the earth.' We have all seen the movies, read the books, or heard the first-hand accounts of the lives of Mahatma Ghandi or Martin Luther King. The bully cannot deal with the power of the one who won't strike back, and, therefore, such people are killed, as the only evident way of stopping them. To err is human, to forgive is divine. We are all familiar with the concept of people being small-minded, big-hearted, narrow-minded, tolerant, bigoted, judgmental, etc. We have seen revolutionaries trying to overthrow the powers-that-be by force of arms. In doing this, many innocent people get killed, and, it often happens that the liberated oppressed become the new oppressors. On the other hand, we have Peace Movements, Civil Rights marches, and candle-light vigils to highlight injustices and oppression. Aggression from one provokes aggression in another. My strength is as the strength of ten, because my heart is pure.

Teaching

Forgiveness is like salt, which is a preservative, and keeps food from going rotten. Before we had fridges and freezers, sections of beef or bacon were packed into boxes of salt, which kept them edible for quite a long time. When a couple get married, it is no exaggeration to say that, if they have enough forgiveness within their hearts, their love will continue, and will grow. Forgiveness is an on-going process on the journey towards total acceptance. This applies equally to my ability and willingness to forgive myself, as it does to the forgiveness of others. Quite a great deal of the violence and turmoil in parts of the world are the results of past injustices, where forgiveness hasn't been given a chance to heal the wounds. There would never be a war if someone, somewhere, was prepared to say 'I'm sorry, I was wrong; please forgive me'.

There is great power in forgiveness. The one who forgives is the one who has the greatest strength. Not to forgive is to harbour resentments, and resentments are always harmful to the one who carries them. If I have a resentment against you, it is like me drinking poison, and I'm expecting you to die! The only one who is harmed is myself. Not to forgive is to allow someone else have power over me. They are in my thoughts, and my thoughts about them disturb and disquiet me, and I am in a state of dis-ease, and I cannot possibly be at peace.

The whole story of salvation and redemption is one of loving forgiveness. It is about forgiveness of sin, and about freeing from debt. God is love, and, therefore, God is a forgiving God. Jesus asks us to love one another as he loves us. The only condition laid down about forgiveness is that I be willing to forgive others. Jesus taught us to pray 'Forgive us our sins as we forgive those who sin against us'. What comes to me from God must go sideways to those around me. Previous generations made constant use of the Sacrament of Reconciliation, in their desire to receive God's forgiveness, and there may not have been sufficient stress on the simple teaching of Jesus 'If you forgive, you are forgiven'.

Response

If I am to live a Christian life, then I have to place forgiveness of others fairly and squarely in the middle of the package. Nelson Mandela says that we make peace with our enemies, not with our friends. Jesus says that if we love those who love us, what reward is in that, because even the pagans do that. Forgiveness of our enemies is the hallmark of the Christian. As he was dying on the cross, Jesus prayed for those who were killing him. 'Father, forgive them...'

Nowhere is it more evident that, by myself, I just don't have what it takes to live the Christian life. Without the Spirit of God within my heart, the whole thing is impossible for a mere human. I never actually become a Christian. I am always in the process of becoming. That is the direction in which my life is going. It is peace on earth to those of goodwill, not to those who are perfect. If I have a resentment towards another, I should pray for that person, day after day, no matter how difficult I may find it. Only in this way will the resentment gradually melt and disappear. Of course, this is difficult, and, when I begin to do this, my heart won't be in it. In fact, the very words may stick in my throat. However, in blind faith, I just have to make the effort, and, after some time, I will begin to see the results.

There but for the grace of God go I is a very wise and true statement. I didn't choose my parents, my place of origin, my social background, etc. I could have been born into any circumstances, and, given the right ingredients and conditions in my upbringing, I could have become the biggest criminal, or the most evil person in history. Being deeply conscious of my own sinfulness is a necessary condition for holiness, and for the capacity to have a forgiving heart. There are two conditions for getting to heaven. One is to be a sinner, and the other is to know it. Let the one among you who has no sin throw the first stone, says Jesus. If I was deeply convinced of my own sinfulness, then I would leave you alone, and stop pointing a finger at someone else. (When you point a finger at someone else, please note that there are three fingers pointing back at you!) When we began this Mass, we stood together and confessed to God and to each other that we are sinners. Have you noticed that the first person singular is used only three times in the whole Mass? I confess … I have sinned … Lord, I am not worthy … All the rest of the Mass is in the plural form. When it comes to sin, however, each one of us has to speak for ourselves.

Practical

How would the following exercise appeal to you? You sit in front of a mirror, reflect on all of the failures, brokenness, and sin in your life. You take as much time as you need for this. You are going to ask God's forgiveness, you are going to try to make amends wherever possible, and you want to move forward from here. Ask yourself one simple question: How willing are you to give yourself absolution, to forgive yourself totally, before you dare ask God to forgive you? Is there any point in asking God to do something for you that you are unwilling to do for yourself? Guilt is not from God. Rather is it your own inability to forgive yourself. A leading psychiatrist said that he could discharge two-thirds of his patients immediately if he could get them to forgive themselves.

To forgive is not necessarily to forget. I cannot press a button and erase the memory of some hurt or injustice. I can forgive, though, and, through the work of God's Spirit, the memory will be healed, and will no longer hurt. Is there anyone who has really hurt you, and against whom you have every reason to have a very great resentment? Sometimes I may have to forgive God for what I see as the unfair hand I got in life. We all have received our own share of hurts in life, but there is usually one or two in particular who have hurt us more than others. Do you think you could hand over that hurt to God in the Offertory of this Mass?

Jesus taught us one simple prayer, which we call the Our Father or the Lord's Prayer. It is a simple prayer, and it is quite short. One of the petitions is where we ask God to forgive us our trespasses as we forgive those who trespass against us. We can rattle off this prayer, and fail to realise the bind in which it can place us. We are putting a condition on God's forgiveness, and that condition is that we are willing to forgive others. Please take time out sometime today to reflect on the ramifications of saying this prayer.

Story

Corrie Ten Boom was a Christian Jew living in Holland during the Nazi occupation of that country. She has written some beautiful books, filled with the spirit of the Christian gospel. One of those books is her own story. She tells of what happened to herself and to her family. One night a man came to their door in great panic and terror. He told them that himself and his family were going to be taken away by the Nazis. The only hope he had was that he might be able to bribe the police, and they might be left unharmed. He begged for some valuable objects to effect the bribe. He was given whatever they could possibly give, and then he left. It was a trick, because he went straight to the Nazi police, and reported them for assisting in his proposed escape. Corrie and all of her family were arrested, and they ended up in a German concentration camp. All of her family died there, and she was the only survivor. Later, when she returned home, she spent a considerable length of time tracking down the man who had betrayed them. She eventually did so. Her only reason for wanting to meet him was that, for her own peace of mind, she needed to forgive him. She felt that it was only through forgiveness, and not through resentment, that she could continue to live in freedom.

EIGHTH SUNDAY OF THE YEAR

Gospel: Luke 6:39-45

Theme
Today's gospel has some simple clear messages, that are easily understood. Jesus speaks about how it is so much easier for us to see the faults in others, and he gives us a simple test to show whether a person is good or not.

Parable
'From what delusions it would free us, if we could see ourselves as others see us!' Point your finger at something right now, and then look at your hand. What you see is that, while there is one finger pointing at something, there are three pointing back at yourself! I remember a friend of mine telling about a confrere who spent one full hour with a camera to get a close-up shot of a bee in flight. My friend considered this a serious waste of time. What he failed to realise, of course, was that while the photographer was busy trying to get a good photo, my friend was standing watching him, doing nothing! At least one of them was doing something!

Teaching
Jesus is teaching us to know our place. When a pupil considers himself greater than his teacher; when I take the liberty of pointing out to you what I think you should change in yourself,…in such ways, we are getting too big for our boots, and are out of place. Jesus says that if the student works hard he will become like his teacher.

It's so easy for us to see the faults of others. For years I was wondering what was wrong with other people! Then, one day, I made a simple discovery. I discovered that what was wrong with them is that they were different from me! They all seemed to do things I wouldn't do! Upon further reflection, I discovered that the reason they were different from me is that God, in his infinite wisdom, had made them different from me. For his own good reasons, he decided that one of me was enough, and so he broke up the mould and threw it away!

'Whatever is in your heart determines what you say.' There has never been a bomb planted, or a bullet fired that did not begin in the heart of some human being. By the heart I mean the

144

core of our being, that part where we are most ourselves. 'A pure heart create in me, O Lord, and put a steadfast spirit within me.' On a physical level, we can have angiograms, ECGs, stress tests, etc. all to find out the condition of the physical heart. We ourselves should run a check on that inner being which we call the heart, to ensure that our thinking, our attitudes, and our inner dispositions are life-giving and healthy.

Response
Before I offer to remove the speck from my brother's eye, I should have a long hard look at myself in the mirror. Quite often, what I condemn in others can be part of my own behaviour. A parent lecturing a son or daughter about drugs, may be a constant user of alcohol, nicotine, etc. I remember seeing a young lad, who had hit his little sister, being lifted off the ground with a smack by a very hefty mother, with the warning 'I'll teach you not to hit anybody smaller than yourself!'

The best way to lead others is by example. Of course, I can help another remove a speck from an eye, or a resentment from the heart, or a destructive bias from the mind. I can do this by example, when my own behaviour does not contradict the advice I give to others. Others benefit both directly and indirectly, every time I make an effort to cleanse my own heart.

A tree is judged by the fruit it produces. I have seen people seriously ill in hospital, and their very illness was bringing out the best in them. Their concern for relatives and friends was most impressive, and their determination not to be a burden on others was most edifying. While not pretending to understand this fully, I have often thought that whatever is causing this illness must be from God, because the only results I can see are good ones. On the other hand, I have seen people in hospital, and it was an ordeal to visit them. There was nothing but complaints, as the staff tip-toed around the bed. The tea was too hot, the porridge was too cold, etc. There was no concern for how the visitors were fairing, and anything that may be amiss with others was dismissed as trivial. I could not see any good fruit coming out of this sickness...

Practical
It is easy to get practical directives from the teachings in today's gospel. The only problem, of course, is that, by myself, I can do nothing about it. All the transformation spoken of is the work of the Holy Spirit. 'Spirit of God, please open my heart and my

eyes to truth, and let me see things as they really are.' To say that prayer constantly, and from the heart, will surely bring wonderful results.

'Lord, let there be truth, justice, and fair play in this world, and let it begin with me.' It's so easy to sit back and wait for others to change. I watch the television to monitor progress in the peace process in Northern Ireland, the Middle East, etc. All the while, of course, I myself may not have peace within my own heart. If I really want to see peace in the world, then I know where to start.

When the Holy Spirit comes to dwell in our hearts, he brings the gifts of the Spirit with him. These gifts enable us do the work of God, something, that, of ourselves, we never could do. As I write these lines, I expect the Spirit to inspire me, and I pray that, as you read them, you, too, will be touched by that same Spirit. There are times when we badly need wisdom, discernment, knowledge, faith, etc., and these are all gifts of the Spirit. When the gifts are allowed work in and through me, this produces the fruits of the Spirit. Jesus speaks of producing good fruit today. Each of us has a choice as to what kind of tree we choose to be.

Story
It was a Saturday, and the weather was very bad. The mother had gone off for the day, and the father was minding several young children. He was a top business executive, and he was well experienced in management of people, of time, and motion, etc. However, because of the weather, which confined the children to the house, he soon felt the pressure of all the hyper-activity going on around him. He came up with a plan that he thought would solve his problem. He took down a magazine from a shelf, flicked through it, and found a map of the world. He tore out the page, got a scissors, and cut the page into many pieces. He jumbled up the pieces, and put them on the table, and told his ten-year-old to put that jigsaw together again. That would keep him quiet for a while!

He proceeded to make out other assignments for each of the others. In a short while, however, he looked over and saw that his son had completed the jigsaw. He was amazed, and partially annoyed. 'How did you do that so quickly?' he asked. 'Dad, I didn't know how or where to start. I never saw one of these before. There were lines going in every direction, and I was going to give up. But, dad, guess what? I turned over a piece of the paper and I found that there was a man on the other side. I turned over all the pieces, put the man together, and the job was done'!

Man or woman, you are the person on the reverse side of the world...!

NINTH SUNDAY OF THE YEAR

Gospel: Luke 7:1-10

Theme
This is a clear and simple lesson in faith. It is a fascinating story, and there are so many lessons to be learned from it. The story of the Roman centurion has always had a place of special significance in the gospel story.

Parable
Several years ago a niece of mine, aged 7, arrived at Dublin airport from New York with her mam. She had been violently sick throughout the flight, and, before she set foot in Ireland, she was already dreading the return flight. Some hours after she arrived, I brought her to one side, and I told her that I was going to entrust her with a very important secret, which nobody else must know. Through a friend of mine, I had succeeded in getting a tablet which was guaranteed to prevent travel sickness, but my problem was that it was not available on the public market, and my friend would get into serious trouble if it were known that he had given one to me. This cheered her up no end, and any chance she got during her vacation, she would come to me and whisper that she didn't worry at all now about the flight back home. I left them at Dublin airport for their return journey. I brought her over into a corner, where I slipped her half an aspirin, with a sup of water. Within seconds she was telling me that she felt much better already! She had a most enjoyable flight home. I use this example to show what can happen when there's faith and trust. The comparison ends there, in so far as the power Jesus used was very far removed from the deception employed by me!

Teaching
This gospel is rich in teachings. One of the first things we notice is the kind of person the centurion was. It was Jews who came to Jesus, because he was so good to them, and he built their temple for them. He was concerned about his servant who was a slave, at a time when slaves were another form of property, to be disposed of at the will of their master. He was truly a remarkable man.

One of the most striking things about the man, of course, was the strong faith he had. How he came to this level of faith we can only surmise. He must have been a very humble man, because centurions in his day were people of authority, and things happened because they said so. He considered Jesus so superior to him that he did not consider himself worthy to have Jesus come under his roof. It is interesting to note that, following his example, after all these years, we, too, declare 'Lord, I am not worthy…'

'All things are possible to those who have faith' were the words of Jesus to the man whose son was possessed by the demons. 'There is nothing impossible with God' was the message to Mary. Jesus pays a remarkable tribute to the centurion 'I tell you, I have not found faith like this in all of Israel.' The centurion was certainly a remarkable man.

Response
A miracle like the one in today's gospel is one that puzzles me. We are used to preaching, teaching, catechism, articles of faith, etc., etc. The centurion, however, was a pagan, and he had none of our formation or religious inheritance. The one thing he had going for him was he was a good man. Although he was on the side of the conquering Romans, he liked the Jews, was a friend to them, and he built their synagogue. He also cared deeply about his slave, which was even more remarkable for those times.

The centurion was a man who had love in his heart. Therefore, he was someone who had God in his heart, even if, officially, he was a pagan. He was what we might call today an 'Anonymous Christian'. Because he was a caring person, he was loved by those around him. He was a man who made a deep impression on Jesus, and his story will live as long as the gospel is preached.

The centurion would be expected to be cast in an authority mould. He was part of the occupying power. He spoke of the authority he had over others, and how others reacted when he gave the orders. It is most impressive, therefore, to see the respect he had for the authority of Jesus. We are told that he had heard about Jesus, but he must have been a humble man to recognise in Jesus someone who had power to do things he could not do. He certainly had no problem bowing to superior authority.

Practical
It is worth trying to get inside the head of the centurion. As a

Roman officer, one would expect him to be rough, uncouth, un-feeling, and over-bearing. Within this man was a gentle giant, and a heart that had a great capacity for love. He respected peo-ple, whether they were the Jews, or one of his slaves. He had a sense of morality that was highly developed, and a humility that made him very unique. One of the simplest, most sincere com-ments I have heard at funerals is when the deceased is described as 'a very decent human being'.

The story has to do with a centurion, a slave, and Jesus. If I personalise the story, and place myself in the part of the centurion or the slave, how would that feel? I don't have a slave, but I could easily have someone in my life who is less important to me than a slave ever could be. Do you know the kind of person who really means nothing to me? Of course, I have friends that mean more to me than others, but are there others to whom I am completely indifferent?

Do I have authority in my life? All authority comes from God. 'The greatest among you are those who serve.' Humility is the ground-stone of all authority. We are told that Jesus spoke with great authority; in other words, he knew who the author was, because he never said anything unless the Father told him. People in authority positions have a greater responsibility for service. Their authority is based on love and service, rather than fear and power. A husband asked his wife one time 'Do you know how many truly great men there are in the world today?' 'I don't', she replied. 'But I know that there's one less than you think there is!' As a result of reflecting on today's gospel, I could do well to search my heart for arrogance, pride, domineering, haughtiness, and impatience.

Story

It was a hospital ward. Over in the corner was a man lying on the broad of his back, looking up at the ceiling. He was unable to sit up, or lift his head. Over by the window was another man, who spent most of his time looking out the window. For over an hour every day, the man by the window regaled the other man with graphic descriptions of everything that was happening out on the road. As he spoke about the clouds, the children playing, the vehicles flying past, the other lay there with his eyes closed, trying to imagine in his mind's eye everything the other man was describing. One day, the man was describing a parade pass-ing by, while the other could almost see the band marching and

playing. Listening to the descriptions of what was going on outside was the highlight of his day, and it helped him enormously
to deal with the frustration of being so powerless.

One morning the nurses came in and found that the man by
the window had died during the night. His body was removed,
and, later that evening, the man in the other bed asked if he
might be transferred to the bed next the window. The nurses
readily acceded to his request. After a few days, the man made a
Herculean effort, and, with the help of a few pillows, he managed to get into some sort of sit-up position, so that he could
look out the window, and see all the things the other man had
described to him so often. When he looked out the window he
got a great surprise. There was a blank wall outside the window,
and there was nothing to be seen. He called the nurse, and asked
her how was it that the other man had given him all those daily
details, when, in fact, there was nothing to be seen outside the
window at all. The nurse replied 'He was one of the kindest men
I have ever met. He was actually blind, and he did that every
day just to help you deal with your boredom.'

Like the centurion, a man like that is himself a miracle, and
miracles happen wherever they are ...

TENTH SUNDAY OF THE YEAR

Gospel: Luke 7:11-17

Theme

In this account of the heart-touching story of restoring life to the dead son of the widow of Naim, is to be found a truly beautiful insight into the heart of Jesus.

Parable

There have been many occasions when I was involved with families who came face to face with the death of a child. While, in several cases, the child made a remarkable recovery, and I was able to share in their great joy, I will never forget the darkest moments, as we all sat around awaiting the worst possible scenario. To be a parent in such a situation must be one of the most painful, and most powerless situations anybody could be in. The euphoria and joy when a child made a full recovery was somewhat proportionate to the pain and the agony that had preceded it.

Teaching

'Learn of me, for I am meek and humble of heart', says Jesus. He certainly, also, was very soft and kind-hearted. We are familiar with the phrase 'Oh, my heart went out to her'. Jesus was in that situation on many an occasion. He was always ready to weep with those who wept. It is certainly no exaggeration to say that Jesus was the most kind-hearted person that ever walked on this earth.

When I was growing up, we were all familiar with what we called devotion to the Sacred Heart. In the picture, the heart of Jesus was presented at the very front, and there were rays of warmth and love shining forth from it. In our language of today he was 'all heart'. Witnessing human suffering, and seeing others marginalised touched him very deeply. That is why he always sought out the outcast and rejected of society. When Jesus saw the poor widow, we are told that 'his heart overflowed with compassion'. There was no way he could pass her by. Her situation just drew a response from him.

We are told that great fear swept the crowd. They were in the presence of some awesome power, and fear is a very normal response in such circumstances. They were obviously not afraid of Jesus, but being in the presence of such a person must surely have greatly heightened a sense of their own powerlessness. As they themselves put it 'A mighty prophet has come among us. We have seen the hand of God today'.

Response

'Learn of me, for I am meek and humble of heart', Jesus tells us. He certainly is full of compassion and love. We have many examples in the gospels where his heart was filled with pity, even to the point of weeping. Compassion is the sharing of a common grief; even if the grief is yours, it is one that I also share. The whole story of salvation and redemption is one of compassion.

As you reflect on the scene facing Jesus, as he met the funeral, and saw the sorrowing widow, I'm sure most of us have come across such a scene, or, at least read about it in the papers, or saw it on television. We are profoundly touched with a sense of powerlessness to do anything; a deep awareness of our personal failure to comprehend what the other must be feeling at this time. Somewhere within our hearts we may whisper a prayer, if only a 'God help her'. God is never far away from such grief and suffering.

Against the background of the very dramatic event, there are some very simple human touches in the story. Jesus saw the situation, and, rather than have a long conversation with the mother, he went straight to those carrying the dead body, and asked them to stop. He then took the young man by the hand, and spoke directly to him. We are then told that the young man sat up immediately, and began to talk. (A nice human touch there). The next thing is that Jesus gave him back to his mother. Jesus didn't make any demands. He didn't ask the young man to follow him. He reunited the boy with his mother, and he went on his way.

Practical

Unfortunately, it is common-place in today's world to be confronted with scenes of horror and atrocities every day. Because these may be happening many miles away, it is easy to remained detached, and not have any sense of involvement. When I was growing up, we were praying for the conversion of Russia. That was safe enough, because it was far enough away! When I begin to let these scenes touch my heart, and draw a response from me, then I am beginning to accept my own responsibility. To look on, and remained detached, is to be part of the problem.

The widow of Naim was going through her darkest hour.

She must have felt totally alone in the world. Hers was a unique
loneliness, that only time, support, and friendship could fill. We
all have our dark hours from time to time. We sometimes call
this depression, but that is not always the case. We can genuinely
feel totally alone in the midst of throngs. It is at such times that
we should invite Jesus to enter that emptiness, and fill it with his
love and healing. He is only too willing and pleased to do this,
and is always delighted to be invited.

Jesus came that we should have life, and have it more abundantly. There can be many areas in our lives that are quite dormant, inactive, and fruitless. There are times when we can feel as
dry as the Sahara. It is at such times that we can reflect on the
Spirit being like a fountain of living water, rising up from within
us. Beneath the driest desert there is plenty of water, but it is
only the rare spot that allows the water reach the surface. We
can be an oasis in the lives of others. We all encounter the widow
of Naim in our own lives from time to time.

Story
One night a man had a dream. He was walking along a beach
with the Lord. Across the sky flashed scenes from his life. In
each scene, he noticed two sets of footprints in the sand: one belonging to him, the other belonging to the Lord. When the last
scene of his life flashed before him, he looked at the footprints in
the sand. He noticed that many times along the path of his life
there was only one set of footprints, and that, every time that
happened, he was at the lowest and saddest times of his life.
This really bothered him, and he questioned the Lord about it.
'Lord', he said, 'you said when I decided to follow you, you
would walk with me all the way. Why, then, in the most troubled times of my life, are there only one set of footprints? I don't
understand why you should leave me when I needed you most'.
The Lord replied 'My precious precious child, I love you, and I
will never leave you. During your times of trial and suffering,
when you see only one set of footprints, it was then that I was
carrying you.'

ELEVENTH SUNDAY OF THE YEAR

Gospel: Luke 7:36-8:3

Theme

Today's gospel tells the moving encounter in the house of a Pharisee between Jesus and a sinful woman. It gives us a 'close-up' view of the friend of sinners in action.

Parable

I knew a Religious Sister some years ago, who was retired, and who was free to use her time as she pleased. Every morning she set off with a shopping bag, and no one seemed to know where she was going, and what she did all day. She never spoke about her work, and nobody asked her. One day she was knocked down and killed by a car as she attempted to cross a busy road. Her funeral took her community completely by surprise. Every 'drop-out', wino, and homeless person in Dublin arrived at the convent for her funeral. She had been their friend, and they came to pay their own tribute to her. It was quite a revelation for her community, who were embarrassed, humbled, and profoundly moved by the outpouring of grief they witnessed.

Teaching

The setting is perfect. It is the house of a Pharisee, one of the religious leaders, who placed total emphasis on a love of law rather than a law of love. Such a house was certainly no place for a public sinner to show her face. She was outside the pale, and must not be associated with by a religious Jew. It is almost as if Jesus had prearranged the scene, to enable him stress the whole purpose of his mission. He frequently said that he had come to call sinners, and to befriend them.

Not only did Jesus befriend the woman, but he even allowed her minister to him. There was something about him that stirred a profound reverence within her, and she showed that reverence and respect by the anointing with oil, which was the highest expression of reverence one could show to another. Jesus had a ready-made, real, living object lesson right there, and he took full advantage of it. He was aware of the shock and horror among the onlookers, and he used the occasion to drive home a very central point of his teaching.

Sin is the absence of love. Many sins were forgiven her, because she loved much. Charity covers a multitude of sins. The conclusion of the gospel speaks of many among his followers who had been transformed like this woman, and who followed him, and ministered to him. They were his friends, and he was never ashamed of them. This would eventually contribute to his death, because he was condemned 'for being friends with sinners, and even eating with them'.

Response
To try to get some sense of what Jesus is about, it is essential that I get in touch with my own brokenness and sinfulness. There is little point in speaking about a Saviour to those who are not convinced that they are sinners. This woman is an extraordinary lesson to us all. Yes, of course, she was a sinner. Even she herself would not deny that. She also, however, had a very deep awareness of what kind of person Jesus was. She came into his presence with confidence, and without fear of being rejected. What an extraordinary lesson!

Pouring out her tears, and pouring the precious ointment, was a powerful example of an outpouring of the heart. It was a letting-go of much pent-up emotion, pain, suffering, and loneliness. Her tears were as precious as her ointment. Even using her hair to dry his feet was a symbol of doing what she could with what she had.

It is not possible for a human being to fall on her knees, cry out to God, and not be heard. This was a perfect setting for a practical lesson in the compassion and love of Jesus. Without a direct miracle from God, it would be impossible for a Pharisee to cross the divide between his vision of the woman, and the person that Jesus saw, as he looked at her. He was deeply moved, and, in another account of the same incident, Jesus said 'Wherever the gospel is preached, what this woman has done will be spoken of.'

Practical
It is easy to get very practical lessons from today's gospel. Right here, right now, I can fall at Jesus' feet, and acknowledge my sinfulness. I can pour out all my pent-up guilt, regret, remorse, and self-condemnation. I can expect the same acceptance as the woman in today's gospel. The only thing that can hinder that is a failure to appreciate the boundless nature of Jesus' love. It would be failure to comprehend the very reason for his coming.

Any expression of my own remorse, or any acknowledgement of my own powerlessness is proportionate to my openness to grasping the prodigal generosity of the Lord's acceptance. Faith has been well defined as 'having the courage to accept his acceptance'. The only limitation of what the Lord can do in my life are the ones I set.

If I am to change, and to walk with Jesus, then I must be prepared to come under the Niagara of his love, to come within the circle of his acceptance. Just as the woman walked right into the house where Jesus was, so must I come, without fear, into his presence, and open out the canvas of my life before him. His unconditional love is the divine initiative, and when I am willing to begin with that, then I will be ready to respond to that. Jesus offers me unconditional love, and he awaits my response to that offer.

Story
Graham Greene wrote a powerful novel called 'The Power and the Glory'. It involves a priest who decided to remain with his flock, despite the great danger of the persecution of Catholics in that country. Whether it was the pressures of his situation, or just an inherent personal weakness, he took to the bottle, and was alcoholic. He was in his prison cell. It was the morning of his execution. He was lying on the floor, reaching out in vain to an empty brandy bottle that was just beyond his reach. Suddenly, the situation in which he was, swept over him like a tidal wave. Here he was about to face his Maker. This was not going to be the kind of death he had hoped or prayed for. He was a failure, an alcoholic, a disgrace to his calling. He tried to mutter an Act of Contrition, but the words just wouldn't come. From where he was now, it was easy to see that his life would have been so much better, and his death so much more peaceful, if he had only made an effort to be a saint, instead of a drunk, and a failure. At that moment he believed that the only thing that should ever have concerned him was his attempt to become a saint. It all seemed so simple and easy now that it was too late. All he would have needed was a little courage, and a little self-control.

He must have been filled with amazing joy at the hug of welcome he received when he came face to face with Jesus.

TWELFTH SUNDAY OF THE YEAR

Gospel: Luke 9:18-24

Theme

Today's gospel contains a central question in the gospel: 'Who do you say that I am?' If we reply that he is someone we are prepared to follow, Jesus leaves us in no doubt as to what that will imply.

Parable

Imagine, if you can, Jesus posing that same question to a group of intellectual theologians. The answer would go something like this: 'You are the eschatological manifestation of the ground of our being; the kerygma in which we find the ultimate meaning of our interpersonal relationships.' I could well imagine that Jesus' reply would be: 'WHAT?'!

Teaching

The first question is 'Who do people say that I am?' He is not particularly interested in the reply, because he goes right to the core, and asks 'And you, who do you say that I am?' Jesus is a personal God, who asks personal questions. 'Will you also go away?' 'Do you love me more than these?' The question is addressed to me personally, and the answer must come from me personally. I will not find that answer in a book, but in my heart.

The complete answer to the question is 'You are my Saviour, my Lord and my God.' 'You are Saviour in the room of my past; the Lord of the room of my future, and you are God in the room of today.' God is totally a God of now. 'I am who am.' If he is Saviour, then I don't have to be back in the past, with regret, guilt, or self-condemnation. If he is Lord, then I don't have to live in the future, with worries, anxieties, and fear. I need have no fear of the future, if I believe that he holds the future. If he is God today, then 'there is nothing impossible with God'.

If we are to follow him, then we must join him on the journey. We must take up the cross of daily living, and of fidelity to his call, so that he can lead us into the fullness of life. If we choose to follow him, there will be little in the way of earthly glory involved in the journey. Just as he was rejected, misunderstood, and alienated, because he refused to conform to the standards of this world, so we, too, can expect the same, if we take him seriously.

158

Response

The cross is not too well understood. Someone suffers a misfortune, and may be looked upon as someone who has a great cross to bear. That is not true, because misfortunes also happen to pagans as well as Christians. The cross is always a blessing, and it does not crush or destroy. 'My yoke is sweet, and my burden is light.' The cross is made up of splinters. The cross is anything I have to do because of my decision to follow Jesus. If I follow him, then, I must forgive, I must share, I must live in a certain way. 'The greatest among you are those who serve.' Those who serve are the happiest people on earth.

Travelling in the Christian way is to grow in my relationship with Jesus, so that I turn my will and my life over to him. If he is Saviour, then I trust him to save me, and I can entrust to him with total confidence every moment of my life up till now. If he is Lord of my future, then I can be totally certain that, as he gives me the gift of each new day, he also gives me the Spirit to live that day with peace and confidence. Each day comes with batteries supplied! It is called my daily bread. If he is God, then 'if God is for us, who can be against us?' 'Having given us Christ Jesus, will the Father not surely give us everything else?'

I said already that I can find the answer to today's question within my own heart, and not anywhere else. Travelling with Jesus each day brings me into a personal conviction about the reality of my answer to his question. It is a question of letting go, and letting God. I have to open one hand, and let go of the past, open the other hand, and let go of the future, open my heart, and accept the gift of today.

Practical

If the gospel is now, and I am every person in the gospel, then, of course, I must face up to this question right now. I have to be careful with the word 'say', because it is not confined to what I might put in words. I could say one thing, and believe something else. Who actually is Jesus to me? What difference does he make in my life? What do I think my situation might be now, if he had not come on earth? I should seek the answers to these questions in my heart, and not in my head.

'No cross, no crown.' Easter Sunday is always preceded by Good Friday. 'Happy are they who dream dreams and are prepared to pay the price to make the dreams come true.' 'You're either for me or against me', says Jesus. A willingness to embrace the cross of service is a very good indicator that I am for him.

Following Jesus involves a constant dying to self. Death is like a pile of sand at the end of my life, which I can take and sprinkle a little every day along the road of life. If I do that there will be nothing at the end but my ascension. On the other hand, if I wait till the end of my life to die it could be too late.

To live the Christian life is to be an eternal optimist. Life faces me with opportunities rather than problems. 'God loves a cheerful giver.' To willingly embrace the cross of Christian service is to develop a generosity of spirit, and a great capacity for love. The secret of Pentecost is to die quietly. I can do the good without fanfare, or without acting the martyr. By my acts and attitudes I am letting the whole world know who I believe Jesus to be.

Story
Wilma Rudolph was a disaster from birth. She was a tiny premature baby, who caught pneumonia, then scarlet fever, and finally polio. The polio left one leg badly crippled, with her foot twisted inward. Until the age of eleven, Wilma hobbled around on metal braces. Then she asked her sister to watch while she practiced walking without braces. She kept this up every day, afraid that her parents might discover what she was doing, and she would have to stop. Eventually, feeling guilty, she told her doctor, who was flabbergasted. However, he gave her permission to continue as she was, but only for a short period of time. Anyhow, to make a long story short, Wilma worked away at it until she eventually threw away her crutches for good. She progressed to running, and by the time she was sixteen she won a bronze medal in a relay race in the Melbourne Olympics. Four years later, in the Rome Olympics, she became the first woman in history to win three gold medals in track and field. She returned to a tickertape welcome in the US, had a private meeting with President Kennedy, and received the Sullivan Award as the nation's top amateur athlete.

It is facing up to the daily carrying of the cross that releases within us our full potential.

THIRTEENTH SUNDAY OF THE YEAR

Gospel: Luke 9:51-62

Theme
Jesus is on his way to Jerusalem to pay the ultimate price of love. He challenges those around to declare where they stand. Are they coming with him or not?

Parable
A few years ago I asked a tradesman to do a job for me, and he promised that he would be along the very next day. When he failed to show, I phoned him again, and, once again, he said he definitely would be with me on the following morning. I let a few days go by, before I got another tradesman to do the job. A few days later my friend arrived all ready to go. He got a bit of a shock to learn that the job was completed, and he had missed the opportunity of some business. In today's gospel Jesus is telling us that he has no intention of hanging around, waiting on others to make up their mind...

Teaching
The opening sentence in today's gospel is quite expressive. Jesus set his face resolutely towards Jerusalem. In other words, this was it, he was going forward, fully aware of what lay ahead. They had attempted to arrest him before, and had even tried to kill him on occasions, but he always walked away, and they were powerless. He said 'No one takes my life from me. I will lay it down, and I will take it up again'. When they came to arrest him in the garden he told his apostles 'The hour has come...'

Once again, we see the contrast between Jesus and those around him. He was going to Jerusalem, so the Samaritans refused to accept him, as they saw him as one of 'the others'. (Reflections of Northern Ireland?) The apostles are angry with the Samaritans, and they want to demolish them with fire from heaven! Once more Jesus had to pull them back on track. His patience was constantly being tried and tested, because the others either did not listen, or they did not understand.

Excuses, excuses! All diets start on Monday! Never do today what you can put off till to-morrow! Jesus calls now, and he expects a response now. It is like the story of Bartimeus, the blind man, who, as he sat by the roadside, was told that 'Jesus of

Nazareth is passing by'. Bartimeus cried out immediately, because the moment of grace was now. Jesus would not be there
to-morrow. One man wanted to return home to bury his father.
There is no hint in the story that his father was dead. Perhaps it
was a question that, many years later, when his father did die,
that he would be ready to follow Jesus. Jesus knew only too well
that, by that time, there would be someone else who needed to
be buried!

Response
To follow Jesus is to accept a whole new way of being, and of
looking at things. It is to take on his vision, as he looked at the
world. It is to be a light, or salt, or leaven, whose presence does
make a noticeable difference. When Jesus had completed his
mission, he returned to the Father, and he entrusted us with the
task of completing his work on earth. This is made possible
through the presence of the Spirit within us.

Jesus calls us to action. He himself came 'to do, and to teach'.
He taught by his example, as well as by his words. He calls for a
commitment, for a covenant, for a life-long unity with him. He
promises to be with us always, but we must choose to stay, and
to travel with him. The call to be a Christian is the greatest possible call for any human being. We use the word 'vocation', and
that word is only now being given its proper meaning. For
years, it was confined to those called to the clerical or Religious
Life, and it is only now that it is conceded that each and every
Christian has a very special vocation.

There is nothing more powerful than an idea whose time has
come. Excuses come easy when we want to avoid action. The
test of our sincerity is our willingness to mediate our commitment down to the smallest detail. There is not one 'maybe' or
'might' in all the promises of Jesus. 'Heaven and earth will pass
away before my word passes away.' He wants our response to
match his offer. With his call comes the grace to respond to the
call.

Practical
There is much talk today about racism, bigotry, and what is
called xenophobia. This betokens an intolerance of others because of their difference from us. It betokens an arrogance, and a
sense of superiority that is self-conferred. It is a despicable quality, and it is destructive in every way it shows. Jesus had no 'no-
go' areas in his life, but others were constantly trying to contain

him within the constraints of their own narrow-mindedness. The Jews were scandalised because he spoke to Samaritans; the Samaritans refused him entry to their town, because he was on his way to Jerusalem. It would, indeed, be a wonderful and fruitful exercise to exorcise my heart of all such attitudes. God has no grandchildren; we are all children of God.

When two of Jesus' disciples asked for favoured status in his Kingdom, he asked them if they were prepared to drink the cup from which he was going to drink. In other words, to follow me has its privileges, but it also has its responsibilities. In involves the short-term pain for the long-term gain. Do I have what it takes to answer the call? There is always a natural tendency to seek an easier and simpler way. Jesus is THE WAY, and this does not allow for 'going my way', or 'I did it my way'! His offer is a take-it-or-leave-it deal, and he awaits my response.

When Jesus spoke about the bread of life, in John's gospel (chapter 6), some of his disciples turned and walked away, saying 'This is a hard saying, and who can take it?' Jesus let them go. He didn't run after them to offer them some easier simpler deal. He even challenged those who remained, as he turned to them with the words 'Will you also go away?' Today's gospel calls for a personal renewal of our Baptism commitment from each one of us. Nobody else can do that for me. My response must be my own personal response.

Story
A group of Christians were holding a Prayer Meeting in Russia, when such a thing was completely forbidden. Suddenly the door was broken down by the boot of a soldier, who came into the room, faced the group, with a machine gun in hand, and asked 'If there's any one of you who doesn't really believe in Jesus, then get out now, while you have a chance.' There was a rush for the door. The soldier then closed the door, and stood in front of the remainder of the group, with machine gun in hand. He looked around the room, as the people were beginning to think that their end had come. Then he smiled, and said 'Actually, I believe in Jesus too, and you're better off without those others!'

FOURTEENTH SUNDAY OF THE YEAR

Gospel: Luke 10:1-12, 17-20

Theme
Today's gospel has Jesus sending his disciples out to do his work. He instructs them, and gives them very definite directions. We then read what happened when they returned to him to report on how they got on.

Parable
We are all familiar with election times. We get the literature in the post, through the mailbox, or we have someone call to the door. Those who call to the door usually travel in twos. They have been well briefed, and they have their presentation ready. They are representing the one seeking election, and, therefore, they ensure that they remain faithful to the political manifesto of that person or party. If not every day, then certainly every week, they return to headquarters to report on how they got on. Today's gospel, of course, is about much more than seeking votes in an election, but there are some similarities.

Teaching
There is so much teaching in today's gospel that I am forced to be very selective. Firstly, it is important to note that he sent them out in pairs. He called each one individually. He never asked the five thousand to follow him, after he had fed them with the loaves and fish. While he called each one personally, he never sent an apostle out alone. There are but two incidents in the gospels when an apostle went out alone: one was to betray him, the other ended up denying him. Community support is essential to living the gospel. Even a hermit has to be commissioned by a Christian Community, and must continue to be in touch with that group.

Jesus told the apostles that he was sending them out like lambs among wolves. That wasn't very encouraging! His disciples had a choice. They could conform to the world, and preach a message that made people more comfortable in their complacency; or they could preach the message of Jesus, that was bound to be opposed, because it called for fundamental change. Many years later St John wrote in his first letter 'The people who belong to this world speak from the world's viewpoint, and the world listens to them. But we belong to God; that is why those who know God listen to us. If they do not belong to God they do not listen to us. That is how we know if someone has the spirit of truth or the spirit of deception.'

It is encouraging to listen to the enthusiasm of the disciples when they returned. They had obeyed Jesus, and it worked. His promise to them was vindicated. They discovered that the call to mission contained the power to effect that mission. Jesus went even further in assuring them that he had given them full authority over all the power of the evil one, and that their names were registered as citizens of heaven.

Response
The gospel is in between two phrases. The first is 'Come and see', and the last is 'Go and tell.' If I have come and seen, I will want to go and tell. There is a difference between witnessing and evangelising. We are all called to witness, but not all are called to evangelise. Many of us would die a thousand deaths if we were called to stand on a box in Hyde Park, and preach to the passers-by! We can all witness, however, through the example of our lives. Christianity is about attracting, rather than about promoting.

To be involved in the work of the Lord is to be involved with others of a similar vision. If there is no involvement, there will be no commitment. I cannot be a member of the Body of Christ, and fly solo. My foot cannot go off for a walk on its own. The whole body must be involved in the exercise. This does not mean that everybody should be doing the same thing, or that all should be involved in each single undertaking. There are ministries and missions; there are gifts, talents, and charisms. The gift of some is in organisation; of others in prayer ministries; of others in ministering to the sick, the marginalised, or the least of the brethren.

The words at the end of today's gospel are addressed to each one of us. Jesus does give us his power. We are empowered to do his work, and to work in his name. His call is an anointing call, and we are sent with his authority. We have the power if we are willing to supply the goodwill. Jesus assures us that we have a passport, visa, and 'green card' for heaven. Our names are already registered there. We are saved, and our mission is to proclaim the good news of salvation to others.

Practical
Look around at the situations and circumstances of your life. Is
this where Jesus wants you to be? Are there situations and circumstances of my own making that are incompatible with giving Christian witness? If I am to proclaim salvation to others, I
must open my own heart to the grace of salvation. 'Let there be
peace on earth, and let it begin with me.' I am not implying that I
myself must become perfect before I can give effective Christian
witness! I am saying, however, that my very change of heart is,
in itself, my best witness. The greatest witness a recovering alcoholic can give is to walk sober down the main street of his own
town.

Jesus advises us today against playing God. I do what I can, I
say what I have to say, and I leave the rest to him. The most I can
do for another is to heal sometimes, to help often, and to care always. If others don't want my help, or refuse to follow my example, I am totally free to continue, and leave the outcome to God.
Parents do what they can for their children, but they begin to
play God when they hold themselves responsible for how their
children turn out.

Have you ever consciously claimed the power and authority
of Jesus in your life? Were you ever in a situation where you
were totally powerless and helpless, and you had nowhere to
turn? Would you consider calling on the power, the name, and
the blood of Jesus in such a situation? We have sacramentals,
like holy water, blessed oil, blessed salt, etc. for protection from
the presence of the powers of evil. We have been given that authority by Jesus, and it would be a serious mistake not to use it.
Jesus has already attained the victory, and he shares that victory
with us. It is up to us to use it.

Story
In a way I believe that Christianity is on trial in today's world.
Let me put it this way, by using figures from a seminar on evan-
gelisation in Switzerland a few years ago. Imagine there are only
100 people on this earth, all in one village. On today's facts, 67 of
them would be poor, while 33 of them would be at various levels
of being well off. 93 of them would have to watch while 7 of
them spend half the money, have half the bath-tubs, and eat one
third of the food, and have ten times as many doctors looking
after them than the 93 put together. That is not the real problem,
though, from our point of view. The real problem is when the 7

have the nerve and the gall to attempt to evangelise the 93! They tell them about the wonderful Saviour they have, who talks about sharing, feeding the hungry, etc., while the 7 throw out more food than would feed all of the 93! They build bigger and better basilicas and cathedrals for this God of theirs, while the 93 find it increasingly difficult to find a place to live. They transfer monies, and open new and better bank accounts, while the 93 find it more and more difficult to get something to eat. The bottom line must surely be this: If the 7 are so stupid and so blind that they cannot see the frightful contradiction of their situation, then, surely, they cannot expect the 93 to be that stupid, to be that blind!

FIFTEENTH SUNDAY OF THE YEAR

Gospel: Luke 10:25-37

Theme
This is a very enriching gospel, containing the two great commandments, and an excellent story to illustrate exactly what the two commandments are about. To reflect on this gospel is to get to the core of the message.

Parable
Several days after the Titanic sank in the North Atlantic, a newspaper carried two pictures side by side. The first showed the side of the ship slashed open by a massive iceberg. The caption read 'The weakness of man, the supremacy of nature.' The second picture showed a passenger giving up his place on a lifeboat to a woman with a child in her arms. The caption read 'The weakness of nature, the supremacy of man'. Today's gospel points to a balance between God and neighbour, between a vertical religion, that includes only myself and God, and an horizontal religion, which includes only me and my neighbour.

Teaching
It is important to notice that the questioner was trying to catch Jesus, to see if he would say anything that was contrary to the law which they held with such intensity. Jesus' reply was 'What does the law say?' Jesus is prepared to meet him on his own terms. The man quoted the law about loving God and loving neighbour, and Jesus said 'Fair enough. Do that, and you're OK'. Later on, of course, Jesus would further refine the commandments to one new commandment: 'Love one another as I love you'.

Jesus was a born teacher. He usually began with something that was quite familiar to his listeners, and he used that to bring them to a new insight into what he wanted them to learn. The road from Jerusalem to Jericho was infamous for bandits and robbers, and any one who travelled that road on his own was certainly taking a great risk. He told a story about this road to highlight what he meant by love of one's neighbour. A neighbour is not just someone who happens to live on the same block. It is someone who is regarded as one who should be friendly. A true neighbour can always be depended on. It is not a question

168

of where the other lives. When I come into your presence I become your neighbour, and I am in a position to help, should such be needed.

One thing we must notice about the Samaritan in the story: When he began something, he saw it through. It is easy to throw a few coins into the hat of a beggar, and then pass on down the road. It is different when I share a compassion for the other, feel the pain and isolation, and I want to accompany the other to security and healing. That is love, which is more personal and 'touching' than mere charity, which can be quite cosmetic and sanitised.

Response

Today's gospel certainly calls for a response. Notice the quality of the people who passed the man by on the roadside. They were very religious people, who were so engaged in their religious practices that they hadn't time to stop and help. Also their kind of help was so conditioned and limited, that it certainly was not open to just anybody. If you conformed to their definition of a good person you would be included in the club. If you dared to be different, then you don't belong to the club.

It is more than interesting that Jesus chose a Samaritan as the central character of his story. The Samaritans were despised by the Jews. It was both morally courageous, and possibly slightly foolhardy for Jesus to risk a vicious backlash to such provocation. He said what he said, however, because he was determined to underline the message that love is love, wherever it comes from, or whoever expresses it. God is love, and they who live in love live in God, and God lives in them. This is true, whether the person be Jew, Samaritan, Christian, Muslim, or pagan. God has no grandchildren. We are all children of God.

God is not bound by racial barriers, colour, or creed. Religion without spirituality is dead. Christianity is about witnessing to love in all its forms, on all occasions. It does not differentiate, it does not discriminate. To be so busy praying to God that I have no time to serve my neighbour is an abomination to God, and gives him no honour or glory whatever. The religious people in the story could have been in a hurry on their way to a religious service, or to some study session of Scripture that they just couldn't possibly stop to help the injured man. It is this kind of contradiction and hypocrisy that Jesus is anxious to root out.

Practical

A good way of looking at my life is to check on the balance between the vertical and the horizontal, between how I approach and see God, and how I approach and see my neighbour. 'Whatever you do to the least of these, that's what you do unto me.' 'If you bring your gift to the altar, and there you remember that someone has been hurt by you, go first, and be reconciled with that person, and then come and offer your gift.'

I must surely pass people in need just because I fail to notice the need, or I have so many things on my mind that I'm not open to the needs of others. We all know what it means to have a friend who is very 'thoughtful'. Implied in this is that the person is very kind, the person remembers, and I figure among that person's thoughts and concerns. Unwittingly, I can be quite hurtful, simply because 'I didn't think'. I tend to remember the things that matters most to me personally, and, when I forget something important in the life of another, it is just another way of showing that I wasn't too involved one way or another, and my interest wasn't very real.

We all have come across people whom we might describe as those who are always helping lame dogs over stiles. There are continually doing acts of kindness for others. I have a relative, and I'd be afraid to admire any item in her house, because she would have it wrapped and ready at the front when I go to leave! We don't all have to be like that, because there are those who meet their own needs through their helping of others. We all, however, can minister to those we find along the road of life who have been battered by events, and who have been wounded and discarded by life. There is no time limit to an act of kindness. It can be a once-off, or like the Samaritan, it may entail a follow-up. The very fact that it might entail a follow-up is what could deter me from helping in the first place. I can learn quite a lot about myself by looking closely at how I respond to the needs of those around me.

Story

A king who had no son to succeed him posted a notice inviting young men to come along and apply for adoption into his family. The two qualifications were love of God and love of neighbour. A poor peasant boy was tempted to apply, but felt unable to do so because of the rags he wore. He worked hard, earned some money, bought some new clothes, and headed off to try his luck at being adopted into the king's family.

He was half-way there, however, when he came across a poor beggar on the road, who was shivering with the cold. The young lad felt sorry for him, and he exchanged clothes with him. There was hardly much point in going any further towards the king's palace at this stage, now that he was back in his rags again. However, the young man felt that, having come this far, he might as well finish the journey.

He arrived at the palace, and, despite the jeers and sneers of the courtiers, he was finally admitted into the presence of the king. Imagine his amazement to see that the king was the old beggar-man he had met on the road, and he was actually wearing the good clothes the young man had given him! The king got down from his throne, embraced the young man, and said 'Welcome, my son!'

SIXTEENTH SUNDAY OF THE YEAR

Gospel: Luke 10:38-42

Theme
Today's gospel is one of my favourite passages in the gospel story. It is the story of Martha and Mary, and it shows very clearly the two possible approaches of two good people in their response to Jesus. It is a simple but very important lesson.

Parable
Prayer and work can be both sides of the same coin. If I am in a boat, and rowing across a lake with but one oar, I may find myself going round in circles. On the other hand, if I wish to get to the other side, I will need a second oar to keep the boat moving forward, and in the right direction.

Teaching
Martha and Mary were both good people, and dear friends of Jesus. Like any other two human beings, they were different, of course. The main difference was in their point of departure. Mary began by listening to Jesus, and she then would have prepared the dinner. Martha began in the kitchen, and, if she had time, she would then come to listen to Jesus. It is possible that I can become so busy with the work of the Lord, that I don't have time for the Lord of the work.

St Francis de Sales says 'Each Christian needs half an hour of prayer each day, except when we're busy; then we need an hour.' When I speak about prayer here, I'm not necessarily speaking of saying prayers. I could teach a parrot to say a prayer, but I could never teach a parrot to pray. Prayer is not so much me talking to God who does not hear, as God speaking to me who may not listen. While listening to Jesus, Mary's heart would be deep in prayerful reflection. Like the disciples on the way to Emmaus, she could say that her heart burned within her as she listened to his words.

'There is only one thing worth being concerned about.' That is quite a statement from Jesus, especially when he goes on to say 'Mary has found it, and I won't take it away from her'. There is a hunger in the human heart that can only be filled with the divine. To discover that secret is all that matters. 'Seek ye first the Kingdom of God and its righteousness, and everything else will be added to you.' Going aside with Jesus was always a special time for the apostles. It was at such times that he explained the parables, taught them to pray, and explained the mysteries of the Kingdom. To discover this is, indeed, the pearl of great price.

Response

Today's gospel is one that any of us could read, reflect on, and gain a great deal from it. The message is self-evident, and it is very simple. If I don't listen to Jesus, I have nothing to say as a Christian. He is the vine and each of us is a branch, and, separated from him we cannot survive, but will wither, and end up on the rubbish heap. This does not require any strenuous attempt on my part. All it requires is the goodwill to be open to him, and allowing the Spirit do the rest. I don't go round all day conscious of my unity with Jesus. That is a fact, whether I am conscious of it or not. There are times, though, when I am conscious of this, and I respond to this. These are times of prayer.

Martha a was good woman. She loved Jesus, and Jesus loved her. She wasn't wrong as in being wilfully wrong; it was simply a question of priorities. She was a doer, and she wanted to do her best for Jesus. In shifting the stress, she turned the divine initiative into human endeavour. This is a frequent trap for the Christian. Only God can do God's work. It is never a question of muscular Christianity, or being a member of the 'white-knuckle Club'!

One dimension of today's gospel that might not strike us straightaway is that all three persons in the story are being true to themselves. Martha was a natural worrier, who tended to fuss a lot over things to be done. Mary was naturally a contemplative soul, who could easily 'waste time' with God, with others, or with herself. This is a rare gift, because many of us can be driven by a compulsion to activity, or we begin to feel guilty. Jesus was totally at home with both Martha and Mary, and he probably would have said nothing if Martha had not made an issue of the situation. His reply was not a put-down for Martha, but a typical response of Jesus, which was always gentle, fair, and totally honest.

Practical

If I want to get a suntan, I have to go outdoors, and make myself available to the sun. (I'm not even considering the artificiality of the sunbed!) I go out into the back garden, get out the deck-chair, lie back, and let the sun do the rest. Prayer is like that. It is always a question of showing up, and letting the Lord do the rest. I cannot train a swimmer unless we go to a swimming-pool, or to the sea-shore. It is never a question of will-power; rather is it a question of having the will, and trusting God to supply the power. I cannot take a photo if there's no film in the camera. Today's gospel challenges me to examine my heart when I put myself in the presence of the Lord.

If I'm too busy to pray, then, I'm too busy. I should examine any twenty-four hour period in my life, and see the priorities it shows. How I spend my time and my money gives me some indications of my priorities. I myself notice that if there is an important football game on the television, I either get to see it, or I record it for later viewing. Where there's a will there's a way. For the person who has a genuine 'Why?', there will always be a way of dealing with the 'How?'

There is a Martha and a Mary within all of us. This is good, and it only becomes a problem when the Martha takes over, and fails to appreciate the value of the Mary. The longing of the heart of Jesus is that the self-righteous brother might accept and hug his prodigal brother, that the Pharisee might embrace the Publican, and that Martha might accept Mary. This is the reconciliation that must take place within all of us. At the beginning I said that work and prayer can be two sides of the same coin. It is not a question of heads or tails, but a realistic acceptance of the completeness that comes from inner balance, and from inner tranquillity.

Story
Down in southern California is Mount Palamor mountain which is topped by a giant observatory. There are massive telescopes that can scan the distant spaces. One of the facts that I heard from experiments there is the following: If you put a photo-sensitive plate into one of the telescopes, and open it to outer space for a few seconds, when the photo is developed, it will show many hundreds of bodies in outer space. On the other hand, if the telescope is left open for up to half an hour, the developed photograph will show many thousands of bodies in outer space. In other words, the longer the exposure, the greater the results.

The longer I spend in the presence of the Lord, the more of his light is reflected through me...

SEVENTEENTH SUNDAY OF THE YEAR

Gospel: Luke 11:1-13

Theme

There are many thousands of books written on prayer, and there are many times that number written as prayer-books, yet today's gospel teaches as much about prayer as any of us need ever want to know.

Parable

Around early October, John was asked what he wanted for Christmas. He thought for a while, and then he very casually said 'A bike'. He never mentioned the word 'bike' after that. He talked about the latest CDs, the latest computer game, etc. When Christmas came, he didn't get a bicycle, and he still never once mentioned the word. It would appear that he never really wanted one. If he had, you can be sure that his parents would have received constant reminders, would have been brought down to the bike shop to examine the model he wanted, etc. When I ask God for something, he knows whether I really want it or not; he also knows whether I need it; and he also knows whether I believe that my prayer means anything to him.

Teaching

When I was growing up I was taught many prayers, but I don't remember anyone teaching me to pray. The apostles saw Jesus walk on water, calm the storm, and raise the dead; yet when they came to him with a request, it was 'Lord, teach us to pray'. They saw that prayer was such a powerful force in his life, and they felt that the secret lay there. He often slipped away on his own, and spent a whole night in prayer. He did that before he chose his apostles, before his sermon on the Mount, before he faced Calvary. They saw this as the source of his strength, and they wanted what he had.

When he was asked to teach them to pray, he gave them a very simple prayer. It is well worth examining it in detail, because it summarises what Jesus himself would say to the Father. It begins with praising God, and praying that life around here might become more compatible with his presence, and more according to his will. We are told to ask just for what we need today, and we make a commitment about forgiveness, accepting the fact that we must forgive others if we want God to forgive us. We ask for protection against the evil that surrounds us, acknowledging our inability, of ourselves, to overcome the trials and temptations that come our way.

Jesus lays great stress on taking prayer seriously. Prayer is not just some form of wishful thinking, but it involves a sincere stance before God. It involves a constant call on God for his help, and a constant attitude of praise for his goodness. Of course, God knows our problems and struggles only too well, but he will not take over and run the show for us unless he is asked. He is very protective of our free-will, and his help is readily available only when we ask for it.

Response

Let me put the 'Our Father' into different words, which might help us in our understanding of it. 'Father, Father of each and all of us, you live in a state of complete happiness and holiness. May you be praised and reverenced for that. May your kind of life and living come among us, when we do as you want us to do, just like the angels and saints in heaven. Give us today what we need to live this day, and forgive us what we do wrong, just as we promise to forgive those who do wrong to us. Please prevent us wandering into situations with which we cannot cope, and protect us from evil, and all evil influences. Amen.

Prayer is an attitude that is translated into action. It is something that requires my full attention, something in which I put my whole heart. Because it comes from the heart, it reaches and touches the heart of God. The organ God gave me with which to pray is my heart, not my mouth. If the heart is not praying, the tongue is wasting its time. 'These people honour me with their lips, but their hearts are far from me.'

It is good to pray with the heart of a child. God is my Father, and, like any good and kind father, he will always listen to the cries of his children. It is not possible for a human being to fall on her knees, cry out to God, and not be heard. In our prayer to the Father, we can even ask for his Spirit, and expect that prayer to be answered. St Paul says 'Having given us Christ Jesus, will the Father not surely give us everything else?' There is nothing impossible to God, and prayer can become the key to the treasuries of heaven.

Practical

I learn to pray by praying, just as I learned to walk by walking.

There is a vast difference between praying and saying prayers. I could teach a parrot to say a prayer, but I could never teach a parrot to pray. If I ask the Holy Spirit to be in my words, then the Spirit will turn my words into prayer. I pick up the telephone and dial a number before I begin talking to someone elsewhere. I turn to the Spirit, and invite him to be in my words, before I begin to pray.

I can pray a lot, while not necessarily saying prayers. I can develop a praying heart by being wide awake, alert, and conscious of what's going on around me. If God asked me 'Did you enjoy my creation?', I might well have to admit that I never really had time to smell the flowers. Prayer creates a sense of wonder within the heart, and it heightens the awareness. It puts me in touch with reality, because, as Jesus put it 'Watch and pray' ensures that I am not just mouthing words as in a dream. A call to prayer is a wake-up call. To live in a Muslim country would make it easier to understand this concept, as the call comes forth from the mosque several times a day. In Ireland, we have the Angelus bell.

Prayer is as much nourishment for the soul as food is for the body. It is very easy to become malnourished spiritually, and, in the affluent West there can be a real Third World. If I am too busy to pray, then I'm too busy. Prayer is quite a personal encounter between God and myself, therefore, it is not possible to define it. Ideally, prayer is much more of 'Speak, Lord, your servant is listening' than 'Listen, Lord, your servant is speaking.' Prayer is not me talking to God who doesn't hear, as God speaking to me who won't listen. It is about giving God time and space in my life, and it is about working on my relationship with God.

Story
I got up early one morning,
And rushed right into the day;
I had so much to accomplish
That I didn't have time to pray.
Problems just tumbled about me,
And heavier came each task.
'Why doesn't God help?' I wondered.
He answered, 'Because you didn't ask'.
I wanted to see joy and beauty,
But the day toiled on grey and bleak.
I wondered, 'Why didn't God show me?'

He said 'Because you didn't seek.'
I tried to come into God's presence,
I used all my keys at the lock.
God gently and lovingly chided,
'My child, you didn't knock'.
I woke up early this morning,
And paused before entering the day.
I had so much to accomplish,
That I had to take time out to pray!

Each Christian needs half an hour of prayer each day, except when they're busy; then we need an hour. (St Francis de Sales)

EIGHTEENTH SUNDAY OF THE YEAR

Gospel: Luke 12:13-21

Theme

In today's gospel Jesus speaks of the riches of heaven, as compared to earthly riches. 'There's no pocket in the shroud' is a good old Irish saying. As with the Beatitudes, he is speaking about the poor in spirit. In other words, I could have a lot of wealth, but it does not possess me, nor am I enslaved by it.

Parable

It took me many years to distinguish between being rich and being wealthy. I was confusing riches with money. I didn't understand that riches and richness has nothing to do with money. As a family, I thought we were fairly poor, but it was many years later when I discovered just how rich we were. When I came to work with people who were wealthy, and I discovered just how poor they were, it was quite an eye-opener for me.

Teaching

Ireland has had its share of family disputes over property and inheritance. I am not in a position to say where we come in the international league, but to evidence a family being torn apart over a few acres of land is something very sad. Of course, I respect and expect justice and fair play, but, I believe there comes a time when the property is not worth the destruction it costs. It presumes wonderful maturity and personal freedom to be able to walk away, and shake the dust off the feet. One would have to have a very enlightened understanding of what possession of property and wealth contains before being able to let go, and walk away. When the property takes over and possesses me, then I am in bondage.

In his story Jesus tells us about something we all know too well. The first million will never satisfy! It may be the most difficult to make, but it can generate a compulsion to accumulate, and I can become driven with the needs to go one better. Once again, it is a failure to distinguish between wealth and riches. Some of the richest people I know have very little of this world's goods. There is no greater riches than a loving, kind heart. Money couldn't buy the gifts that bring happiness.

It is such a simple lesson, but I will never learn it if I refuse to open my heart. When I die, I will have to let go of everything. I was at the bedside of a very wealthy woman when she died. She had a well-merited reputation for minding the pennies; she had no family of her own; and there was no shortage of interest as to where her wealth was going to go. ('Where there's a will, there are relatives!'). One of the staff asked me 'I wonder how much did she leave?', and, with a slight hint of cynicism, I replied 'She left everything'.

Response

To put a modern translation on the final sentence of Jesus in today's gospel would be: 'Yes, a person is a fool to store up earthly wealth, but not have a rich relationship with God'. The only riches worth pursuing are those that have an eternal value. 'Lay up to yourselves treasures in heaven, where the moth cannot consume, nor the rust corrupt.'

It is only by growing in appreciation of the wonderful gift of my Christian vocation that I can hope to come into an awareness of my real riches. 'If God is on our side, who can be against us?' 'Having given us Christ Jesus, will the Father not surely give us everything else?' 'What does it profit a person to gain the whole world, and lose themselves in the process. Or what price can a person put on a soul?'

It is not possible for me to be grateful and unhappy at the same time. If I am grateful for what I have, then, I will be happy also. To be happy with what I have, to do the best with what I have; that, I believe, is an act of thanksgiving to God. I have known individuals during life who epitomised this to a unique extent. They were always content, always grateful, and always quick to confirm another. The surest sign that I have had a Pentecost is my willingness and ability to confirm another, and make that person feel worthwhile. The greatest gift you can give another is not to share your riches with her, but to reveal her riches to herself.

Practical

It is a very worthwhile exercise, from time to time, to do some sort of moral inventory of ourselves. To take the last twenty-four hours, and see how we spent our time and our money. To try to discover what our priorities are in life. Many people have to do something akin to this once a year in their business dealings. They have to check on the pluses and the minuses, the success and the failure, the good and the bad. They have to check the balances, and see what changes have to be made to correct an imbalance. We all need such an exercise in our lives.

Each one of us is uniquely gifted by God. God gives each of us certain gifts according to his wisdom, and he lets us know what those gifts are by sending people to us, requiring us to use those gifts. If someone asks me to give a Retreat, to write an article, etc., it is God's way of telling me what gifts I have. God gives me nothing for myself. He doesn't give me my gift of speech to do around talking to myself! I do not discover my own gifts. If I do, I am like someone at a party who insists on singing, and he's the only one there who thinks he can sing! On the other hand, there is someone else at the same party, and everybody is calling on her to sing. She had better heed the call...

Imagine you were to write your own obituary notice! What would you write, beyond the mere biographical facts? What would be the legacy of your memory? Even among your mourners, how would the investment of your time with them be showing a return? You cannot save time; you can only spend it wisely. Time is one of the many riches we now possess, and we should be investing it wisely. 'Seek you first the Kingdom of God, and everything else will be added onto you.' We still have time, we still have choices, we still can make decisions.

Story
A rich man heard that a certain priest had a 'hot line' to God, and he came to him in search of a favour. He wanted the priest to pray, and find out if he, the rich man, was going to heaven when he died. It was a strange request, but when the priest heard that the man was prepared to contribute generously towards the completion of the church repairs, he decided to give it a go.

A week later, the rich man returned. 'Did you find out?' he asked. 'Yes, I did', replied the priest. 'Well, then, what's the answer?' the rich man asked, very anxiously. 'The answer is in two parts', replied the priest. 'There is good news, and there's bad news. Which would you like to hear first?' The man was quite nervous, but he ventured to hear the good news first. 'The good news is that you are going to heaven when you die.' The rich man was thrilled, and excited, and it was a few seconds later when he spoke. 'That's great. That's the good news. Surely what could be bad news after that? What's the bad news?' 'The bad news', replied the priest, 'is that you're going tonight!'

NINETEENTH SUNDAY OF THE YEAR

Gospel: Luke 12:32-48

Theme
Jesus speaks very plainly about the importance of taking our responsibilities seriously. We have been entrusted with a very special task. 'The Lord gives, the Lord takes away.' He can come at any time and demand an account of our stewardship. Like sentries or night-watch men, we must always be on duty.

Parable
I remember giving an assignment to a class one time, asking them to work on it for a while, as I had to go down to the principal's office to consult about something. I had just gone down the corridor when I remembered that I had forgotten a folder. I returned to the class-room, and, as the door was open, there was no advance warning of my arrival. Imagine my amazement to find myself standing right behind a pupil, who was standing out in front, facing the class, and doing a very good impersonation of me! I put my finger to my lips to signal to the other pupils to remain silent, as the parody continued. I thank my God that I had the ability to laugh at what was something really funny, even at my expense.

Teaching
Life is a gift that is given us for others. The first time I was carried into a church I was not consulted. The next time I'll be carried into a church I will not be consulted either. To try to run the show in the meantime is crazy. I own nothing. Everything is given to me on loan, and can be taken back from me whenever God decides. God is not a tyrannical God, but he does impose certain expectations. My role is simple, but it is real, and must be taken seriously.

Jesus tells us to 'watch and pray'. There is a certain way in which we must remain alert. Any one of us would be amazed if we could really discover just how much of ourselves is dormant and inactive. The Advent liturgies calls on us to 'arise from your slumber', to waken up, the Lord is coming, and, like the shepherds, we should be on duty when he comes. We all know only too well that we will die one day, but, because it won't happen today, there is no sense of urgency. We also know people who didn't believe it was going to happen that day, and it did. It came 'like a thief in the night'.

We are called to be responsible. We will have to give an account of our stewardship. 'To whom much is given, of him much will be expected.' I cannot accept the privilege without accepting the responsibility. I will be held responsible for how I invested the gifts and talents that God has entrusted to me. Whether it is one talent, three, or five, the return will have to be commensurate with the treasure entrusted to me.

Response

It is interesting to hear Jesus' comment about those who are ready when he comes. Instead of demanding anything, he will sit them down, put on an apron, and minister to them. The apostles experienced this when he washed their feet, or cooked a meal for them on the sea-shore. He is grateful for our loyalty, and for our service. He is grateful that we are grateful, and that we appreciate his love and generosity, and his call to be part of his plan for others. His gifts are given us for others, and what we do to them he takes as having been done to him.

God is not a demanding God. He does not ask for what is impossible for us to supply. His talents are gifts and blessings, and, in using them, we are at our best, and at our happiest. 'It is in giving that we receive.' The happiest people on earth are those involved in the service of others. He himself came to serve, and the greatest among us are those who serve. He always wants what is best for us, and that is why he urges us to use the gifts we have, and to live life to the full.

Jesus speaks of a servant 'who knew his duty, but did not do it'. It is said that procrastination is the thief of time. All diets begin on Monday! There is nothing more powerful than an idea whose time has come. St Augustine prayed 'Lord, make me chaste, but not yet'! The only 'yes' that God is interested in is my 'yes' of now. God is completely a God of now, and his call of now is to be answered now. 'Jesus of Nazareth is passing by.' Each moment is a moment of grace, and I cannot live today on a decision I made yesterday.

Practical

Jesus tells us at the beginning of today's gospel 'Don't be afraid, little flock, for it gives your Father great happiness to give you the Kingdom'. I must accept my place in that Kingdom, and accept the responsibilities that go with that. The response to this offer must come from my heart, and nobody else can make that response for me. We all would do well to pause right now to renew that response within our hearts. In case anyone might have a question about what words to use, I might suggest something like the following: Lord Jesus, I accept you as my Saviour, and I ask you, please to establish your Kingdom in my heart, and become Lord there. I turn all that I have and am over to your care, and I trust your Spirit to guide my feet, my thoughts, and my actions according to the ways of your Kingdom.

Each new day is a gift; it is a gift that not everyone receives. It comes complete with batteries, or what we call 'our daily bread'. I must accept the gift with gratitude, and make the most of that gift. It is given to me for others. At the end of this day others should have benefited because of the gift that was given to me this morning. The Kingdom of God is built by tiny acts, most of which are hidden. Any one of us can be involved in building the Kingdom right here, right now.

It is good to live life, with a view to the end of life. We are a pilgrim people, and we are on our way home. God will not send me anywhere when I die. Rather will he eternalise the direction in which I choose to travel now. The decisions I make now have eternal repercussions. I hold the future in my own hands. God has been lavishly generous with me, but there comes a time when he stands back and allows me take responsibility, and make a personal response to his offer, to his gifts. That moment is now…

Story
Let's pretend this actually happened. I enter a second-level college, and I go into one of the Senior classes. I have a bunch of envelopes in my hand, one for each pupil in the class. I hand out the envelopes, asking them to do two things: 'Don't open the envelope till you get home; and don't tell anyone else what is in the envelope.' So far, so good. Whether they waited till they got home or not before opening the envelopes, when they did so they discovered that I had given them every question that was going to be on their final exams at the end of the year. I would have friends for life!

Do you imagine that each kept the secret? I feel certain that a country cousin would get a phone call that night! Imagine what would happen for the rest of the year. Some poor English teacher is trying to enthuse them about the extraordinary literary treasure that is 'Tintern Abbey', but, because it is not on the exam paper, all attempts fail to evoke the slightest interest. The same would happen with every other subject, when the subject is irrelevant to the questions on the exam paper. Unless it is on that paper it is seen to have no importance.

When the exams come along, there is one thing the pupils must agree about. If they don't do well, they just have themselves to blame!

In today's gospel and in his account of the general judgement, Jesus gives us the questions we will be asked at our Final Exam. If we don't do well...

TWENTIETH SUNDAY OF THE YEAR

Gospel: Luke 12:49-53

Theme
In today's gospel, Jesus really comes to grips with his mission, and he pulls no punches when it comes to acknowledging the enormity of it all, and how it effects all of us as well.

Parable
At the time of writing there are plans announced about a parade in Dublin city of Orangemen from the north of Ireland. They have been invited to come down for the march. The reaction is so predictable. Many are delighted to see this gesture of tolerance, while others are highly incensed at what they see as an insult to the people of Dublin. When the US president visited Dublin, there were thousands went out to welcome him, to wave banners, and to cheer, while other groups gathered with protest banners, and tried to create a riot. Jesus certainly divides people into those who are for him, and those who are against him.

Teaching
Jesus tells us that he has come to bring fire to the earth. Fire can heat, purify, provide facilities for cooking, or it can totally destroy. When we pray to the Spirit, we ask him to 'enkindle within us the fires of divine love'. My own initial understanding of the word 'fire' in today's gospel is the fire of divine love. To inflame us with the fire of enthusiasm. The opposite to love is indifference, not hatred.

We seldom had to light a fire in the winter, when I was a child. The last thing at night was what was called 'clamping down the fire'. A bucket of dampened turf-mould was packed tightly all over the fire. When we got up in the morning, the ashes were removed, and there in the centre were the bright hot coals. A few sods of turf, and the fire was off again for another day. (Incidentally, I think of today's church in much the same way. The hot coals are still there, but there is great need for the ashes to be cleared, and for the fire to be poked into flame again.)

To understand what Jesus means about families being split apart because of him, it is easier to understand when I consider that even I myself encounter differing pulls within myself when

I consider taking him seriously. 'The spirit is willing, but the flesh is weak.' It is no surprise, therefore, that, in certain cultures, a family member risks death by becoming a Christian and forsaking the religion of the ancestors.

Response
There is a restlessness within Jesus in today's gospel. There is a task ahead that must be faced, no matter how unpleasant or unsavoury it is. He longs to complete the work entrusted to him by the Father. With his dying breath on Calvary he says 'Father, I have finished the work that you gave me to do'. The task ahead is called a 'baptism', except that it is a baptism of blood. He began his journey with the baptism of water by John the Baptist in the Jordan. He would complete that journey on Calvary. At the Jordan, we are told that 'the heavens were opened'. On Calvary we are told that 'The veil of the Temple was rent in two'.

Jesus says that he did not come to bring peace on earth. At first reading, this may surprise us. It is only when we understand the nature of the conflict and combat that Jesus had to face on this earth, before the evil one was overcome, that his peace would be available to us. Every time he appeared to his apostles after his resurrection, his first words were 'Peace be with you'. He had achieved the victory, so he could share the peace that follows a victory, when the battle is over.

'I have come to bring strife and division'. Once again, this seems strange, until we reflect seriously on it. If Jesus landed among a group of people anywhere on this earth right now, he would create division. The reason he would create division is that, once he begins to speak his message, the crowd will become divided, some agreeing with him, and some opposed to him. If Jesus waited for everybody to listen to him, he wouldn't have started yet! He divides people into those who are for him, and those who are against him. The 'in-betweens' are against him, because 'if you're not for me, you're against me'.

Practical
The first conflict I myself must face up to, and deal with, is the conflict within myself. If I decide to take Jesus seriously, there will be all sorts of voices coming at me. Voices of prudence, of reason, of intellectualising. If I were to fast, my friends will express concerns about my health, while, if I eat too much, they may well remain silent!

I remember, years ago, when I gave Retreats in schools, I always had one word of advice for the pupils before the Retreat ended. 'Don't go home full of enthusiasm, and overpower your family with your new-found excitement! That will surely cause them to throw cold water over everything you speak of. Because they were not here for the Retreat, it would be unreasonable to expect them to understand what you're saying.' I advised them to let their kindness, helpfulness, and thoughtfulness do their speaking for them. Your family will not be able to deny the evidence of their own eyes.

Today's gospel is not the easiest gospel to understand. It does, however, call for some practical responses. 'You're either for me or against me.' It calls on me to state my position, to declare where I stand. This is something that I must do on a regular basis. Even on a daily basis. Of course, I can expect to be tested, even by those closest to me. I will draw the snide remark, or the cynical comment. If I am convinced and convicted about my position, such attacks will go right over my head. I have nothing to defend. The words and promises of Jesus speak for themselves. If I become defensive, it could indicate that I'm not totally convinced about what it is I believe in.

Story
The little girl inherited her mother's stubbornness, and there was often a flare-up, when the little one stomped her foot, and just refused to do what she was told. One day, it had gone too far, so the mother decided to get the better of her in some other way. She put a stool in the corner, and told her daughter to sit down there, and stay until her dad came home. She refused to sit, despite all the threats. Eventually, in frustration, the mother put her hand on the child's head, and pushed her down until she was sitting on the stool. Shortly after that, the dad came in, saw her sitting on the stool, and asked 'Well, what are you doing over there?' To which he got the teeth-clenched answer 'Outside, I'm sitting down, but inside I'm standing up!'

TWENTY-FIRST SUNDAY OF THE YEAR

Gospel: Luke 13:23-30

Theme
Jesus speaks of the need to know him, to do his will, and thus to belong to him. If he is the only way back to the Father, then no one can attempt to slip in any other way. Eternal life in heaven is a logical follow-up to living in the Kingdom now.

Parable
I am often puzzled by the temerity of some people who think little of taking chances, and who don't go in too much for planning and preparation. I have known people who go along to an All-Ireland football final without a ticket, just in the hope that they might get one anyhow. I have seen the same at International games, where the tickets are like gold-dust, and people come along and try to enter the turnstiles. This, indeed, has led to riots when hordes of hooligans followed a team to the continent, and created great destruction just because they were denied entrance.

Teaching
Christianity is about a person, Jesus Christ, and it is about knowing him, and walking with him. The disciples on the road to Emmaus were walking with Jesus, but they did not recognise him. They even told him they had heard a rumour that he was alive, but they obviously had paid no heed to it. At that very same time, a group of women were racing to tell the apostles that he was alive, because they had actually met him, and he spoke to them.

Jesus tells us 'I am the Good Shepherd. I know mine, and mine know me.' In today's gospel he tells the people 'Go away, I do not know you'. In other words, you never knew me. Oh, of course, you knew all about me, and you had heard about me, but it didn't make any difference to your lives. If you were mine, if you belonged to me, you would know me.

There are three things that will surprise you when you get to heaven. You will be surprised at some of the people you see there. You will be surprised at some of the people who won't be there. And, lastly, you'll be amazed to find yourself there! 'Some who are despised now will be greatly honoured then; and some

189

who are greatly honoured now will be despised then.' He is a
God of infinite love, but he is also a God of infinite justice.

Response

Once again, Jesus speaks of the need to heed his call now.
Tomorrow could be too late. This is a moment of grace. I sin in
what I do, and in what I fail to do. It is only right that I should
have to account for the moments of grace that come my way. 'To
whom much is given, of him/her much will be expected.' Two-
thirds of the people in today's world never heard of Jesus, beyond, perhaps hearing his name. They will have it easier at the
pearly gates, because they will have an excuse. It has been put
forward as a possibility that, at the moment of death, each and
every one of us will come face to face with Jesus, and will be
given one final chance to say 'yes' or 'no'. Whether the person is
Hindu, Buddhist, Muslim, or pagan, there is no other way into
heaven except through Jesus.

When I am out of the body, and I can see myself clearly
against all other realities, free of the body, and, for the first time
in my life, able to make a free decision, I will come face to face
with Jesus. Every human being, from Adam till the end, will
come face to face with Jesus, at least once, and will have to decide for or against him. Many will say 'yes', even if they never
heard of him before. Jesus tells the story of the man in the vine-
yard who hired workers at various hours throughout the day,
and, when the day's work was over, he paid each one of them
the same wages.

It is hard to imagine Jesus telling anyone to 'Go away; I do
not know you'. However, it does seem just, if we consider that
these people actually had every opportunity to know him, and
they chose to neglect every moment of grace that came their
way. Jesus told his disciples, when he sent them out to preach 'If
people in a town do not receive you, shake the dust of their town
from your feet, and go on your way ...' They were offered a gift
and they chose to reject it.

Practical

Today's gospel, and the gospels of the past few Sundays keep
bringing us back to the NOW. 'If today you hear his voice, harden
not your hearts.' 'This is the day of salvation, this is the day of
the Lord.' St Paul gave a long sermon in Athens on the statue
they had erected 'To the Unknown God'. He told about the God
he knew, and he spoke at great length about Jesus, and about his

message. At the end of it all, they said to one another 'That is interesting; we must hear him again sometime'! In other words, we're not going to do anything about it now!

There is a common phrase in football commentaries today called 'ball watching'. It is about a fullback watching the ball, and is totally unaware of a forward slipping in behind him. While it is important to keep your eye on the ball, it is also important to be aware of what's going on around you. Time and time again, in the gospel, we are called to waken up, to be alert, to be ready. As a Christian, I am never off duty, and I certainly never retire. The Lord can tap me on the shoulder in the most unlikely places, and at the most unlikely times.

There is a vast difference between knowing Jesus and knowing about him. One is experiential knowledge, and the other is academic knowledge. It is a long journey from the head to the heart. The task of knowing Jesus is uniquely the work of the Holy Spirit. 'He will tell you all about me, and remind you of all that I have told you.' If I really want to know Jesus, and have a deep personal relationship with him, then I can depend on the Spirit to ensure that that is so. If I am in touch with my brokenness, I will certainly come to know Jesus as my Saviour. The deeper my awareness of my own powerlessness, the greater will be my openness to his salvation, and to his love.

Story

A wealthy man lost his wife when his only child was very young. A housekeeper came to work in the house, and to take care of the boy. The boy died tragically at twenty years of age. The old man was without kith or kin, and he died of a broken heart some years later.

He had no heir to his enormous estate, nor could one be found. Neither was there a will, so the whole property passed to the state. In due course, there was an auction to dispose of the personal effects of the mansion.

The old housekeeper attended the auction, not because she could buy anything, but her grief was too strong to keep her away. There was only one thing in the whole collection that attracted her attention. It was a photo of the son. She had loved him as her own. No one wanted the photo, so her few pence were enough to buy it.

She brought it home, and proceeded to take it from the frame. When she opened the back of the frame some papers fell out. They looked important, so she brought them to a lawyer.

The lawyer looked at her and laughed, saying 'You sure have landed on your feet this time. The old gentleman has left all his estate and all his money to the person who loved his son enough to buy this picture.'

TWENTY-SECOND SUNDAY OF THE YEAR

Gospel: Luke 14:1, 7-14

Theme

Today's gospel is a simple teaching on humility and on generosity. It is a very typical gospel teaching, because it flies in the face of all worldly wisdom.

Parable

I have a friend who is a Christian, and to watch him live his Christian life is quite edifying. He is very quiet about the whole thing, and he certainly would never trumpet his good deeds in public. He always invites one or two for Christmas dinner; people who would not be in a position to repay the favour. He is a handy-man, and, now that he is retired, he is always doing odd jobs for people who could not afford to pay a tradesman. He has a natural ability to keep in the background, and, were I to mention him by name here, it would surely test his Christianity beyond the point of strain!

Teaching

Humility is not too well understood. I suppose the fact that pride is so prevalent has something to do with it. We live in a world which encourages self-promotion, and it is all too easy to get sucked into the rat-race. There is something extraordinarily powerful about humility, because of the disposition of character that is required to discipline the ego, and to know my proper place. Pride is so endemic in our natures that it goes undetected by those who display it. On the other hand, I always find myself deeply touched while in the presence of someone who displays genuine humility.

Jesus calls for selfless service in today's gospel. This is at the heart of Christianity. It consists of putting others before self. This is not easy, because selfishness is very much part of our human nature. It is part of our human instincts to look out for number one. If we were to line up God, others, and ourselves as being the proper order of things, then sin consists in mixing those up in any way, e.g., putting others in front of God, or putting myself in front of others.

Jesus tells us that 'the greatest in my Kingdom are those who serve.' He showed this by example when he washed the disciples' feet, when he sent them away to rest, while he took care of the crowds. He took a child, put the child in the centre, and told his disciples what real greatness was. His message was a sign of contradiction to this world, because his values are completely different. There is no way that his message could be accepted or understood by someone with a worldly mind-set.

Response
Humility is truth. It is the work of the Spirit of truth, who leads us into all truth. When we know the truth about ourselves, it is easy to be humble, because it simply means accepting things exactly as they are, and not as we would prefer to see them. 'From what delusions it would free us, if we could see ourselves as others see us.'

Have you ever found yourself in a tizzy over Christmas cards? You receive a card from someone to whom you hadn't sent one? You sent one to someone but did not get one in return? There's a condition on everything; every gift has a hidden price-tag. When I buy something in a shop which is a gift for another, I ask the person serving me to please remove the price tag before gift-wrapping the present. The idea is correct if it is followed through to the extent that it really is a gift, with no strings attached.

At the time of writing there is a world-wide crusade to persuade the rich countries to scrap the debts of the poorer nations. Mozambique is the number one priority at the moment, after very devastating floods. It is difficult to argue this line with hard-headed financiers, whose god is money. In today's gospel Jesus speaks of God's reward for those who give to the people who cannot repay. Not only is this difficult on an international level; it is difficult for you and for me, with what little we have. Because of our flawed nature, generosity doesn't come naturally to us.

Practical
Today is a day for each of us to examine our consciences. If I give some serious reflection, I will surely recognise if there is a tendency in me to dominate conversation, to tell all the world of my successes, to flaunt my goods for the world's admiration and approval. In my heart, I probably despise myself for doing this, and I am probably in full flight of ego-boosting before I realise what I am doing. To be aware of it is good, and could well be the beginning of a journey into truth, into humility.

There is no implication here that I am not worth attention, or that what I do is not of value. What matters is that I leave the judgement of that to others. If they think I do a good job, they will call upon me. Self-praise is no praise. If others choose to praise, that can serve as confirmation and encouragement. There are people who are so good at what they do that they never have any need to self-advertise. They let their work speak for itself.

It would be good to reflect on how I treat strangers, and those who hold out a hand for help. In coming in touch with the poor, I may discover just how poor I myself am. I may have plenty of money, but the outstretched hand puts me in a position to decide whether I own the money or it owns me. In today's world, half the world is dying of hunger, while the other half is on a diet, trying to get down the weight.

Story

A priest began his homily by holding up a huge triangle. He said he was going to use the triangle to illustrate the main points of his homily. He pointed to one of the angles and said 'Half the world is dying of hunger, in a world in which there is plenty of food. I will deal with that at some length'. Pointing to the second angle he said 'The problem is that most of us don't give a damn about the poor, and I will develop that point at some length also'. Pointing to the third angle, he said 'It is possible that some of you listening to me now are more concerned about the fact that I used the word 'damn' than you are about all those hungry people, so I will have to deal with that third point also'!

TWENTY-THIRD SUNDAY OF THE YEAR

Gospel: Luke 14:25-33

Theme
In today's gospel, Jesus spells out very clearly the price of discipleship. He doesn't put a tooth in it, and he repeats most of it for better effect.

Parable
The young lad got a violin, and he had ambitions to be a concert violinist. He was in his room, and the squeaks and wrong notes were driving his dad crazy, as he tried to watch something on the television. Finally, he could take it no longer, and he went out to his wife in the garden, and he asked her 'I know he wants to be a concert violinist, but, my God, does he have to practice?'!

Teaching
It is very easy to turn the gospel into some sort of a la carte menu, when I pick and choose the parts I like, and that suit me. Jesus makes wonderful promises of power working through us, of his peace, and of the Father's hug when we return to him. Part of the gospel story is the cross, whether we like it or not. No cross no crown. Everything that Jesus did in his life was gearing him towards that final showdown which was before him.

In a gospel of a few Sundays ago, Jesus speaks of being impatient to come face to face with the cross. 'I have a baptism with which I am to be baptised, and how can I be at peace until it is completed?' It would be through the cross that the victory would be won. Happy are they who dream dreams, and are prepared to make the effort to make those dreams come true. Up till the time of Jesus it was an animal that was sacrificed for the forgiveness of sins. He was now going to become that Lamb of God, and it would be he who would take away the sins of the world.

Over the years I have seen students entering seminaries, young men joining the army, or others beginning work in some financial or government institution. There was always a testing time, to discover if this person had what it takes for this way of life, or this kind of work. That is what Jesus asks us in today's gospel. 'Don't follow me if you don't have what it takes to do so...'

Response

As a follow-up to that last sentence, let me say quite clearly that I do not have what it takes to be a Christian. I am like a car without an engine. It is only when I have received the Spirit that I have any hope of following Jesus. Jesus called the apostles to follow him. They saw him walk on water, calm the storm, and raise the dead, and, at the end of all that, they denied, betrayed him, and deserted him. It was not until the Spirit came upon them at Pentecost that they were prepared and equipped to take up the cross, and follow him, even to dying for him.

The cross is not like some misfortune or calamity that occurs to people. When I decide to follow Jesus, and to walk in his footsteps, everything I do as a result of that decision is a cross. It is the cross of service. It is not heavy, but it does make demands. It leaves us with no options. If I am a Christian, I am obliged to forgive, to share, and to bring goodness to others. 'Make me a channel of your peace. Where there is hatred let me bring your love. Where there is hunger, let me bring your food…'

Because Jesus so much wants to give us everything, he is anxious that we should be willing to give up everything for him. If my hands are full of my own possessions, I will not be able to receive anything from him. I need an open heart, and open hands, if Jesus is to pour his gifts into me. There is absolutely no comparison between the all too limited comforts and resources I may be asked to surrender, and the prodigality of his generosity in return. I watched somebody heading off to Mozambique recently, where his living conditions will be very primitive, and he will not have any of the common comforts that we take for granted here at home. While I might not be prepared to imitate him, I certainly admired him, and, in a way, I envied him.

Practical

Today's gospel requires much reflection, because it doesn't make for easy reading. There is a danger that I may fail to grasp just how serious and central it is, and I can settle for something less than what it demands. It is here when I need prayer. 'Spirit of God, please reveal to my heart the full implications of what Jesus is saying to me. Let his words find a welcome in my heart, and, please give me the courage and the generosity to respond to his call.'

Jesus tells me that, if I want to be a disciple of his, I should love him more than anybody else in my life, including myself. He is not telling me not to love anyone. He wants to love me so much, that he wants to be free to fill my heart with love; then, and only then, will the others in my life receive the proper love from me. I cannot give what I haven't got. If he is free to pour his love into my heart, then that love, in turn, is poured out into the lives of others.

It is essential that we reflect on the cross, and see it as a necessary reality in our lives. It is not something I can pick and choose. I can even come to love and embrace the cross, as the Spirit melts my heart, and touches others through me. 'Lord, may your Spirit within me touch the hearts of those I meet today; either through the words I say, the prayers I pray, the life I live, or the very person that I am.'

Story
A very rich man died and arrived in heaven. He looked around at the beautiful buildings, and he already had his eye on a building that would become someone of his stature. However, Peter beckoned him to follow, so he went along. The choice of beautiful buildings was breath-taking, but he was led past the whole lot. Finally, they came to an area where there was a little hovel, with just the bare essentials, and no creature comforts of any kind. When the man discovered that this was for him, he was furious, and demanded to know why he was given a hovel, when all the others had mansions. 'Well, you cannot blame me', says Peter. 'You see, all we do is build with whatever material you sent on ahead when you lived on the earth. With what you sent, this is the best we can do!'

TWENTY-FOURTH SUNDAY OF THE YEAR

Gospel: Luke 15:1-32

Theme
Today's gospel is a collection of parables about people and things that were lost and found. The story of the Prodigal Son is at the heart of today's gospel, and, in itself, it is a summary of the whole gospel.

Parable
Emigration was the norm when I was growing up. One after another my own brothers and sisters left for England or the US. This was a heart-wrenching experience all 'round. As time went on, however, and the first ones began to return on vacation, the joy of that home-coming was enormous. Thankfully, they all were very faithful in returning whenever they possibly could. It seemed as if the time of emigration was over, and the time of home-coming arrived. Four of those who left, later got married, and some years later, returned to live in Ireland. Their home-coming made them much more important to us than they might have been had they never left!

Teaching
Today's gospel tells us about the lost sheep, the lost coin, and the lost son. Any one of these stories would provide more than enough material for reflection. In Jesus' day, the idea of a sheep being lost was a serious situation. A lost sheep would not survive too long out there among the desert wolves. The role of the shepherd was to be willing to die, if needed, in defence of his sheep. Money was not very plentiful in Jesus' time, and for someone to lose a coin was also a tragedy. There could be no let-up until the coin was found.

And then we have the story of the Prodigal Son, or, as it is sometimes called 'The Story of the Forgiving Father'. He just had two sons, and one was gone, without leaving a trace behind. The father was heart-broken, and the safe return of his son was the only thing he lived for. Day after day, his eyes searched the horizon, in the hope of seeing a figure approach in the distance.

All of these stories is Jesus' way of telling us about the happiness in heaven whenever someone turns back to God, and forsakes evil. God wants this more than anything else. He loves us,

he longs for us. 'Come back to me with all your heart. Don't let
fear keep us apart. Long have I waited for your coming close to
me, and living deep within my love.' Because of our free-will,
God cannot compel us to do anything. He can wait patiently, or
he can hope that we allow him find us. The door of our hearts
has but one handle and that is on the inside. He cannot enter unless I open the door.

Response
Despite the length of today's gospel, and the amount of material
in it, there is but one message, i.e. God wants us to turn, and to
return to him. We belong to him, and he knows that we cannot
find happiness apart from him. If we are not living within his
love, then we are lost. It is difficult to live outside of God's love
because his love is everywhere. However, I can live without reference to his love, and I can be driven by self-love, and by a self-
will run riot.

The whole gospel can be summarised in the story of the
Prodigal Son. Jesus was on this earth for thirty-three years. If,
however, he were here for just three minutes, he could have told
us this story, and we would have an insight into our own condition, and the heart of God. There is always a hug waiting for us
at the end of the journey home.

I am every person in the gospel, and the gospel is now.
Therefore, in turn, I can be the prodigal son, his self-righteous
brother, and I am called to become the forgiving Father. A lot of
the guilt I experience is the result of that self-righteous brother
within all of us. How God would love to see reconciliation here
between these two. 'Make friends with your shadow.' Only
when I am prepared to look in a mirror, and give myself forgiveness, am I ready to come to God for forgiveness. Otherwise, I am
asking him to do something that I myself refuse to do.

Practical
There is no scarcity of practicalities coming out of today's
gospel. I myself can often feel lost, and am not sure which way
to turn. It is then that I can call on the Lord, like the bleating of
the lost sheep, and I can be sure of his coming to my rescue.
Being lost like this is when I feel cut off from those around me;
when I feel very alone in the midst of crowds; or when I am completely devoid of motivation, enthusiasm, or *esprit de corps* of
any kind. It is not possible to call out to the Lord at such times,
and not be heard.

The Prodigal son 'came to his senses'. He opened his eyes to see, his ears to hear, and he reached out, and got in touch with reality. He fully comprehended his position. For the Jew, even to this day, the pig is unclean, and must not be touched, eaten, or befriended in any way. For the son to end up wanting to share their food with the pigs, and, even that was denied him, that was skid row with a vengeance. For a Jew, that was rock-bottom. Can you identify a time in your life when you hit rock bottom?

The father's welcome was extraordinary. Everything came to a stand-still. All stops were pulled out to celebrate his son's safe return. The best of clothes, the best of food. It is interesting to note that the father ordered sandals. Sandals were worn only when people went on a journey. Giving his son the sandals was telling him that he was free to leave again, should he decide to do so. Are you willing to let the Father hug you, and are you prepared to experience that hug? It is there for any of us who turn to him with all our hearts.

Story
A teacher asked her class to rewrite the parable of the lost sheep in a way that would make sense to the rest of the class. One student wrote: Suppose you had just finished typing a 100-page term paper. You had worked long hours in drafting it, and typing it. You were exhausted, but deeply relieved that the job was finished. You were collecting the pages to staple them, and bind them, when you discovered that there was one missing. Imagine the horror, the panic, the sick feeling in the pit of the stomach. You drop the other 99 pages, and begin the anxious search. Everything in you is longing and aching for a sight of that missing page. Without that page, the whole project falls limp. Suddenly, there, away in the corner, is the page. You excitedly push a chair aside, sending the 99 pages on it flying in all directions, and you are on your knees, reaching into the corner to touch and to grasp that page.

TWENTY-FIFTH SUNDAY OF THE YEAR

Gospel: Luke 16:1-13

Theme

In today's gospel, Jesus acknowledges the mind-set of the world, and how such people think and act. He acknowledges that this is not all evil, but he points out that there are lessons to be learned from such 'worldly wisdom'. The riches he offers are so much more precious than the riches of the world, and, therefore, should be handled with much greater care.

Parable

Two boys found a purse in a parking lot. It probably belonged to the elderly lady who had just driven out of the lot. The purse contained the lady's name, her address, and a ten-dollar bill. One of the boys said 'It's not right to keep the purse and the money. But, before we return it, let's change the ten dollar bill into ten single dollars'!

These boys had not yet accumulated the wisdom of the world, which would have prompted something more devious...

Teaching

Jesus speaks about the wisdom of this world, and he says that it can actually be used for good. 'Use your worldly resources to make friends. In this way, your generosity stores up a reward for you in heaven.' Not everything in the world is evil. It can, of course, become corruptive, if it dominates and controls our actions and our thinking. He speaks of a wisdom which is so much greater than earthly wisdom.

Wisdom is a truly wonderful gift. It is a gift of the Spirit, and it enables us discern between what is true and what is false. We speak about the three wise men from the East, or the wise and foolish virgins. As well as being inspired, it also is helped by experience, and by knowledge. Life involves many many decisions, and it is so easy for us mere mortals to make hasty decisions that have not been thought through; and then we find ourselves on the rocks of disaster.

Jesus tells us that we cannot serve God and money. Money is not an evil, but it can take over, and it can preoccupy to the exclusion of all other interests. Money can be a hard task-master when it takes control of us. Unless it is treated as a servant, as something to be used for good, it can become a bully, and take over our lives. 'Blessed are the poor in spirit.' There is no merit in being poor. The merit is in the detachment, and the ability to part with my money, for the sake of others. At this moment of writing I have just returned from down-town. One of the things that struck me were all those who held their hands out. Some of them were selling daffodils for World Cancer Day, others were selling a magazine that helps the unemployed; while others were simply begging. It is interesting to stand watching the passers-by for a few moments...

Response
With reference to that last sentence, I remember one occasion when I stood with a few friends to study this phenomenon. We were trying to guess, as we watched someone approaching, whether he/she looked like a person who would probably contribute something to the out-stretched hand. It was interesting to discover that we were often wrong in our decisions about those who would give, but we were seldom wrong when we said that 'this one won't even look'!

The liar has to have a good memory. Once I begin down that road, it will take another lie to cover up the last one. The man in today's story was dishonest, and, when he was found out to be dishonest, he proceeded to being dishonest in another way. He didn't seem to know how to act uprightly and fairly. His offers to the other servants were not out of any sense of generosity, but simply to save his own skin. He would make a deal with the devil to save himself, and ensure that he would be OK.

Jesus does see a place for worldly wisdom in the scheme of things. He advises us to be as wise as serpents and as simple as doves. To be a Christian does not imply being a doormat for anyone. To be a Christian is to believe in justice, to advocate it, and to practice it. I also have a right to expect justice from others. I am not expected to be treated like a fool, or to be seen to act like a fool in my dealing with the wise and clever of this world. There is a time to speak out, and a time to remain silent. The wisdom of the Spirit will give me the discernment, wisdom, and knowledge as to how to act best in each circumstance.

Practical
With the gift of life comes my own personal quota of gifts and talents. These are entrusted to me, with the idea that I should invest them in the service of others. Jesus tells a story of servants

who are called to give an account of their stewardship. The person who was given five talents was expected to have invested those talents, and gained five more. The same with those who received three talents, or just one. 'To whom much is given, from him will much be expected.' Can you identify some particular talent that you accept that you do possess? How do you think you are doing with it, in the living of your life?

'Unless you are faithful in small things, you will not be faithful in large things.' The Kingdom of God is built by tiny acts of kindness, most of which are hidden. It is through the ordinary and everyday events of life that holiness happens. Holiness is something that happens to us; it is not anything we do. Just as the newly-born baby will get hair and teeth, and this process cannot be controlled or rushed in any way, so it is with the work of God's Spirit within us.

We are told that we cannot serve two masters. We need to look at our lives for our priorities. What is it that takes up most of my time and my money? I always seem to find time and money for the things I really want to do, or to have. I could spend four hours playing a game of golf, and I could begrudge the Lord ten minutes of quiet time. This is something I should look at very seriously, and, if needed, make some serious decisions about it.

Story
There was a company which built houses, and their business was on a very large scale. There is a story told about one of their building contractors, who was approaching the age of retirement. He had become very careless and carefree, and his working standards were constantly slipping. He began cutting corners, using inferior material, and taking short-cuts. He was quite pleased with himself, and he felt he was onto a good thing here.

As time progressed, so did the standard of his work disimprove. The houses were new, so the faults would not show up straightaway, and he would be well out of the business by then. The time of his retiring arrived, and it coincided with what was possibly the most shoddily built house he had ever built. Imagine his surprise, at his retirement party, when his golden handshake was to be presented with the keys of that last house he had just completed!

TWENTY-SIXTH SUNDAY OF THE YEAR

Gospel: Luke 16:19-31

Theme

In today's gospel we learn that, while riches, in themselves, are not an evil, possession of riches, without being willing to share with those who have nothing, is something for which I will be held responsible.

Parable

Some years ago, the government here came out with a whole new selection of legal tender notes, from £5 up to £100 bills. That night, on the news, a roving reporter was out on the streets to get the reaction of people to the new notes. There was one old man who was stopped, and asked what he thought of the new £5 note, and if it were an improvement on the old one. He thought for a while, then shook his head, and said 'I'm afraid I would not be able to answer your question. My problem is that I never saw many of the old notes, so I'd have no way of comparing.'!

Teaching

The problem with the rich man was not that he was rich. There is nothing wrong with being rich. The problem was that there was a poor man right outside his door, and he refused to share anything with him. If the poor man were elsewhere, the rich man might have the excuse that he didn't know of his existence or his condition. In this case, however, there was no such excuse, and that is why the rich man is held answerable for his neglect.

We own nothing, not even life itself. Everything is given us on loan. One heart attack, and it's all over. As a Christian, my vocation in life is to be at the service of others. In sharing my riches with others, I am investing them in the bank of heaven. Everything I give away takes on an eternal value; while everything I keep for myself, when I die, it dies too. 'Lay up to yourselves treasures in heaven, where the moth cannot consume nor the rust corrupt.'

It appears to me that Jesus told this story in such a way that his message could not be misunderstood by anyone. We are given the dialogue and the details. We are shown the emotions and the attitudes. The contrast is constant between one man living it up, while the other has nothing, until the roles are totally reversed, and the rich man is asking that the poor man come to his assistance. It is quite dramatic in its presentation, and we are left in no doubt about the message.

Response
One point about today's story is that it is happening in this world right now. Half the world is dying of hunger in a world which has plenty of food. A few years ago, I read where millions of tonnes of wheat were burned and buried in Canada, just to keep up the price. There had been a good crop, and the more wheat available the lower the price will be.

It can be easy to miss the core of today's message by confining it to a global world event. What is in today's gospel can happen in my own home. There are different ways of being poor, and of being deprived. There is a hunger for recognition, and a great thirst for praise and for approval. There are many ways in which a person can feel marginalised. I can become so busy about my own work that I fail to notice the other who is made to feel left outside the door of success.

God is a God of love, but he is also a God of infinite justice. Jesus always showed a preferential love for the poor and the outcast. At the time of writing there is much debate about the plight of travellers and immigrants in our society. There is a lot of talk, but when all is said and done, there is much more said than done. There is a lot of greed and selfishness in the world, and we all can become infected by it. On the other hand, there are many shining examples of generosity and goodness. My own experience is that when the Irish are asked to contribute to an area of disaster (like the floods in Mozambique), they are extraordinarily generous.

Practical
I like to think that any one of us could read today's gospel, and be moved to make a response. If you were to say to me 'If I ever come across a group which is radically living the gospel, I will join them'; I could very well respond 'No, that is not so. When you are ready to radically live the gospel, you will find that group. If you are not, you will never find that group, even if they were right in front of you. If you were ready and willing, then, if there is no such group around, you yourself, would begin one.'

If I have a surplus of anything, money, clothes, food, etc., and I know of those who do not have enough of these goods, then, as a Christian, I am under an obligation to do something about it. Many of us could clear out a wardrobe and find items of clothing that we have not worn for years. We might even find clothes that we would no longer fit into! Why should we hoard, while others do not have the necessities?

Unlike the rich man in hell, we still have time to do something. When he had the time and the opportunity, he did nothing. There is nothing more powerful that an idea whose time has come. There is no scarcity of ideas. For those of us who want to, there is no scarcity of opportunities to help our less fortunate brothers and sisters. If the heart is right, the eyes will see and the ears will hear the cry of the poor. The rich man in hell was told that if his brothers did not heed the words of the prophets, they would not heed the word of someone risen from the dead. This was prophetic about what is happening today, when the word is spoken by one who was raised from the dead. 'Happy are they who hear the word of God, and keep it.' The word of God must be acted on...

Story

A man came home from work late and tired. He found his five-year-old son waiting for him at the door. 'Daddy, may I ask you a question?' 'Yeah, sure, what is it?' replied the dad. 'Daddy, how much money do you make an hour?' 'That's none of your business! What makes you ask such a thing?' the man said angrily. 'I just want to know. Please tell me, how much do you make an hour?' pleaded the little boy. 'If you must know, I make $20 an hour.' 'Oh,' the little boy sighed, head bowed. Looking up, he asked 'Daddy, may I borrow $10 please?' The father was furious. 'If the only reason you want to know how much I earn an hour is just so you can buy a silly toy or some other nonsense, then you can march yourself straight to your room, and go to bed. I work hard hours every day, and don't have time for such childish games.'

The little boy went quietly to his room, and closed the door. The man sat down, and began to get even more annoyed about his son's attitude. How dare he ask such questions, just to get some money. After an hour or so he calmed down, and began to think that he may have been a little hard on his son. Perhaps there was something his son really needed to buy with that $10, and he really didn't ask for money very often. The man went to the door of the little boy's room, and opened it. 'Are you asleep, son?' he asked. 'No, daddy. I'm awake,' replied the boy. 'I've been thinking. Maybe I was too hard on you earlier,' said the man. 'I've had a long day, and I took my annoyance out on you. Here's that $10 you asked for.'

The little lad sat straight upright, beaming. 'Oh, thank you, daddy!' he exclaimed. Then, reaching under his pillow, he pulled out some more crumpled notes. The man, seeing the boy already had money, began to get angry again. The boy slowly counted out his money, and then he looked up at his dad. 'Why did you want more money if you already had some?' the father demanded. 'Because I didn't have enough, but now I do,' the boy replied. 'Daddy, I want to give you this $20, if you'll spend an hour with me.'

TWENTY-SEVENTH SUNDAY OF THE YEAR

Gospel: Luke 17:5-10

Theme

Jesus speaks of faith as the minimum he expects of us. It is his blood and our faith. Faith is our response to love. It is something that he has a right to expect, and if we have faith in him it is only what he expects and what he deserves.

Parable

I taught swimming during my years as a teacher. Whether I called it 'faith' or not, I was continually asking someone to trust me. 'Let go of the bar. Come on down here into the deep end ... etc.' They had everything they needed to swim – except confidence in me and in themselves. When the breakthrough was made, it was no thanks to anyone. They did what they had always been able to do. They did what both myself and themselves asked them to do.

Teaching

What a simple request! 'We need more faith; tell us how to get it.' How often most of us could make that prayer our own. Faith is a response to love; since God is love, there can be no limits to faith, except the ones we set. Like a child learning to walk, we can learn to trust. Faith is not in the head, like some sort of mental assent. For example, I know that Jesus is Lord. That is just knowledge, and even Satan knows that. Faith has to do with my response to God's love, and to the promises Jesus has made.

I grew up on promises. Every New Year's Day, every Ash Wednesday, every Annual Retreat, etc. there were more and more promises. (Probably the very same promises of the year before!) It is only in the second half of my life that I woke up to the fact that it is Jesus who makes the promises, because he is the only one who can keep promises. 'Heaven and earth will pass away, before my word passes away.'

It helps in our understanding if we remember that the whole idea of creation, salvation, redemption, etc., is the divine initiative, and we must never turn it into human endeavour. It is very easy for us to do this. We can even end up trying to have faith in our faith. We are not doing Jesus any favour by believing in him, because that is what is expected of us. His love is poured out upon us, and, if we are aware of that at all, then our response is one of love, gratitude, and ever-growing faith.

Response
Our faith can grow. Jesus compares faith to a tiny grain of mustard seed, which can grow into a huge tree. I remember getting some grains of mustard seed one time, and they were so tiny that I was unable to pick them up with my fingers. The only way I could control them was to pick them up with a piece of cellotape, and stick them inside the cover of my Bible. I was in the Garden of Gethsemane at the time, so I could look around at the huge mustard trees that surrounded me, and compare them to the tiny seeds. I was also touched by the thought that these same trees were in this Garden for many hundreds of years before the time of Jesus. Something like that helps us to know our place!

'I believe, Lord; help my unbelief.' 'Lord, increase my faith.' These are among the most beautiful prayers in the gospel. Paul tells us (Romans 3) that we are saved 'by his blood and our faith'. Therefore, our faith is a necessary part of our salvation. 'The sin of this world is unbelief in me... When the Son of Man comes, will he find any faith on this earth?' Asking the Lord to increase our faith is a simple, but a very central prayer.

It is extraordinary how very definite Jesus is about faith; I mean faith that moves mountains. Anything can happen for those who have faith. I said earlier that it is a response to love. It must also be a direct outcome of humility; out of being certain that only God can do God things, and that what I seek is beyond all possibility for me on my own. It is certainly the basis of miracles in the gospel. When Peter had fished all night and caught nothing; when the little woman in the crowd had spent every penny she had for twelve years, and was getting no better; when the man sat at the pool for thirty-eight years,... then, and only then, were they ready to concede defeat, and let Jesus take over. 'At your word, I will let down the net... If I can only touch the hem of his garment, I will be healed... Say but the word, and my servant will be healed.'

Practical
Seek out the 'impossibles' in your life. Ask yourself if you are ready to hand them over to Jesus? Faith means handing them over, and keeping your hands off them. There are questions to be asked, and to be answered. Do I believe that he can do for me

what I cannot do for myself? Do I believe that he wants to do this for me? Do I believe that he cares enough about me that he wants to be a power for blessing in my life?

Jesus says 'Seek first the Kingdom of God, …and all these things will be added to you'. In today's gospel, we are told that our first work is to be humble servants of the Lord. This is both our responsibility and our privilege. We do not do this to get a return, but, we can be sure and certain that, if I give the Lord his rightful place in my life, that everything I need will be taken care of. There is a distinction between what I need, and what I want. If God were cruel and sadistic, he would give us everything we ask for, and then have a good laugh, because we often ask for things that are not for our good.

'We are servants who have simply done our duty.' Jesus even thought of himself that way, when he stood before the Father. 'I have come to do your will… My very meat is to do the will of him who sent me.' He had no other reason for living. He had a total and unswerving faith and trust in the Father, and that's what kept him going. 'As the Father sent me, so I am sending you … live in my love … for, apart from me you can do nothing.' Faith is to have one hand in his, as I reach out the other hand to another.

Story

Before modern radio and TV became so sophisticated, a telephone operator used get a call every afternoon asking for the correct time. She was always able to give this information with great confidence. The reason for this was that she always checked her watch, and adjusted it when needed, when the whistle blew for closing time in the local factory.

One day her watch stopped. The telephone rang, inquiring for the correct time. She explained her predicament. Her watch had stopped, and she had no way of ascertaining the correct time until the factory whistle sounded some time later.

The caller then explained his predicament. He was calling today, as he had done every other day, from that same local factory, and he had always adjusted his clock, when necessary, to agree with whatever time it was in the telephone exchange.

Be careful in whom you place your trust!

TWENTY-EIGHTH SUNDAY OF THE YEAR

Gospel: Luke 17:11-19

Theme
This is a rich gospel, because it not only tells us of a wonderful miracle, but it also lets us get a glimpse into the heart of Jesus, when he receives or does not receive gratitude.

Parable
I have the occasional day when I am in a 'cleaning mood'. The desk gets cleared, the bin gets emptied, the books are put back on the shelves. Every time I clear the desk I always notice the same thing. I always come across letters thanking me for something I did, said, wrote, or inspired. It is only recently I have noticed that I tend to hold on to letters like that for a while after receipt. Maybe, it's pride, but I like to receive affirmation and acknowledgement for what I do. When that comes in the form of a letter or card, I tend to put those on my desk, and they don't get 'binned' until that special day arrives!

Teaching
The lessons of today's gospel are very simple. The ten lepers were total outcasts, and should not have been anywhere near where 'ordinary' people frequented. Yet, such was their trust in this man Jesus that they dared to come within shouting distance of him. I could well imagine the horror among the religious leaders, who were so particular to avoid contamination of any kind. 'Jesus, Master, have mercy on us.' It is not surprising that their cry reached the ears and the heart of Jesus.

His response was immediate. He could have healed them right there, but he proposed a test for them. 'Go, and show yourselves to the priests.' (In those times, if someone was cleansed of leprosy, that person had to get permission from one of the priests before returning to live in the community). As the men left, they still had their leprosy. They were taking a frightening risk. Supposing they still had their leprosy when they arrived at the priest's house? However, they took Jesus at his word, and he did not disappoint them.

From a casual reading of the text, it appears that nine of the men were Jews, and the tenth was a Samaritan, or a pagan. In other words, there was only one of them who had no 'religion'.

It is interesting to note that he was the only one who returned to give thanks. Is it possible that the others had been brought up in the Jewish religion, and, therefore, they thought that God owed them something?! The Samaritan had no doubt whatever that what happened to him was pure gift, and he just had to express his gratitude.

Response
It is not possible for me to be grateful and unhappy at the same time. To be a grateful person is to be a happy person. I have heard it suggested that maybe Jesus punished the other nine by allowing their leprosy return, but I wouldn't consider that for one second. Jesus was sad when they did not return, but he probably was more sad for them than for himself. 'How sharper than a serpent's tooth it is to have a thankless child.'

Jesus consistently did things that were outside the strict law of the religious regime. When there was a choice between a law, and the welfare of a human being, the person always came first. There is another occasion recorded in the gospel when he even touched a leper, at a time when lepers were called the 'untouchables'. Jesus had the ability to see through the outer walls, right into the heart of the individual. He knew that, beneath the surface, we all share a common humanity.

I sometimes meet a parent who is concerned about a son not going to Mass, or a daughter living with someone to whom she is not married. While I can understand and empathise with their concern, I tell them about Mary, the mother of Jesus. She was reared with every little iota of the law, and she held her religious leaders in awe. The law was sacred, and the list of 'untouchables' was endless. She had one son, and, when he grew up, he did every single thing she was told not to do! He touched lepers, befriended Samaritans, talked to tax collectors and prostitutes, and even went as far as calling her religious leaders a bunch of snakes and vipers! I continue to speak of this situation, and, by the time I'm finished, I always feel that the parent feels much better!

Practical
Have you ever cried out from your heart to God? It is not possible for a person to fall on his knees, cry out to God, and not be heard. The cry, of course, must come from the heart. The heart is the organ God gave me with which to pray. If you think about the lepers in today's gospel, what makes your situation so different?

Have you ever tried to walk in faith? Just think about the lepers making their way to the priest. How do you think you'd feel? (Sit down on the road, and not budge till the leprosy was gone?!) Faith is in our feet, not in our heads. Faith is what enables us to step out in trust, and to take on the impossible. 'There is nothing impossible with God.' 'If God is for us, who can be against us?'

Do you consider yourself a grateful person? Do you appreciate what you have? (I heard of an old lady who said that we should never be off our knees thanking God that we're able to stand up!) One of the surest signs that I've had a Pentecost is my ability and willingness to confirm others. I cannot give confirmation if I myself do not have the Spirit. The greatest gift I can give another person is, not to share my riches with her, but to reveal her riches to herself. It is wonderful to meet grateful people; people who appreciate what others do for them.

Story
There is a huge fortress on a hill overlooking the town of Weinsberg in Germany. One day, far back in feudal times, the fortress was surrounded by the enemy. The commander of the enemy troops agreed to let all women and children leave the fortress. He also agreed to allow each woman take one valuable possession with her.

Imagine the amazement and frustration of the commander when he saw each woman leave the fortress with her husband on her back!

Charity begins at home. The hardest place to practice the gospel is at home in my own house.

TWENTY-NINTH SUNDAY OF THE YEAR

Gospel: Luke 18:1-8

Theme
A simple lesson in prayer without ceasing. There is a way to pray with the heart which God cannot but hear, and he cannot but answer. To speak from the heart is to speak to the heart. God can read the human heart, and that is more important than any words I might say.

Parable
It is early October, and the family were sitting around eating their dinner. For whatever reason, Christmas came into the conversation. In the course of the conversation, the mother asked young John what he wanted for Christmas, and, after a long pause, he said 'A bicycle'. The months went by, and the word 'bicycle' was never mentioned again. Not even when the mother bought roller blades for John at Christmas, with which he was delighted. She had decided that, if he really wanted a bicycle, she would have heard about nothing else for all the weeks coming up to Christmas...

Teaching
The purpose of the story in today's gospel was to show the disciples that they had a need for constant prayer, and they should never give up. Prayer is being in touch with God, whether he is speaking to me, or I am speaking to him. It is part of building the relationship with God, and it is the source of our spiritual nourishment. Without prayer, we become malnourished, and unable to resist the infections of this world. There are many pagan gods and idols out there, and they are only too ready to replace my interest in God, and to preoccupy my intention.

There was something that the widow wanted, and, despite all his toughness, the judge just had to give in to her eventually, because she had no intention of letting go, or giving up. If I met an alcoholic who wants to get sober, my initial question is 'How badly do you want it? Do you want it bad enough that you are prepared to do what it takes to achieve sobriety?' I knew a young lad who wanted to work for a particular firm, and they had no vacancies. So we went back there eleven times in one month, until the personnel officer threw his hands in the air, and gave him a job!

Jesus goes on from speaking about the evil judge to speaking about his Father. If even the judge gave in, how much more certainly will our heavenly Father respond to our prayers? As I said earlier, God can read the heart, and he knows whether I really want what I ask. I don't pretend to understand this, because I know parents who, at this very moment, are begging for the life of their daughter, and it is not likely that their prayers will be answered. I like to think that God gives us what we ask for, unless he has something better to give us. For these parents, they cannot possibly see how God could have something better to give them than a daughter whom they dearly love.

Response

The prayer that is the subject of today's gospel is the prayer of petition. It is a very important form of prayer, of course, but it is not the most important. Prayer of praise is the highest form of prayer; but, of course, that is greatly augmented, when my prayers of petition are granted. There can be some confusion around the whole area of prayer. If my prayers are always prayers of petition, I run the risk of being selfish and self-centred; except, of course, when the prayers of petition are for others. Like one of the ten lepers, I can ask, and, when my prayer is answered, I can return to give thanks.

The persistency of my prayer is always determined by how seriously I seek what it is I pray for. If I want something bad enough, I will pray without ceasing until God answers my prayer, even if that answer be 'No'. 'No' is also an answer to prayer. Be careful what you ask for in prayer, because you might receive it! We often ask for things that are not for our good, and, if God were sadistic and cruel, he would answer such prayers!

'When the Son of Man comes, will he find any faith on this earth?' After all I have told you, says Jesus, is there anybody who really believes me? A gospel like this morning's needs to be read several times, to try to understand the mind-set of Jesus. He is speaking with conviction and with authority. He knows what he's speaking about, because he himself experiences this all day long. The Father of whom he speaks is a Father whom he knows and trusts. Even before calling Lazarus forth from the tomb, he prayed 'Father, I thank you that you have heard me.' Before multiplying the loaves and fish, he thanked the Father. In other words, the Father to whom he prayed is a Father that always listens.

Practical

What is it you're asking from God these days? Are you convinced that you really want/need it? God reads your heart, and he knows you through and through. God will never disappoint you. If you don't expect him to answer your prayer, then, you can be sure that he will not answer. The old woman read about the faith that moves mountains, so, one night, before going to bed, she prayed that the mountain in front of her house should be moved by the following morning. The next morning she got out of bed, went over, pulled back the curtains, and exclaimed 'Hum, I just knew it wouldn't!'

The poor are used to waiting. They wait in queues for social welfare; they stand at bus-stops for ages; they wait for a shelter, or a free-meal place to open. If I understand my poverty as I stand before God, I would find it much easier to be patient with prayer. Day after day I can pray for something, and there seems to be nothing happening. Is it possible that some of us give up the praying just a day or two before the answer was due to arrive? I don't pretend to understand this, but I imagine that if I kept praying, and did not cease until the prayer was answered, I would understand much better what Jesus is talking about.

I remember getting a woman to attend A.A. meetings one time, because of her alcohol addiction. I begged her to make one big act of faith, and just go to meetings day after day; and not to stop going till the miracle happened. There were many times when her faith wobbled, and when her resolve weakened. However, thank God, she kept going, and, yes, the miracle happened. Nobody can explain how the system works, but it certainly does for those who stick with it.

Story

A group of botanists were exploring almost inaccessible regions in search of new species of flowers. One day they spied, through binoculars, a flower of great rarity and beauty. It lay in a deep ravine, with perpendicular cliffs on both sides. To reach it someone would have to be lowered over the sheer precipice by means of a rope, and it was certainly a very dangerous undertaking.

Approaching a young lad nearby, who was watching them with great curiosity, they said, 'We'll give you twenty dollars if you let us lower you down below, to obtain that beautiful flower for us'. The young lad took a look down into the ravine, and then he said 'Wait here; I'll be back'. When he returned, he was accompanied by an older man. Approaching one of the botanists, he said, 'I'll go over the cliff, and get that flower for you, if this man holds the rope. He's my father.'

Faith is a direct response to love...

THIRTIETH SUNDAY OF THE YEAR

Gospel: Luke 18:9-14

Theme
This is one of the most well-known stories in the gospel. If I could get this one right, I would be helped enormously in my over-all understanding and practice of the gospel. It spells out how to come before God, and how not to come before God.

Parable
A newly-commissioned colonel had just moved into his office. A private entered with a tool box. To impress the private, the colonel said 'Be with you in a moment, soldier! I just got a call as you were knocking.' Picking up the phone, the colonel said 'General, it's you! How can I help you?' A dramatic pause followed. Then the colonel said 'No problem. I'll phone Washington, and speak to the President about it.' Putting down the phone, the colonel said to the private 'Now, what can I do for you?' The private shuffled his feet, and said sheepishly, 'Oh, just a little thing, sir. They sent me to hook up your phone'!

Teaching
My generation was reared in the Holy of Holies! We were given all the rules and regulations, and we were told to remain faithful to those, and not deviate in any way, and that we would thus merit heaven. The religion I had growing up was to keep people from going to hell. Spirituality, on the other hand, is the only thing that frees those who have already been in hell. Ask anybody in recovery from addictions, compulsions, etc. Religion is about externals, it's what we do, and it's about control. Spirituality, on the other hand, is what God does, it is internal, and it's about surrender.

Holiness is to discover that I'm a much bigger sinner than I ever thought I was! The closer I come to God, the more obvious the sin is. It is a long journey from the Pharisee at the front to the Publican at the back. It is a journey of repentance, and of facing up to the truth. It is a journey that Life will provide if I have the courage and honesty to find it. If I still think that I should be still up at the front with the Pharisee, then my life will be riddled with guilt, and I will never find peace.

The Publican knew his place before God. God is the Creator, I am the creature. I am a sinner, Jesus is Saviour. Unlike the Pharisee, I have no right to compare myself to anyone else. All judgement is to be left to God. I can look at the most hardened criminal, and say 'There, but for the grace of God, go I'. I have no reason to boast whatever. I could have been born to any parents, in any country, at any time. I did not select my sexuality, the colour of my skin, or my religious beliefs. With total conviction, I can stand before God, and pray 'Oh, God, be merciful to me a sinner'.

Response
Today's gospel gives us a simple and practical example of two ways of coming before God, one is wrong, the other is right. Instead of saying 'Praise the Lord', the Pharisee was saying 'Praise me, Lord.' Original sin is the result of a lie. It is only the truth that can set us free. How can I possibly hope to stand before God, and think that, somehow, I can hide, and cover up what I'm really like? When I stand before God, I must open out the canvas of my life fully before him. He knows me through and through, anyhow, and I should not insult him by practising some sort of charade before him, and call that 'prayer'.

To judge myself superior to others is ignorance; to boast to God about it, is arrogance. We are all children of God, and the most disabled person is on this earth with as much right as the greatest genius. 'The greatest in my Kingdom are the ones who serve.' The Pharisees were very good people, in that they did all that they believed to be right. Unfortunately, as with Religion generally, this can create a superiority complex when it comes to looking at us lesser mortals. Religion has always tended to be destructive, and there is not a war in today's world that is not a religious one.

We often use the phrase 'to know where he's coming from'. The Pharisee and the Publican were coming from opposite ends of the spectrum. In essence, there was no difference between them, in so far as both were Jews, both were sinners, both went to pray in the Temple. The religious pride of the Pharisee, however, blinded him to the reality of his situation. Religious pride is a contradiction in terms, and it involves assuming to myself something that is not mine. There are many ways of playing God, and all of us can fall into that role from time to time.

Practical
The gospel shows us two men coming before God. I am given a

very clear distinction between their different attitudes, and I am forced to examine my own attitude before God, in the light of today's gospel. Falling on my knees, and crying out to God for mercy and forgiveness, is not self-denigration, or implying that I am worthless, and beneath contempt. Far from it. It's to tell it like it is, to face up to the truth, and, thus, to be set free. Only God is perfect, and to come into the presence of the all-holy God, must show up a very glaring contrast. When I come into the glare of a spotlight, I can see the slightest speck on a shirt, a jacket, etc. things which I had never noticed before.

Check your own attitude before God. It is like going out into the back garden on a warm sunny day, lying back in a deck-chair, and getting a sun-tan. The only thing you did was to make yourself available; the sun did all the rest. Don't ever over-emphasise the importance of your contribution when you stand before God.

If there is ever a time when you have no choice but to be totally open and honest, it is when you stand before God. Reflect on the fact that, at death, you will come face to face with God. No more hiding, no more games, no more pretences, no more excuses. You have a choice right here, right now. You can have a full dress rehearsal for such an occasion right here today. It is good to face up to reality, rather than letting reality catch you by surprise, when you waken up too late.

Story

A clergyman had reached the end of his rope, and he decided that he was swimming against the tide trying to get any response from his congregation. He decided to try some other way of life that might give him a greater personal satisfaction. He was very disappointed to discover that a job was hard to come by. In fact, he got to the point that he was prepared to take any job at all that came his way. At last, he landed a job in the local zoo. Unfortunately, when he went there, the job was not exactly available just yet, but the manager asked him to consider taking a temporary job, until the other one was vacant. As it happened the chimpanzee had died, and had not yet been replaced. The chimp was a great favourite with the children, and the cage could not be left empty for long. They had a chimp suit, and the man was asked if he would mind getting into the suit, and taking the place of the chimp. All he'd have to do was to roll around a few times, eat a banana, go back in the back for a rest, etc. He decided to give it a go.

He was an instant success. The children gathered around his cage. Every movement he made was greeted with cheers. He soon discovered that he was now getting much more attention than he ever got in the pulpit. One day, he decided to really get into the act. He jumped up, grabbed an over-head bar, and began to swing to and fro, to the delighted screams of the children. The cameras were flashing, and the crowd was gathering, so he got carried away with himself, and he really began to swing with full gusto. Unfortunately, after one huge effort, his hands (paws?) slipped, and he went flying over the partition into the cage next door. A huge tiger approached, and, forgetting that he was supposed to be a chimp, he screamed 'Help! Help!', to which the tiger whispered sharply, 'Shut up, you fool; I'm a minister too!'

We are all the same when we stand before God ...

THIRTY-FIRST SUNDAY OF THE YEAR

Gospel: Luke 19:1-10

Theme
The story of Zacchaeus is so simple, and has such a simple message, that it is frequently used in the preparation of children for their First Communion. Zacchaeus is anxious to see Jesus, and Jesus rewards him by offering to visit his house, and spend some time with him.

Parable
There were some raised eyebrows when John XXIII was elected pope. He was in his seventies, and there was no great hope that he was going to shake the church. One of the first things he did, however, made people sit up and take notice. He went in person to visit prisoners in one of Rome's prisons. He met them as equals, and he chatted very informally with each. He even disclosed that he himself had a relative in jail! The work and short pontificate of this man was going to open many doors, and set many prisoners free.

Teaching
The first thing that is obvious in today's gospel is that Zacchaeus was both anxious and determined to see Jesus. Notice that he was a 'big shot' in the town, being a very rich man, and certainly not very popular with the Jews, as he was at the top of the tax-collecting business for a foreign oppressor. He accepted his limitations, and, although he was a grown adult, he reverted to his boyhood days, and climbed the nearest tree to get a good look. He certainly caught the attention of Jesus, much more than he ever dreamed of. Not only did he see Jesus, but he was even invited to meet him, and to have Jesus as a guest in his house.

Jesus responded to Zacchaeus' enthusiasm, and he decided to go one better. He told him to come down out of the tree, and bring him into his house for a while. This sent shock waves through the surrounding religious leaders. Zacchaeus was a public sinner, someone to be despised, and, certainly not someone who would be visited by any self-respecting Jew. Once again, of course, Jesus was consistent, in that he said he had come to seek and to find the lost ones.

Immediately upon entering Zacchaeus' house, we can see the results of Jesus' action. Without saying a word, Zacchaeus is deeply moved, being in the presence of Jesus, and he makes some radical decisions about his life-style, and his manner of treating others. Salvation had come to his house, he was in the presence of the Lord, and his heart was touched in a profound way. He determined to right the wrongs in his behaviour. A personal contact with Jesus always evokes conversion.

Response
Once again, we have a very good example of the Lord rewarding our goodwill, and our limited human endeavours. Zacchaeus made an effort, he did his best, and Jesus was prepared to meet him more than half-way. His desire to see Jesus was obviously inspired, and it provided a moment of grace, which Zacchaeus was prepared to take.

Jesus, yet again, declared his mission. 'I have come to seek and save those like him who are lost.' Jesus was prepared to enter any house, to face up to any amount of scorn from his enemies, if it meant that he made contact with a sinner, or demonstrated to everyone where his preference lay. Far from making an apology, he reinforced his determination, and he restated his intentions regarding sinners.

It is interesting to see how Zacchaeus melted, as it were, in the presence of Jesus. Jesus didn't preach any sermon, he made no call for conversion and change of heart. His very presence was enough. Zacchaeus was in the presence of Truth, and he could not remained unmoved. This is quite a commentary on Zacchaeus himself, because many many others were in the presence of Jesus, and their hearts remained unmoved.

Practical
It is easy to suggest several practical little exercises, as a result of reading today's gospel. Once again, we are challenged to examine how deep our desire is to actually meet Jesus. 'Deep down in my heart the Spirit is moving', is a line of a song. It is down there that the hunger must be generated, and that the longing must be nurtured. This is prayer, which is more about going aside, going down into the heart, and crying out from there. I couldn't imagine myself finding a prayer in a book that could replace that call from the heart.

Jesus said to Zacchaeus 'Come down, because today I wish to dwell in your house'. When I waken up in the morning, I can hear the Lord say 'Get up, because today I want to live in you, and act through you. I want this to be OUR day, you and I together, as we walk the way for friendship's sake, and for the joy of us being together'. What an invitation at the beginning of any day!

It is easy to imagine myself alone, in the presence of Jesus. I can take a few moments any day, and construct such a situation in my creative imagination. I can just sit and listen. Most importantly, I must be prepared to listen. I have to learn to listen, so that I can begin to listen to learn. Prayer is more a question of the Lord speaking to me, than me speaking to him. Prayer can be risky, because I may hear something I don't want to hear. Jesus came to comfort the afflicted, but he also came to afflict the comfortable!

Story

I remember, some years ago, when the Irish national soccer team became to come into prominence. It was the European Championships, and they were doing very well. The whole country was behind them. I was befriending a man who was terminally ill with cancer at the time, and he was in a Hospice here in Dublin. He was a totally committed football supporter, and, sick and all as he was, he watched every single game.

I had some work to do down the country, and when I returned, the Championship was over, and Denis was very low, with no interest in anything. He knew he was dying, and he was prepared to speak about it. One day I suggested to him a possibility of what might happen, at the very moment of death, when we come face to face with Jesus. He would sit us down in front of a big screen, just like the ones that became so popular for watching the football matches during that summer. He would put on a video called 'This is Your Life'. He pulls over a chair and sits beside you. The first part of the video is simple enough, but, as it gets on with your life, you become uncomfortable, because you're not sure just what's going to appear next! It takes some time before you become aware of something else that is happening. Blanks begin to appear, some quite frequent, and some quite long. You glance sideways at Jesus, but he is not looking at you, so you cannot get his attention to ask him any questions. It is almost at the end of the tape that you guess for yourself what is happening. Every time you did something wrong, and admitted it, he pressed the erase button, and it was wiped clean. Even if you asked him now, he would not remember. You then settle back in your chair, relax, and realise that you are in the presence of your Saviour, who came to save you, not to condemn you.

Gospel: Luke 20:27-38

Theme

Jesus is usually at loggerheads with the Pharisees, who are demanding strict adherence to the law. Today he comes up against the Sadducees, who do not believe in the possibility of resurrection, and it is interesting to see how he deals with them.

Parable

I am writing these lines in the spring-time of the year. Nature is bursting out all over. Like Wordsworth, no matter where I look, I see a crowd of golden daffodils. What must it look like through the eye of a worm in the ground, though? He is surrounded by death. Withered, shrivelled bulbs all around him. From where he is, there is no sign of life, and he could have no idea what things look like from above the ground, where there is a different perspective on the very same situation. The worm may not believe in an after-life!

Teaching

I remember a time in my life, during my student years, when we had 'Harte's Christian Doctrine', and 'Sheehan's Apologetics' in generous daily doses. My one desire, at that time, was to accumulate so much information that I would be able to confound all the atheists, the agnostics, and all other forms of unbelief! I was on a crusade of conversion, so I needed to have all the answers! Things have changed a lot since then, thank God. If I met the Sadducees in today's gospel, I wouldn't enter into discussion with them at all. 'For those who not understand, no words are possible, and for those who do understand, no words are necessary.'

Thank God, it was Jesus they met, and not me! He accepted them where they were at, and he taught them about the conditions prevailing in the life to come. We cannot judge it from our limited understanding of life here now. Jesus' teaching is gentle and firm; not berating or condemning. These people just did not believe in life after death, and all Jesus could do was teach them what he knew. Perhaps his words touched some hearts, and left others unmoved. All I know is that it certainly is much easier to believe in life after death than not to believe. I carry that thought in my heart at every funeral I attend.

The example the Sadducees use is exaggerated, and humorous, but it was the best they could come up with by way of a hypothetical case, to test how Jesus would respond. In the after-life, the Kingdom and family of God will be complete. We will be free of the constraints and appetites of the body that are part of our present experience. We will all be children, and we will all be complete in love, no longer needing human love and lusts to sustain us.

Response

I often wonder if belief in an after-life is not part of the instinctual life of all of us, no matter how some people may try to deny that fact. The most primitive tribe believed in an after-life. They 'crossed the Jordan', went into 'the spirit world', or entered Valhalla. There is a resilience within the human spirit which tells us that, even if today is bad, to-morrow will probably be better. There is some sort of inherent resurrection-hope within the human heart.

There are three stages in life. The first is the womb-life. After that comes a breaking, a wrenching, as we enter the womb of life. This is followed by one last wrenching when we break through into the fullness of life. As soon as a baby is born, the only thing we can be certain of is that, one day, this person will die. We are born to die, and, after death, we become what we were created to be. If you ever waken up some morning and your life is exactly the way it should be, don't move, just stay as you are, until the undertaker arrives!

There is a vast chasm between the three stages of life, and, at any stage, it is absolutely impossible to imagine what the following stage might be like. If an unborn baby could hear you, there is not one word you could use that the baby would understand. There is not one thing you could mention – flowers, sun, etc. – that the baby would understand. That is why nobody comes back to tell us. 'Eye has not seen, nor ear heard, nor has it entered into the heart of any person to imagine what God has in store for those who love him.'

Practical

Some people don't know how to deal with death! Do I face up to that reality now, or do I keep my head down, and wait till it comes?! One thing is certain: We shall all one day die. 'I shall one day die' can be too close for comfort. Under normal circumstances, it's always the other guy's funeral! (If you don't go to other people's funerals, how can you expect them to come to yours?!) An elderly couple agreed that, when one of them died, the other should mourn for a short time, and then take the insurance money, and have a good holiday. After a few moments of thoughts, the husband casually remarked: 'Do you know what I was thinking? When one of us dies, I think I'll go to Paris'!

My own experience has shown me that, when I faced up to death, and put it in its proper perspective, life took on a whole new meaning. I am no longer concerned with life after death. I am much more concerned with life before death. Everybody dies, but not everybody lives. Some people settle for existing, and, when they eventually die, a doctor is called to certify that fact, because there was never much life there in the first place! You could write on the tomb-stone 'Died at forty, buried at eighty'!

The first time I was carried into a church, I was not consulted; and the next time I'm carried into a church, I will not be consulted either. To try to run the show in the meantime is crazy. We are coming to the end of the church year, and, in two weeks time, we begin a new church year. This is a good time to do some serious thinking about life in all its dimensions. 'If Jesus had not risen from the dead, then our faith is in vain.' We are not like the Sadducees. We have had two thousand years to reflect on the teachings of Jesus. The Sadducees had a genuine excuse, and were probably good people. We cannot claim that we didn't know, that nobody told us...

Story
There were twin boys in the mother's womb. After some time, they became aware of each other, and they began a conversation. They noticed the cord, and they decided that their mother must love them very much, when she was prepared to share her very life with them. After a while, they noticed little nails appearing, and several other changes in their bodies. One of them asked what this might mean. The other replied that they were probably getting ready to be born. The first one shivered. 'I don't want to be born. I want to stay where I am.' 'But you have to be born', said the other. 'We can't stay here forever.' 'How do you know there's any life after birth? Have you ever seen anyone who was born? Has anyone ever come back to tell us? How do you know we have a mother, anyhow? I'll bet we only invented her for our own consolation.' 'I really don't know', said the first guy, ' but it doesn't make any sense to me that this is it,

and there's nothing after this.' One of them was already a little atheist(!), while the other was a person of faith, which means that he has proof for nothing! After some time they were born. When they felt safe to do so, they opened their eyes, and looked up into the face of their mother. They then looked at each other with a look which spoke volumes. 'Weren't we two right fools. Sure how could we possibly understand something as beautiful and as wonderful as this.'

THIRTY-THIRD SUNDAY OF THE YEAR

Gospel: Luke 21:5-19

Theme
We are drawing towards the close of the church year. It is fitting, therefore, that today's gospel should deal with the final days of our world. It is almost as if to say, 'Well, if you haven't been listening too well up till now, this should make you sit up and listen.'

Parable
With the growth in communication technology of recent times, one would begin to expect to buy to-morrow's newspapers today! Supposing you could actually buy to-morrow's newspapers today, what difference do you think it would make? In today's gospel, we are told about the future, about the end of the world, about the end of our own lives. In recent times there have been several cults totally preoccupied with the final days. In a few cases, when the end did not come as they expected, we have had mass suicides. If the end of the world wasn't coming, then they decided it was the end for them. It's a great pity they didn't listen to the final few sentences in today's gospel.

Teaching
You cannot save time; you can only use it wisely and well. Each moment is unique and unrepeatable. Time and tide wait for no one. That is why the present moment is so precious. To look at the ruins of the Temple in Jerusalem today is to see, in effect, what Jesus speaks of in today's gospel. This, too, shall pass. Life is fragile; handle with prayer. We get one shot at life; there is no dress rehearsal. It is vital that we reflect on life itself, as we live it.

There has hardly been a generation on this earth that did not consider the possibility that the world would end in their day. I remember this being a particular worry of my own, as a child. The wars, the earthquakes, the widespread destruction were all present. All the signs of which Jesus speaks have been present on many an occasion. I have one life to live. My task is to get on with that life, and leave the rest of the world to God. I could die with thousands of worries unfulfilled.

The last paragraph of today's gospel is the most important

one for us. The Spirit will be with us; not one hair of our heads will perish; stand firm, and we will win our souls. As Christians, we are asked and expected to live salvation, and to be witnesses of that salvation to others. If I am saved, I should look saved, and the only real sin I can commit is to lose hope.

Response

We often hear of some people referred to as 'doomsday prophets'. They are completely negative and pessimistic about everything. They may call themselves Christian, but they certainly are not children of the resurrection. 'All will be well, and all manner of things will be well', the words of Julian of Norwich, is the conviction of the Christian. I cannot hope to understand anything of the end of the world, or anything to do with it, nor need I have such understanding. I have now, and I can say my 'yes' of now, and that is the only 'yes' in which God is interested.

The Christian life is not easy, because it involves the cross. Jesus tells us that we may have to suffer for being followers of his. Being a Christian has cost many a person his/her life. It may not cost us our lives, but it certainly should cost us the sacrifices needed to live in accordance with the message of Jesus. We are in the world, but not of it, and we must avoid the danger of being polluted by worldly values and interests.

I referred to a time in my life when the end of the world was a very real concern for me. Thankfully, that is well gone, and my main concern is living today. Today is enough to go on with. I have the privilege of ministering to a small group of very elderly people most mornings. Time and time again, I tell them that the Lord has taken care of them up 'till now, and all he asks is that they trust him to take care of the rest. Several of them are in their nineties, and one is over a hundred. It is obvious they should trust the rest to him.

Practical

The obvious message from today's gospel is that nothing but God is permanent. We are continually changing in a world that is also changing. 'A thousand years in your sight are as yesterday; they are like a few hours. You sweep people away like dreams that disappear, or like grass that springs up in the morning. In the morning it blooms and flourishes, but by evening it withers and fades.' I can enjoy life enormously, but not take it so seriously that I couldn't possibly face up to the fact that 'this too will pass'.

Life, once begun, never ends. It moves and evolves from the womb life to the womb of life, to the fullness of life. 'The best is yet to come.' My whole sanity depends on my belief in the promises of Jesus. There are many promises which deserve my constant reflection. 'I will never leave you in the storm; I will be with you always, even to the end of time ... I am the Good Shepherd ... it is only the hireling who would desert his sheep...'

'You are the salt of the earth; you are the light of the world.' In a world that is so often racked with despondency and gloom, there is need for the witness of the Christian message. At the present time there is an economic boom, and many people never had it so good. However, once again, the prophets of doom warn that the bubble will burst, that it will all come crashing down. The Christian is not supposed to lay up treasure on this earth, as if salvation could be found in that. 'Lay up for yourselves treasure in heaven, where the moth cannot consume, or the rust corrode.'

Story

I knew of an old lady one time who had a great obsession with money. She hadn't married, had worked hard, and she hoarded every penny she got her hands on. Whether it was the fact that she remembered days of poverty from her early childhood, or whether she was just a natural hoarder, I cannot tell; but money was a constant concern of hers. She was in her nineties, and her nephew was appointed to take care of her finances. Every single week he had to visit her, complete with cheque books, bank statements, etc. and she went through everything in great detail. The nephew told me that she never missed a thing right up to the end. She died in a nursing home. The morning she died one member of staff asked another one 'I wonder how much did she leave?' The answer was quick, and to the point: 'She left everything'!

FEAST OF CHRIST THE KING

Gospel: Luke 23:35-43

Theme
Today's gospel shows us our King on his throne of the cross, and the scene contains all the contrasts between the Kingdom of God, and the kingdom of this world. 'And ne'er the twain shall meet.'

Parable
Jesus was an extraordinary composite person. He was both human and divine, God and man, and he represented the balance between the vertical and the horizontal. The meeting of the two beams of the cross represented the meeting of the vertical (God and me), with the horizontal (me and others). His throne of Calvary was the meeting place for God and his people. It was no longer Moses and the burning bush. In a world that lays great stress on success, activity, power and achievement, it is worth noticing that Jesus was most powerful when he was nailed to a cross, and could do nothing, because that is where the father wanted him to be.

Teaching
In his early childhood, Simeon had prophesied that Jesus would be a sign of contradiction. He certainly was on Calvary. From any human perspective this was failure of the worst kind. His enemies had him where they always wanted him, and they appeared to have achieved the upper-hand over him. In this is the whole paradox of the gospels. What the world discards is what God makes sacred. It is when we are weak that God's strength is given the space and opportunity to operate.

It is ironic that what was intended as a token of mockery, a sign declaring him King of the Jews was placed over his cross. Pilate had asked him if he were a king, and he asked very simply 'Yes, I am, and that is why I came'. The problem here is that they are speaking a completely different language. It is not possible for someone with a worldly mind-set to understand the message of Jesus. Human judgement and comprehension is so narrow, so circumspect, so finite, that it is not capable of looking beyond the tangible, the visible, the commercial item. God's ways are not our ways, nor are our values his values.

The final two sentences of today's gospel contain a gem from the message of Jesus. This man may not have said a prayer in his life. However, with his dying breath he asked for help, and he was offered heaven. It is interesting to note how differently people reacted to Jesus. This came from some certain condition or disposition of their hearts. While one man mocked, the other prayed. The grace of the Lord is equally available to all, but the condition of the soil depended on whether the seed grew or not. Jesus had earlier spoken of the sower who went out to sow his seed. He scattered it in all directions, and he left the rest to the ground on which the seed fell. He had done his part.

Response
The only way I can ever hope to get into the scene of today's gospel is through reflection and prayer. I can place myself right there, as I sit silently, and go down into my heart, where the Spirit dwells, and where all prayer begins. I can look at that figure on the cross, and contemplate that scene for any length of time, and become greatly enriched as a result. This is my Saviour, my Lord, my King, and my God. This is the source of all the grace we receive in the sacraments, and in many other ways. The streams of grace begin right there.

I have to check my mind-set against the mind-set of the world. In the Kingdom of Jesus, he is Lord, all of his people are equal, and life in that Kingdom can be lived only through the power of the Spirit. Because of him, my weaknesses can become my strengths, and my failures can be turned into blessings. I learn compassion through my brokenness, and I know his love through acknowledging my sinfulness. Jesus makes a particular point of turning issues on their heads. He can turn failure into victory, and weakness into power.

'Lord, remember me when you come into your Kingdom.' What a simple prayer! It came from the heart, and that is why it drew such a response from Jesus. Jesus had come in search of those who were lost. Within the final moments of his live, this man allowed Jesus find him. Jesus would never intrude, or high-jack anybody into being a follower of his. He is present among us, and the choices are ours.

Practical
This is a day for some serious prayer in the heart. If I want Jesus to set up his Kingdom within my heart, then I have to invite him to do so. 'Lord, let my heart be your throne, and let me worship you there. For all the mockery you received on Calvary, I offer

you the love and obedience of my heart. Lord, remember me, now that you are in your Kingdom. Let my name be registered as a member of that Kingdom.'

I can measure my own life against the backdrop of today's gospel. I collect and gather my sins and brokenness, and I place them at the foot of the cross. The greatest thanks I could give Jesus for dying for me is to accept all that his death earned for me. 'Here I am, Lord. You are my Saviour, and my Lord. I entrust to you all the failures of my past, and I place in your care all that life still holds for me.'

If I put myself in place of the good thief, and look out through his eyes, what might I see? I certainly would be deeply conscious of my weakness, my powerlessness, and my total inability to manage the situation in which I find myself. There is only one way to turn, and that is towards Jesus. Only Jesus can do for me what I cannot possibly do for myself. It is for people like me that he came, and it is up to me to allow him find me. I stand before him exactly as I am, exactly as he sees me, and I cry out to him, 'Lord, remember me...'

Story

God was the composer of the music of the universe. He wrote a symphony of heavenly music, all in perfect harmony. To the birds of the air he entrusted the pan pipes. To the long grasses he entrusted the strings. To the clouds and the oceans he entrusted the percussion. He allocated sections of the orchestra to all parts of his creation. There was one section of his creation that he chose to treat differently, i.e., human beings. He had gifted them with reason and intelligence, and, therefore, there was no need to write a score for them, as they would know how to blend and harmonise, without receiving instructions.

The music began, and it was heavenly. The harmony was enchanting, and the sheer beauty of it all was breath-taking. Things continued like this for some time. Then, one day, there was a shrieking discordant note, that shattered the harmony of the universe. This was followed by complete silence. 'What was that?' whispered the trees. The birds replied 'That was people. They refuse to continue in harmony with the rest of us, and they have decided to do things their way'. 'What will he do now?' whispered the grasses. 'He may tear up the whole score. He may write a new one. One thing is certain, he cannot pretend it didn't happen, because that discordant note will reverberate throughout the universe for all eternity.'

And what do you think God did? He searched among every sound that ever was, until he found that discordant note. He took that note, used it as a theme, and he wrote a whole new score based entirely on that note. Out of that discordant note he wrote a whole new symphony of heavenly beauty, which we now call salvation. The whole story of salvation is based on our weakness and failure. Only God could think of such a thing!